# SOMEWHERE A
# CHILD IS CRYING

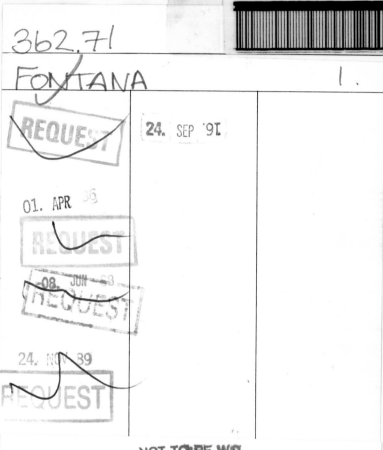

# SOMEWHERE A CHILD IS CRYING

## Maltreatment–Causes and Prevention

**VINCENT J. FONTANA, M.D.**

*Macmillan Publishing Co., Inc.*
NEW YORK

All the names of children, parents, and other nonprofessional participants in the case histories have been changed and are fictitious. Situations in some cases have been disguised to protect the children involved. However, all the facts are true.

*To My Dear Friends*
*Ann and Gene*

# Acknowledgments

THE AUTHOR WISHES to acknowledge Miss Valerie Moolman for her editorial assistance and compilation of the material for this manuscript, which she accomplished with a comprehensive understanding and feeling for the maltreated child. To Mrs. Loretta Carr, my sincere thanks for typing the numerous drafts of the manuscript. Without the dedicated help and support of Miss Anne Dougherty I would have been unable to complete this book.

I am grateful to Constance Schrader, Senior Editor at Macmillan, who gave this project its first impetus and recognized the crucial need for such a book.

Last but not least, this all started with my appointment as medical director of the New York Foundling Hospital by the late Francis Cardinal Spellman. It was his friendship, encouragement, and support that have made the accomplishments recorded in this book possible. I am appreciative also to his successor, Terence Cardinal Cooke, for his friendship and continued encouragement in our efforts to protect children and afford them a quality of life that will insure their future normal growth and development.

# Contents

# The Maltreatment Syndrome

The syndrome itself, in all its aspects, is a
most important symptom of our time. It is a link
in the documentation of my thesis that the
spirit of violence is rampant in our society. It
is a matter not only of the occurrence of these
heartless cruelties against defenseless
children, but of the inadequacy of the steps
taken so far to prevent them. Physicians,
legislators, and child-care agencies have taken
up the question belatedly. Even now no
proper solution has been found. This is one
of those forms of violence which society calls
"incredible" and is unequipped to deal with.
Why, in an orderly society, should this be
such a baffling medical, social,
and legal problem?
—*Fredric Wertham, M.D., A Sign for Cain*

# Preface

IN THE COURSE OF MANY YEARS as a pediatrician and as an activist in the field of child maltreatment, I have been able to observe and come to know countless parents who have battered, neglected, and abused their children. Seeing them, being with them, talking to them, watching their progress or lack of it, I find myself wondering whether our understanding of this problem is even less adequate than most authorities in the field will admit. Perhaps our training in medicine, in psychology, in sociology, in law, and in humanity, is only negligible. Do we really know what we are doing?

A strange note, perhaps, on which to begin a book about child abuse. But it is a matter of great concern that we seem unable to heal many of those who come to us—parents and children alike—and incapable of reaching those who do not.

Often, after treating a beaten, bruised, emaciated child, I go to a meeting of colleagues, in my own and related fields, to encounter disbelief, skepticism, scorn, and even hostility in the face of my persistence that child maltreatment is a major national problem that demands *massive action now*. And I can only think that all attempts to minimize this ugly disease and reduce it to statistics, "proving" it to be of small consequence, dangerously hamper all efforts to find a cure for it and possibly even preclude a solution.

There is no point in pretending, for our own comfort, that it does not exist. It does. Nor is there any point in publishing variously interpretable figures without seeking to apply them to the human beings they reflect. Too many academicians forget that the purpose of social studies is to seek some benefit for those being studied. They are more interested in their statistics than in the sick parent or in the physically or psychologically battered child.

Why this lack of interest, this skepticism, this reluctance to get to the facts behind the figures? I will say for the first time what I find myself obliged to say several times in the pages to come: I don't really know.

But it has something to do with an unwillingness to accept truth, to look ugliness in the eye, to draw upon our reserves of courage, and fight back. *Apathy* is a word that must be used, even though it has become as cheap as "involvement" and "dedication." The many instances of terrible injustices to children—atrocities, battering, starvation, abandonment—in nations that are at peace, just as much as in nations that are or have been at war, should shock all of us for more than a moment or two. But they don't. All too often these crimes are accepted simply as an illness of our society, a mere token of a situation that prevails throughout the world which cannot be solved because that is the way the world *is*. Well, must it be? Human apathy and indifference in the face of cruelty to others, especially to children, is hardly a new phenomenon, but it does not have to be a permanent part of our lives. It had better not be, if life is to be worth living, if the shambles that we have made of our world are ever to be pulled together. Civilized society has, time and again, remained silent, or at least cautiously muted, while millions of people were being tortured or murdered. Today, it does not seem remarkable—in view of the past—that the United States government or the state and local governments or the majority of our private citizens have not recognized and given witness to the rising crime of child abuse.

Thus we minimize the seriousness of the child-maltreatment syndrome, blame the phenomenon upon the illness in our society and tell ourselves that there is nothing we can do about it. At least, not much.

But the impossibility of finding an easy answer does not relieve us of the responsibility of trying to find real solutions. We will find no solution so long as we pretend there is no problem or so long as we sit around hoping for a miracle cure.

We have to seek multidimensional answers. No single, simple approach is going to work, least of all, the approach that nothing can or needs to be done. To date, the medical profession has been largely charged with the task of treating problem parents and their children, but the social and psychological aspects of child battering can no longer be overlooked. Treating an individual patient who neglects, batters, or kills a child is totally insufficient if it is not coupled with a simultaneous effort to ensure adequate rehabilitation of the social-environmental factors responsible for the production of the battering parent and the battered child. The troubled parents must be helped to recognize their intrinsic potentials as human beings. The responsibilty falls on all health professionals to provide the necessary treatment. We cannot continue to ignore this responsibility. Granted, we do not know all the answers to the question of what should be done, but our ignorance does not relieve us of the responsibility for seeking them and attending, to the best of our ability, to the social needs of the battered families. We must seek out what can be changed, what we can do to diminish the incidence of the child-maltreatment disease in all communities.

There is another area of difficulty in our search for a means of helping abusing parents and, through them, their children. In spite of our general apathy, or perhaps because of it, we don't like these parents. We find them offensive. And that's enough reason not to help them. Help their children, fine, but not *them*. Yet this attitude is nonsense. The situation is not saved and the disease is not attacked even if, happily, a child is spared from further maltreatment. We must go to the parents, to the families, to the surrounding circumstances which contribute to the illness. If we ignore the neglectful or battering parents because they go against our moral fiber, the problem does not simply cease to exist. Can we decide that these people are not worthy of help and turn our backs on them? Are we, as physicians or as lay members of society, to help only those whose illnesses we approve of? This is a moral judgment that we have no right to make. Our society cannot be healthy as long as parents and families, as well as children, are unhealthy; and the family units cannot be healthy so long as their social and economic difficulties remain unresolved.

We also have an unfortunate habit of generalizing, I suppose, to make things easier for ourselves. We can, perhaps, bring ourselves to help maltreating parents if we think of them as social problems to be solved in order to improve our own environment and rescue the battered child, but, at the same time, we tend to think of them all as monsters to be put behind bars. All right—some of them do monstrous things. But are we to consider all abusing and neglectful parents as monsters? Or should they be viewed as victims because of what was done to them in their own childhood, because of their own past and present environment, because of their unfortunate life-style and the crises associated with it? They are all victims of sorts, but they are not all alike. From one family to another, the maltreating parents have different backgrounds and different styles of living and different personalities. Their relationships toward their parents, husbands, wives, paramours, or other intimate associates differ. There are abusing parents whose problems surface unmistakably, and there are abusing parents who appear to be well adjusted enough to be indistinguishable (by measures presently available to us) from normal, unbattering parents. The range of maltreating parents is so great that it is a serious mistake to generalize in terms of diagnosis, treatment procedures, and evaluations of the therapy directed at any particular "type" of battering parent.

It has been amply demonstrated that social, cultural, and sexual characteristics are learned in the specific culture and society in which one is brought up and lives. We are, therefore, posed with a very serious, complex, and, at the same time, extremely interesting social and environmental problem in terms of the development of different people and the different ways in which they grow up to establish their roles as fathers and mothers. These individual differences may very well determine whether one type of parent may be helped by one type of therapy and another may not. Perhaps parents with purely psychological problems are easier to help than parents whose problems are environmental and economic as well. Perhaps parents from the ghettos have too many reasons for not wanting to be helped and are even afraid of being helped. They have, perhaps, too many reasons for having gotten into the situation of striking out to permit any hope of solution in their time—especially when they are "treated" by people who do not really care and are only too ready to consign these parents to the trash heap. But we must understand all these differences when we try to treat battering parents.

Those of us who do see the problem are stunned by what we see. We do not know where to turn. We see our efforts failing. We try to challenge the sociomedical disease of child maltreatment, and we see a tendency to ostracize or give up on the "difficult" parents because we tend to regard them as slightly less than human. But we cannot approach them fastidiously with a ten-foot pole. These are *people*—people in terrible need. We should legitimately expect limitations in our treatment and in our results until we know more about our patients and are able to treat the social conditions that have helped to make them what they are. But our ignorance must not prevent us from trying. Giving of ourselves is a very important part of trying. It is not our business to reform or punish but to heal. In this particular disease, there can be no cure without motivation. The one most important aspect of treatment is motivation: what the patients-parents can see as their own need to respond to treatment; what they can understand of how much it means to them; what they can do to look after themselves and their children; what they can realistically hope to achieve in order to better their lives and their futures. If there is motivation and cooperation on the part of the parents to keep the family unit together for the good of all, with the sincere help of professionals and paraprofessionals, the chances of a successful outcome are not bad. But without motivation, there can be little cooperation. Without cooperation, all the professional and paraprofessional efforts in this area are an exercise in futility.

Yet what motivation and what hope do we offer the abusing parents of today, and what comfort do we offer their children? Very little, as long as we insist upon pretending—while the children die—that the problem they pose is exaggerated or even nonexistent.

I find it very strange that a society which professes to care for its children can spend billions on research for cancer, chronic lung diseases, heart problems, and on the Pentagon, while virtually ignoring the greatest crippler and killer of our children—child abuse and neglect.

If the activist youth of today are looking for a challenge worthy of their mettle, here it is. I hope they rise to the occasion.

# Introduction

Vincent J. Fontana, physician, pediatrician, and humanitarian—the author of this significant and informative book—is, without doubt, the most knowledgeable, articulate, and effective spokesman on the shocking subject of child abuse, maltreatment, and neglect. His great interest in and profound concern about this serious medical and societal problem have compelled him, out of a sense of indignation, to do everything possible to publicize the increasing number of almost unbelievable acts of physical and mental cruelty inflicted on infants and children by parents and guardians throughout this country. He discusses the origins and basic causes of child abuse, the patterns of physical injury, and the often prolonged and permanently damaging psychological effects on the young, helpless victims.

Dr. Fontana points up the previous reluctance on the part of the public at large, the medical and legal professions, social service organizations, law enforcement agencies, the judiciary, and the legislature to suspect or believe that those responsible for these criminal acts are generally the parents, many of whom require counseling and psychiatric care. While such overt and covert cruelties occur in some apparently stable families—due to the psychological and emotional inadequacies of one or both of the spouses, related to their own unfortunate childhood disciplinary experiences—most are encountered in disrupted or nonexistent family situations. These are families in which a stepfather or stepmother or natural parent is responsible—including families in which one parent has died or abandoned the family and the other parent cohabits out of wedlock with a substitute, changing the partner for convenience or out of caprice. Narcotics addiction in one or both parents also often results in abuse or neglect of the children.

A substantial number of abused and neglected infants and children die. All such deaths should be reported to an official agency, either a medical examiner's office, or in those jurisdictions in which the ancient system still exists, a coronor's office. Both agencies by law are responsible for investigating all sudden, unexpected, medically unattended, suspicious, violent, and unusual deaths. These official agencies are responsible for looking into the facts and circumstances surrounding and preceding the deaths and determining the cause of death by postmortem examination.

Although the law governing the operation of a medical examiner's or coroner's office does not specifically state that an autopsy must be included in the postmortem examination, it does authorize either official to include one. The medical examiner in New York City, who in addition to being a doctor of medicine is also "a skilled pathologist and microscopist," performs such autopsies himself. The coroner, who is usually a layman, is authorized to see that autopsies are performed by a competent pathologist, whenever there is a reasonable basis and need for their performance. The law also requires and expects prompt and intelligent notification of appropriate agencies—including the police, the district attorney, and the bureau of child welfare—of the existence or discovery of any suspicious injury, evidence of neglect, or obvious homicide which may first be revealed by the autopsy. There is an important basic principle in legal medicine: that a victim of traumatic injury may be seriously and even fatally injured without manifesting immediate disability and without external evidence of violence. The latter may only be discovered by a thorough and carefully performed autopsy. This is especially true in many deaths from child abuse.

In the city of New York, all deaths in the previously mentioned categories, including children and infants, must be reported to the medical examiner's office, but in many jurisdictions in New York State and elsewhere in the United States, reporting is lax, haphazard, and almost optional, depending on the degree of suspicion or concern of the one who encounters the death. In this city, failure to report a death to the medical examiner's office is punishable as a misdemeanor. It is the policy of the medical examiner's office to include an autopsy in every postmortem examination of the body of all infants and children. Because of this, deaths from unsuspected child abuse or maltreatment are not overlooked. In many other jurisdictions. the absence of external gross traumatic injury provides a basis for the assumption and erroneous conclusion that the death under consideration is natural. Such violent deaths escape detection in the absence of an autopsy.

Dr. Fontana emphasizes this failure to report and investigate sudden deaths of apparently healthy infants and children. Many deaths from criminal child abuse remain undiscovered throughout the country, especially in jurisdictions that function under a lax coroner's or medical examiner's system that is not well organized or adequately staffed. Reporting of all these deaths should be mandatory, as should be the official investigation and postmortem examination, with complete autopsy by a competent forensic pathologist. Suspicious and violent causes of deaths revealed in this way must be reported to appropriate law enforcement agencies, police, district attorneys, and social service departments.

Sudden and unexpected deaths of apparently healthy infants, found dead in the home, should be carefully and tactfully investigated at the scene, and this investigation followed by postmortem examination and autopsy—with chemical, microscopic, and other studies—before concluding that the death is natural. In all such cases, it is important that an autopsy is included to reassure the parents that the death was natural, but without evident cause, and to protect them from unwarranted suspicions or accusation of neglect. An autopsy also serves to notify parents if a definite disease entity, such as a congenital malformation or demonstrable infection, was the cause of death.

Dr. Fontana's informative and educational book on child abuse should be read by all concerned citizens and especially by medical students, law students, every physician and pediatrician, every lawyer, law enforcement officer; by social service workers (and others engaged in the field of child welfare), attorneys, and members of the legislative, executive, and judicial branches of government. All medical examiners, coroners, forensic and hospital pathologists responsible for the official investigation of deaths from child abuse, neglect, and maltreatment will find it most helpful in their work. It is their opportunity and responsibility to discover, for the first time, deaths of children from this often unsuspected cause and to confirm and elucidate the findings in the obviously violent deaths.

This book is a tremendous contribution to the knowledge and understanding of the entire subject so essential for effective preventive measures.

MILTON HELPERN, M.D.
Chief Medical Examiner
City of New York

Professor and Chairman
Department of Forensic Medicine
New York University School
of Medicine

# CHAPTER ONE

# The Most Deadly Sin

Some day, maybe, there will exist a well-informed,
well-considered, and yet fervent public conviction that the most deadly of all possible sins is the
mutilation of a child's spirit; for such mutilation
undercuts the life principle of trust, without which
every human act, may it feel ever so good and seem
ever so right, is prone to perversion by destructive
forms of conscientiousness.

*Erik Erikson*
*Journal of the American Medical Association* (1972)

SOMEWHERE A CHILD IS CRYING. Her name is Connie, and she
is six years old. She was stolen by her mother.

Connie hadn't even been born when a county domestic-
relations court took her ten-month-old sister, Bettina, away
from the natural mother, Mrs. Sally Colby, after a finding of
neglect. Bettina had infected injuries about her eyes and ears.
Emergency room doctors felt she might have been abused, but
they had no proof. It was hard to believe that young Mrs.
Colby, a lonely divorcee who appeared to be terribly anxious
about Bettina, could have deliberately hurt her child. Neglected
her, perhaps, while she was trying to earn a living but hurt her,
no. Nevertheless, Bettina was placed with foster parents.

A few months later, Sally Colby became Mrs. Lewis Erhard

and settled down with her new husband in a modest, but comfortable, ranch-style house. They were very happy when Connie was born. Neighbors saw them as a warm little family group in a cosy, well-ordered home.

After a while, the Erhards started petitioning for the return of Bettina, and, when Bettina was four, the court sent her home.

One night, about a year later, an alarmed neighbor heard bloodcurdling screams from the Erhard house and called the police. Erhard was not at home when they arrived, but Mrs. Erhard was home, sprawled out dead-drunk on the sofa. The place was well-furnished and impeccably clean. A few objects had been overturned and broken. The children were found whimpering in their bedroom. Connie wasn't in bad shape, starved, slightly bruised, terrified. But Bettina's belly was swollen with malnutrition. Her body was a mass of contusions, lacerations, puncture wounds, sores, and old scars. There were rope marks around her ankles and wrists, and a gag mark across her mouth. One foot was so severely ulcerated that she could scarcely walk. Her hair was falling out, her skin deathly white, her eyes lifeless and dull.

In the course of the investigation and trial that followed, it was learned that the Erhards often bound and gagged Bettina before going off to their respective jobs. Little Connie had been spared that treatment, but she had not been spared the sight of her sister being tied up and whipped with steel wire or struck with sticks and high-heeled shoes. She had not been spared blows, or having to eat off the floor with her sister, when they were fed at all, or the terror that reigned in the household with the pleasant facade.

A jury sentenced Mrs. Erhard to three years in a women's reformatory. Charges against Lewis Erhard were, for some reason, dropped. One evening a moving van arrived. The contents of the nice little ranch house were removed and taken away, no one knows where. Erhard vanished simultaneously. The two little girls, Bettina, now five, and Connie, three, were placed with a foster family.

Mrs. Erhard served her time and was released, a contrite

and chastened woman. She immediately started proceedings to regain custody of Connie. She wasn't interested in Bettina and didn't even want to see her. It was Connie she wanted.

In a series of hearings, Mrs. Erhard eloquently pleaded her case and impressed the court with her sincerity. As a result, she was permitted visiting rights to the foster home in which her two children lived. At the judge's insistence, her visits were to be unsupervised so that she might have the best possible chance to establish a normal, relaxed relationship with her favorite child.

Bettina screamed, ran, and hid when she saw her mother coming, but that didn't matter. Mrs. Erhard didn't want to see her anyway. She wanted Connie. But little Connie, a bright six-year-old, was wary. She backed away, clutched her foster mother, and looked at her natural mother with dubious, frightened eyes.

But Mrs. Erhard persevered. Once a week, for more than three months, she came to visit Connie. After the first few visits, she would take the little girl out for several hours at a time, and bring her back. Connie seemed to have mixed feelings about these excursions with her natural mother. Before each visit she would be half-fascinated, half-afraid. Sometimes she came back happy, sometimes oddly silent. As time went by, Connie's foster mother began to sense a change in her. The child seemed nervous. Uneasily, the woman wondered what she should do about it.

She started wondering too late. One day Mrs. Erhard took Connie out for a longer trip than usual. Neither of them came back. They disappeared. Perhaps they joined Lewis Erhard. Nobody knows.

Bettina's scars have not yet healed. She limps. She bears the marks of many old wounds. She is withdrawn, timid, confused. Perhaps in time, with love, she will recover.

What scars does Connie have by now? Where is she? Of all those people walking down the street, which one is Mrs. Erhard? What is she doing to Connie? What has she done with her?

Look down any street. Look any day. You will, without knowing it, see a Mrs. Erhard or a Mr. Anyname: a parent with a normal outer face who smiles at passersby and goes home to brutalize a child. Which one is it? It is not one, but many.

Bettina is not just one child. Connie is not just one child. They are both *real* children. But they represent thousands. There are many Bettinas, tens of thousands of them, already scarred, in many cases beyond help or hope. There are many Connies, tens of thousands of them, all in terrible danger, many of them marked for an ugly and early death. Connie may now even be dying.

Whatever may be the public conviction of a seemingly distant future, time and tradition still support the proposition that the mutilation of a child's body, as well as his spirit, is perfectly acceptable adult business.

Tales of children being maltreated and murdered by their parents abound in myth, legend, and literature. The altars of Saturn, merry god of the harvest, were stained with the blood of his own offspring. King Aun of ancient Sweden is said to have sacrificed nine of his sons to Odin at Uppsala in order to prolong his own life nine years at a time. Medea, sorceress-princess of Colchis, murdered her two sons by Jason in revenge for his preference for another woman. In ancient Greece, there were kingly houses of great antiquity in which it was apparently customary to sacrifice the eldest sons when the royal sire's life was threatened or when the royal sire himself was supposed to have been the sacrifice but managed to delegate the terrible responsibility. Throughout the Bible there runs a theme of child murder and abuse, of the destruction of the firstborn, of the laying of a child's bones into the foundation of a new edifice, of a child chosen as a burnt offering to a capricious God. Abraham bound his son Isaac and placed him on a sacrificial altar, with every intent of putting him to death, and was surprised when his hand was stayed. (The divine intervention that saved the boy is rare indeed in the history of child abuse.)

In early times, babies were almost routinely massacred at birth in parts of Polynesia, East Africa, and South America because they were cumbersome on the march or otherwise in the way. Mexicans of ancient days, viewing their maize crop symbolically, perceived the maize as a living being going through a life cycle from conception to death—seedtime to harvest—and represented this being, for sacrificial purposes intended to promote the growth of the crop, as a living person. Thus newborn babies were sacrificed when the maize was sown, slightly older children when it sprouted, and still older children as the maize grew. Logically, old men were sacrificed when it was time for reaping.

But stronger even than the theme of sacrifice is the theme of the child as nuisance to be abandoned or as chattel to be used. Greeks and Romans both abandoned infants, consigning them to death by exposure by leaving them on a cold, wolf-haunted mountainside or casting them adrift on a river. In past civilizations and in various countries—some not long past or far away —children have time and again been deliberately mutilated by their parents, their eyes put out or their hands chopped off, so that they might better inspire sympathy and thus be more successful in their enforced role as youthful beggars.

There are countries today where infants are discarded at birth because the family already has too many mouths to feed, because the soil or home supposedly cannot support more life, because the child is defective in some way, because the child was unwanted in the first place, because the child interferes with an existing life-style. There are still countries in the world in which children are mutilated for a variety of reasons, severely beaten as an overdose of discipline or out of savage whim. There are still countries in the modern world in which children are assumed to be pieces of parental property, to be treated or disposed of at the parents' will. One of those countries is ours.

The child-destructive instincts of the human race do not seem to have changed a great deal with the passage of centuries. In some societies, it was a regular practice to destroy all physically handicapped babies. Although this is not, today, a regular, inevitable practice, it does occur. Infanticide, as a form of birth control, is common throughout history. Countless times through the countless years, mothers—perhaps abandoned themselves, disturbed of mind, made desperate through circumstance—have killed their newborn babies or bundled them up and thrown them away.

Infanticide as we know it—the killing of newborn infants by suffocation, drowning, exposure to the elements, or throwing out with the garbage—was widely accepted in recent societies. It was almost a popular pastime in the seventeenth century when unwanted children were easily and casually disposed of without guilt or recrimination, fear or prosecution. It is less popular today, for reasons which may be no more noble or humane than fear of being caught or prosecuted, but it is still with us as we will see.

Not ancient times or the seventeenth century but the nine-teenth was the nadir in the exploitation of the child. What happened then was not infanticide nor abandonment, but it may well have been then next best thing: the unwanted pro-perty/child was put to work under terrible circumstances. He was scarcely treated better when he had been deliberately crippled for the sake of being a better beggar. In the early decades of the 1800s, he worked in the mines and sweatshops of Great Britain. In this country, around the turn of the cen-tury, he did the same type of slave labor in the same kinds of places. He and his brothers and sisters were little more than babies. They worked long hours, they were chained to their posts, they were permitted to eat but little, and they were urged on to further effort by the blows of their overseers. Of course their abusers were not their natural parents; but the abuse could only have occurred because their parents permitted it and, at least by default, encouraged it. After all, the rest of the family had to live. Let the child work until it had worked itself to death. Then it would no longer bring in any income, but neither would it be a problem.

We might well be astonished by the callous indifference shown these babies and five-year-olds and ten-year-olds if we were not ourselves somehow inured to the horror of it in our twentieth-century world.

But it did not pass unnoticed. The treatment of children in the mines of Great Britain was observed and indignantly des-cribed in 1842 by the Earl of Shaftesbury, who concluded that child labor conditions, as well as the fact of labor itself, were intolerable.

Yet the exploitation of children as laborers continued. The locale changed from the mines to the factories, but the labor and the frightful conditions continued. The hours got longer, the work more intolerable, the children even more slave-driven.

Of these small slaves in the factories, Elizabeth Barrett Browning wrote:

> Do ye hear the children weeping, O my brothers,
> Ere the sorrow comes with years. . .
> They are weeping in the playtime of the others,
> In the country of the free.
> *"The Cry of the Children"*

The child's cry, ineffective then as it is now, was a reproach to humanity—and we may not have listened to it yet. There are ways of exploiting children, of hurting them beyond remedy, that are at least as appalling as working them to death.

We can say that, in the twentieth century, the special needs of children have begun to be recognized. There have been advances to the benefit of children in medicine, science, and social conditions, if not in the human heart. Society has recognized the need to supply children with the care, protection, and education they deserve and must have; but, even though they "must have" these things, the needs of many are still unfulfilled.

A little over one hundred years ago, the few people who paid any attention at all to these things observed that the abandonment of babies had reached crisis proportions in the city of New York. This was 1869, and the country was still in the grip of post-Civil War malaise. Perhaps that had something to do with it; there are always attendant factors to such phenomena as child maltreatment that do not necessarily have to do with human instinct or individual aberration. Wartime and postwar conditions always bring with them considerable stress. New Yorkers of the times called it an epidemic: children were literally being found in the streets after having been left bundled on doorsteps or thrown into gutters or tossed into trash cans. While they were not all dead, the intent was obvious. These were infants. They were incapable of helping themselves. If they were thrown half-dead into the garbage, it was obvious that they were not intended to survive and that those who had abandoned them didn't care.

The newspapers and various public-spirited citizens expressed their horror and demanded that something be done about this wave of infanticide or child abandonment. (The distinction between murder and total neglect, which may take the shape of abandonment, is often blurred. It was blurred during this period and frequently is today.)

It was Archbishop (later Cardinal) John McCloskey who made the most stirring plea for help in salvaging these small victims, and it was the Sisters of Charity of New York who took up the challenge. With two companions to help her, Sister Mary Irene Fitzgibbon managed—in spite of severely limited finances—to acquire a small brownstone. At 17 East Twelfth Street, she laid the foundation of the New York Foundling Hospital. No doubt she had her dreams at the time. Surely she must have had some hope that in the future the Foundling Hospital might be more than a modest home, as yet untenanted, for New York's cast-off babies. But the poverty and privation of the foundling home's early days was such that she could only have had the slightest glimmer of hope.

Sister Mary Irene, Sister Theresa Vincent, and Sister Ann Aloysia opened their doors on October 11, 1869, putting a little crib at the entrance of the brownstone and advertising the function of the home through the editorials of the New York City newspapers. Perhaps, Sister Mary Irene must have thought, some of the desperate mothers would decide to drop their burdens into that little crib instead of into the city's garbage cans; perhaps they would be just as pleased to be rid of them alive as dead. Perhaps it would be possible to save at least a few unwanted infants.

And it was. From the day it was put outside the brownstone, that crib was rarely empty. Often babies were simply left there, nameless, without comment, but often, too, notes would be left with them: "My baby's name is Bobbie. I can't take care of him." "This is Mary. Here is a dollar bill to feed her." "I have no money to look after him. This is Tommy's formula."

Within a matter of months, literally hundreds of children were being brought to the New York Foundling Hospital. Its major aim of attempting to arrest child murder by providing a refuge for unwanted babies seemed to be paying off. It soon became apparent that the prime objective of the Foundling Hospital was being realized: the appalling rate of infanticide in New York City took a downward plunge soon after its doors were opened. Sister Mary Irene was kept constantly busy and was obliged to add two new members to her staff.

On Saturday, November 13, 1869, the *World*, a New York newspaper, carried this story:

## ABANDONED INFANTS
### *The Waifs of Sin in the New York Foundling Hospital on Twelfth Street—Visit to the Institution*

In a select part of East Twelfth Street, between Fifth Avenue and University Place, there is an unpretending mansion which bears the significant sign—"The Home for Foundlings." It is the only institution which has yet been established in this vast city to arrest the crime of child murder, by providing a refuge for abandoned babes. Within the short period of thirty days, fifteen little waifs of sin have been left on the steps and in the area of the building, and they were at once brought inside, cleaned, dressed, and provided with cribs and all the maternal care they required. Yesterday afternoon a reporter of the *World* visited this novel creation of pious philanthropy, and, on reaching the rooms devoted to the nursery, he found thirteen foundlings, whose ages varied from ten to twenty-eight days, quietly sleeping or devoting their attention to infantile bottles, filled with milk. Each babe has had an interesting history. Two of the number had been left, by fugitive mothers, on a stormy night, at the door of the home. One was wrapped in filthy rags, the other in a carriage blanket, and both were drenched with rain. They were taken inside; but the door had scarcely been closed when the bell was rung, and Sister Irene, who had charge of the home, rushed to open it. She found a poor woman extending her child in her arms toward her, and she received it. The mother then fled. The child, when brought upstairs, was examined. Around its neck was a label, giving its name and age; and pinned to its dress was a little package, which, when opened, was found to contain two one-dollar bills.

Four Sisters aid the good founder in her maternal work—and they furnish "the bottle" to the objects of their care every two hours. The home will accommodate about fifty foundlings, and there are thirteen there at present. In order to prevent any possible injury to the babes who may be left, a crib has been placed in the vestibule of the building, where they can be laid by the fallen sisters and destitute mothers who will thus be saved the terrible crime of infanticide. A number of ladies meet twice a week to sew and make dresses for the infants, and an effort is to be made to raise funds to increase its usefulness. So far, the contributions to this noble work have been comparatively few, but when the objects of the home are generally known the funds necessary to sustain it will doubtless be forthcoming.

The sanguine reporter from the *World* turned out, oddly enough, to be right. Child abuse has never been a popular charitable cause, which is somewhat surprising in a nation that supposedly loves children almost as well as animals. New Yorkers of those days did not exactly turn out their pockets for the benefit of the abandoned. But, when called upon and exhorted by the *World*, champion of the children's cause, and offered some entertainment to ease the pain of giving, they flocked to the rescue.

The events of the year October 1869 through October 1870 had graphically brought home the tragic need for an expanded Foundling Asylum. In that first year, the Foundling Hospital had received 1,060 infants, 61 percent of whom were *in extremis* on admission. With the brownstone home capable of accommodating only fifty babies at a time, it was obvious that help was needed. The rate of abandonment, infanticide, and lesser abuse must have been staggering, for over 1,000 dead and dying children were picked off the streets of New York in the 1869-70s. How many maltreated or discarded children did not come to light, were never found—as the case is even today?

A "Fair in Aid of the Foundling Asylum" was held in the last week of November 1870, in a bid to "rescue the innocents." The *World* reported its culmination as follows:

The fair at the Twenty-second Regiment Armory, in aid of the projected asylum for foundlings, closed last evening. The scenes inside the building from 8 until 12 o'clock were very lively. Auctioneers were crying at the top of their voices on every hand, bells ringing, the "wheel of fortune" turning, and the lucky winners of prizes shouting for joy. The band remained in attendance until the crowd deserted the building. All the goods were disposed of, some of them at cost prices. The total receipts of the fair amounted to $55,000. The remaining $45,000 to complete the sum required before getting an appropriation from the Legislature, will have to be made up from concerts and theatrical entertainments. No one doubts the ability of the managers to accomplish whatever they may undertake to do in earnest.

The "managers" evidently rose to the challenge. By the end of 1870, the Foundling Asylum was moved to more commodious quarters in Washington Square Park. In less than a year, however, these new quarters also proved to be inadequate. Another move was made in 1873, this time to 175 East Sixty-eighth Street. Here "The Foundling" settled in for eighty-five years, expanding its services to include a shelter for unwed mothers and a foster-home department. But in the 1940s, well before the end of those eighty-five years, it became apparent that the Foundling's services were again on the verge of outstripping its premises. The facilities were insufficient to meet what was apparently a growing need. A major construction program and yet another move seemed indicated.

But let us go back briefly to the 1890s, when the "epidemic" years were long since past. In 1892, not by any means a bad year in the history of infanticide and abandonment of infants, some 200 foundlings and 100 dead infants were found in the streets of New York City. It was a pattern that seemed to defy change, although it had shown considerable reduction. In the first ninety years of its existence, the Foundling sheltered 107, 286 infants, providing medical care and a temporary home until the child could be placed with foster parents. The initial task of the rescuers was not only to combat the effect of the babies' exposure to the elements but to treat the acute ocular conditions. intestinal disorders, diphtheria, pertussis, and syphilis from which they were often found to be suffering. The characteristics of the abandoned child had, by 1890 or thereabouts, become quite familiar.

In the meantime, another problem had surfaced, apparently distinct from infanticide and abandonment but not, in the long run, so very different. This was the phenomenon of deliberate physical abuse and neglect—not a matter of infanticide but of calculated, inhuman cruelty that had a good chance of seriously damaging or eventually killing the child. (Tragically, the cruelty *is* human.)

In 1874, a nurse named Etta Wheeler was going about her rounds when her attention was called to the plight of a nine-year-old child named Mary Ellen. Concerned neighbors in the tenement house where the child lived told the nurse that, in their opinion, Mary Ellen was being seriously maltreated by her parents. Nurse Wheeler investigated and found the child chained to a bedpost in her parents' apartment. Mary Ellen had apparently been beaten often, for her body gave evidence of severe bruises in various stages of development, and she was pitifully undernourished from her diet of bread and water. Etta Wheeler and interested church workers promptly brought the matter to the attention of police authorities, including the district attorney, only to discover that they could take no legal action to remove the child from her dangerous environment. There was no law to cover such a situation, no agency with the power to interfere. The parents, exercising their absolute right to bring up their child in the manner of their choosing, literally had the whip hand.

Out of desperation, the nurse and her church worker friends appealed to the Society for the Prevention of Cruelty to Animals on the grounds that the child was a member of the animal kingdom and was being accorded worse treatment than the lowest of animals and, therefore, qualified for the society's protection. The society agreed that Mary Ellen's case fell under the laws governing the treatment of animals and had the child removed from her home on those grounds.

Mary Ellen was brought into court on a stretcher. She was weak, ill, and emaciated, with all the signs of vicious treatment still evident in her stunted body; but she was alive and safe. Miraculously, and ironically, she was salvaged through the efforts of a society dedicated to the welfare of animals. It was a shock to the citizenry to realize that the question of cruelty to animals had been regarded as more important than the prevention of cruelty to children. One year later, in 1875, the first Society for the Prevention of Cruelty to Children was organized in New York. Many other societies were founded in various parts of the country in the years to come. For many years, these private organizations and the few foundling homes that began to emerge in some of our major cities were the only institutions dedicated to child protection. City, state, and federal governments were unconcerned as was the public at large. Sombody else was taking care of it, whatever "it" was— and "it" was surely a minor problem.

Unfortunately, it wasn't. Since our initial observation of the fact of cruelty to children, reported cases of severe physical abuse and neglect have shown marked increases annually.

During the close of the nineteenth century and well into the twentieth, small children—newborn infants, tiny babies, toddlers, and growing youngsters—were being brought into hospitals by parents who told tales of bizarre accidents to explain the multiplicity of injuries riddling their children's bodies. The children were "accident prone" (a neat phrase coined by physicians and exploited by abusing parents): they fell off chairs, they slipped on rugs, they tripped and hit their heads against walls, they bumped into things, they leaned against hot stoves, they skidded down the front steps, they got thrown by their roller skates, they caught their legs in the bars of their cribs, they got punched by the kid next door, and anyway, they bruised easily. They did all manner of trivial things and produced upon themselves the most astonishing variety of bruises and bumps, welts and fractures—and they did it again and again.

It was difficult for physicians to believe these stories, but even more difficult for them to entertain the possibility that parents could do anything so abhorrent as to deliberately abuse their children.

Yet the suspicion, slow in arising and reluctantly nourished, received early support from radiologists. As long ago as the turn of the century, X-rays of injured infants revealed a pattern of fractures and other lesions that defied explanation in terms of the children's medical histories. In 1946, radiologist John Caffey first reported in the *American Journal of Roentgenology* the frequency of subdural hematoma in infants who also showed fractures of the long bones—a sinister combination of injuries and scarcely one likely to have resulted from accident. Caffey described six patients with subdural hematoma who exhibited a total of twenty-three fractures and four contusions of the long bones. In not a single one of these cases was there a history of injury to reasonably explain the skeletal lesions or clinical or X-ray evidence of a skeletal disease which would predispose to pathological fractures. Caffey was extremely cautious in the evaluation of his findings, still reluctant to accept the idea of parental responsibility or point the finger of blame. Later he did offer, as a possible cause of this association of symptoms, parental neglect and abuse. How else explain the inexplicable?

Alerted by Caffey and others who also noted the relationship between long bone fractures and subdural hematoma, radiologists began to observe another pattern in the X-rays of mysteriously injured children: a number of inflicted traumas in various stages of repair. This indicated that a series of accidents or incidents of some sort or another had occurred over a period of time and had resulted in injuries at different times; and that these injuries had remained untreated and had been healed, or were in the process of being healed, by the body itself. The question was: Why had the injuries been untreated?

The next and most startling breakthrough was contributed by Dr. C. Henry Kempe of the University of Colorado and the Colorado General Hospital. During a single day in November 1961, Kempe reported, there were four infants in the Colorado General Hospital alone who could be described as battered. Two of the four died in the hospital from injuries to the central nervous system. One was released to his parents in satisfactory condition and died suddenly one month later of undetermined causes—which Kempe and, subsequently, other physicians, found not to be an unusual circumstance with children once-beaten and returned home. The fourth child is presumably alive and well—but three deaths out of four children with the same set of symptoms in one hospital on the same day surely is a coincidence to make one pause and think.

Dr. Kempe did pause and think. He coined a new term to describe his diagnosis of the children's condition: the *battered-child syndrome*. And, with his colleagues, he undertook a nationwide survey—the first of its kind—of hospitals and law enforcement agencies in an attempt to determine how many cases of physical abuse were reported in the course of a year. The results were published in the *Journal of the American Medical Association* (July 7, 1962, pp. 105-112). Seventy-one major hospitals had reported a total of 302 cases of the battered-child syndrome. Thirty-three of these children had died, and 85 had sustained permanent brain damage. Further, 77 district attorneys reported encountering (if not necessarily proving) 447 cases of child abuse. (In that same year, Dr. Harold Jacobziner of the New York City Department of Health observed that some 4,000 cases of alleged child neglect were annually coming to the attention of this city's courts. There is, of course, a distinction between neglect and abuse, but often it is negligible.)

Dr. Kempe and his group of Denver colleagues reported in their landmark paper an alarming incidence of children admitted to hospitals with traumatic injuries for which the parents were unable to provide other than the most specious of explanations. Example: A child upon examination is found to have numerous bruises and abrasions of the head and trunk, laceration of the lip, a healed burn pattern on the buttocks, healed linear scars on the trunk and extremities, a healed fracture (previously unreported) of the femur, a recent fracture of the skull, contusion of the brain, and subdural hemorrhage. Parents are completely mystified as to how the child could possibly have acquired the burn scars and other healed or partly healed surface wounds. But—question—what about the contusion of the brain, the skull fracture, and the subdural hemorrhage? Answer—He fell from his potty chair.

As Kempe pointed out, it is difficult to diagnose the condition in view of the fact that the abuse more often than not is inflicted on children too young to speak for themselves. "If the child could only speak," he commented in his paper, "the physician would be quickly led to the proper diagnosis of abuse. To the informed physician, the bones tell a story the child is too young or too frightened to tell."

As an immediate result of Kempe's initial survey, hospitals were alerted to look out for possible cases of child battering. One hospital in his survey had reported, for the survey year, no cases of the battered-child syndrome; one year later, it reported over fifty. How many might they have missed or not recognized during all the previous years?

The *battered-child syndrome* derived its descriptive name from the nature of the child's injuries, which commonly include abrasions, bruises, lacerations, bites (human bites), hematoma, brain injury, deep body injury, (often with fractured ribs or injuries to the liver or kidneys), "pulled" joints (often of the arm or shoulder), combinations of fractures of the arms, legs, skull, and ribs, burns and scalds, and marks left after strapping or tying up. Roughly speaking, the injuries generally result from knocking the child about, beating or whipping it with the nearest object, throwing it around like a pillow—frequently across the room—pulling and twisting an arm or leg, or slamming the child on the floor or against a wall —literally battering it.

But as time went by and the ingenuity of parents became better known, it was discovered that there is more to battering than battery, that there is scarcely any limit to the weapons used or to what parents are capable of doing to their children. Just about every conceivable type of injury has been encountered, and parents have used almost every conceivable type of weapon.

Parents bash, lash, beat, flay, stomp, suffocate, strangle, gut-punch, choke with rags or hot pepper, poison, crack heads open, slice, rip, steam, fry, boil, dismember. They use fists, belt buckles, straps, hairbrushes, lamp cords, sticks, baseball bats, rulers, shoes and boots, lead or iron pipes, bottles, brick walls, bicycle chains, pokers, knives, scissors, chemicals, lighted cigarettes, boiling water, steaming radiators, and open gas flames.

It was also found that children who came to a hospital with battering symptoms once would almost inevitably be brought back again and again with similar injuries—until the time would come when they were not brought in any more. Perhaps the parents had started hospital shopping, or there was no longer a child to bring in. At the same time, examining physicians and pediatric radiologists were observing that their small patients were seldom victims of only one or two injuries at a time but a multiplicity of them. Commonly, there are multiple bruises. (A British physician, Professor Keith Simpson, has reported finding seventy-four skin bruises on one child.) In one typical case, a child was brought to the hospital with numerous bruises of the face, head and neck, a lacerated lip, a fractured rib, laceration of the liver, and contusions of the lung, mesentery, and small intestine. He died of his internal injuries. In another, the battered child was found to have thirty broken bones. However, she did not die of these injuries; she died of brain hemorrhage. She had, supposedly, "fallen downstairs."

The presenting stories told by parents are another common, almost invariable, feature of the syndrome. "She fell downstairs": Broke thirty bones, covered herself in bruises and lacerations, fractured her skull, and died of subdural hematoma? "He fell from his potty chair." This child, already mentioned, was sixteen months old at the time of his "accident." The mother, when confronted with evidence of guilt for her son's death—even if only by negligence—explained that she had had to discipline the child for having "wet his pants." The discipline consisted of placing the child on a gas burner and beating him vigorously about the head and body both by hand and with a stick.

"He messed and wet his pants" is a common reason given for hurting, even killing, a child. So are "he cried too much," "he had temper tantrums," "he was crying at feeding time," "he wouldn't eat his food," " he messed his pants, and he spit out his food," "he smeared his feces," "he drank from his brother's bottle," and again and again and again, "he wouldn't stop crying . . . he wouldn't stop crying." (In one case he wouldn't stop crying because his arm had recently been deliberately broken, and it hurt.) These trivial excuses clearly refer to that one, final irritation or unbearable crisis situation, the fatal provocation, that precipitated the act of battering. It is equally clear that they have scarcely anything to do with the *real* reason for the violence.

The battered-child syndrome encompasses not only physical injury to the child—often of such nature that the radiographic signs are too specific to be confused with anything else—but also a number of other features. First, the child is usually less than three years old. Second, the violence against the child is almost always a persistent or recurrent rather than an isolated act. Third, the abuse is committed by one or both of the parents (usually just one, with the other bearing passive witness) or a guardian, such as a stepfather, mother's lover, foster parent, older sibling, or baby-sitter. Fourth, the perpetrators often fail to report the injuries or only do so when they become panicky over the extent of the injuries and possible police action should the child die. Fifth, the parents will almost invariably claim ignorance of how the injuries could have occurred or offer some ludicrous explanation; further, the parents frequently attempt to cover their tracks by hospital-shopping (or -skipping, or -hopping), so that physicians in any one hospital would not become suspicious of the many "accidents" that befall the child. Sixth, the parents are tormented individuals of many sorts: angry, compulsive, rigidly authoritarian, lacking in warmth, passive, dependent, aggressive, guilt-ridden, self-destructive, brutal, psychotic, isolated, emotionally immature, unable to relate, of borderline intelligence, often people who were themselves abused as children. Some literally cry out for help, and others don't give a damn—but relatively few are the monsters and maniacs as nonabusers are inclined to think.

And seventh, sooner or later *half* of the abused children returned to an abusing parent will *die* of renewed abuse.

The Kempe survey had uncovered a blockbuster of a child-killing disease. In 1962, the *Journal of the American Medical Association* editorialized that, when the true incidence of child abuse becomes known, "it is likely that it will be found to be a more frequent case of death than such well-recognized and thoroughly studied diseases as leukemia, cystic fibrosis, and muscular dystrophy, and it may well rank with automobile accidents and the toxic and infectious encephalides as causes of acquired disturbances of the central nervous system."

In 1963, it was observed by R. Burns that for every reported case of child abuse, there must be at least a hundred that were not reported—that is to say, at least one hundred untreated, suffering children for each abused child who did receive medical attention.

At the same time, Katherine Bain, M.D. (deputy chief, Children's Bureau, Department of Health, Education, and Welfare) was noting that there were repeated medical contacts in child-abuse cases in which the physician failed to report the case or take any action toward preventing the recurrence of injury to the child. There were several reasons for this:

The first is missed diagnosis. The syndrome of multiple skeletal injuries occurring over a period of time has only recently been the subject of scientific papers. Since few doctors are yet aware of this fairly definite complex, it is understandable that isolated or first injuries are missed. Even when strong evidence of this confronts the physician, he may find the idea that parents could abuse their children so abhorrent that he denies the facts. Often young physicians, interns, or residents especially, finding such behavior too bizarre for belief, try to explain the physical signs as manifestations of some rare disease. A further reason for the physician's failure to act in behalf of the child is the absence in some, fortunately only a few, of a social conscience. . . . . [And] probably many physicians have failed to act because they did not know what to do.
(Katherine Bain, M.D., "The Physically Abused Child" [*Pediatrics*, vol. 31], pp. 895-898.)

For any doctor, particularly a pediatrician, this was challenging material.

# CHAPTER TWO

# The Maltreatment Syndrome

LIKE SO MANY OTHER PHYSICIANS, I read Dr. Kempe's paper on the battered child. It was an eye-opener. He described the children battered by their parents; he discussed the number killed, the number irreparably damaged, the number of cases that went to court. He coined the term *battered-child syndrome* to describe what he had observed, and it quickly got a good deal of attention in medical journals.

I was fascinated and appalled by the content of Kempe's article. It made a dreadful sort of sense, and I hoped that it would alert every doctor in the United States to the disease of child battering. Certainly, I was going to be increasingly on the alert.

By the time "The Battered-Child Syndrome" was published, I had been appointed medical director of the New York Foundling Hospital by Francis Cardinal Spellman. When I became associated with it, some ninety years after its founding, it was still combating infanticide and providing homes for abandoned children, but on a much larger scale. Today, more than one-hundred years after Sister Mary Irene placed the crib in the vestibule, the Foundling Hospital is performing the same tasks for the same reasons. But it is as if we've come nowhere in the course of a century. We read of the baby who was born, unwanted in the bathroom, whose mother stuffed its mouth with toilet paper, slashed the child's throat and eventually tried to flush it away. We read of the hour-old infant crushed in a garbage truck before the sanitation men could turn the grinder off. The latter case was a "particularly grisly incident," observed the *New York Post* (March 22, 1972, p. 39), slightly over a century after the *World* reported on the new asylum for abandoned infants, "but it was not surprising" that: "Infants have been found dead and alive in past years in trash heaps, garbage cans and incinerators. . . . Unwanted children are also abandoned in subway stations, department store restrooms, movie theaters, parked cars, the bus terminal, and numerous other locations." Nothing seems to have changed—except, perhaps, to get worse.

The New York Foundling Hospital, when I joined it, was sheltering approximately 320 children. They had, obviously, not all been picked off the streets but had been referred to us by a number of agencies and brought in by a number of parents, for a variety of reasons, and suffering from a variety of ailments. Some were tiny babies; some were several years old. After reading Dr. Kempe's findings, I found myself looking at them all with slightly different eyes.

In making the rounds, seeing these children, getting to know them, it soon became apparent that, although some had been brought in after having been battered, the great majority showed signs of neglect rather than physical abuse. This, of course, was more readily apparent in slightly older children than in infants; babies who are brutalized or abandoned (or both) when they are only a few hours or a few days old don't get much chance to be "neglected." We looked at these children and wondered about them. We wondered why each child was with us at all. Of course he needed treatment and a place to stay, but—were the parents unable to take care of him? Had they really not wanted to take care of him? Hadn't they known how? Were they desperately poor, or in what other ways could they be desperate? Could they really not feed him, keep him clean, tend to his small injuries, love him?

What my associates and I saw were dull-eyed children who turned their faces to the wall, who could not respond to a friendly touch. Children with infections that had gone untreated. Children with sores that had been unattended. Children who were emaciated. Children who had had lice removed from their hair. Children who were slightly bruised, perhaps had a minor dislocation or two, whose eyes were big in hollow faces. Children who had been dehydrated almost to the point of death. Small children, barely capable of speech, who used the most incredible gutter language. Children who had been fed totally unsuitable foods. Children who showed traces of medication never intended for children. Children who gave every appearance of being physically healthy, yet looked terribly lost, and who never laughed and seldom cried.

Granted, they didn't have much to laugh about; but it wasn't always the physically injured child who sank most deeply into himself. Sometimes the child with burns and fractures responded more readily to treatment and friendly overtures than the child who showed no evidence of inflicted injury. We got the feeling that there must be something more to child abuse than just the battered-child syndrome.

We realized that we had not discovered a brand-new thing called "neglect." We were aware that child neglect was at least as common as deliberately inflicted injury, if not more so, even though it was often less apparent and less dramatic. Interesting and valuable studies of child neglect were under way even then. Later a controversy was to develop between those who considered neglect and abuse as qualitatively different and those who put neglect and abuse in the same category and only quantitatively different. Some investigators found it very difficult to define physical cruelty and neglect separately, while others managed to do so with no difficulty at all. They believed that neglect obviously involved failure to supervise the child properly, failure to feed it appropriately, failure to provide sanitary living conditions, failure to clothe the child adequately, failure to attend to the child's medical or educational needs. And physical abuse, or battering, that was. . . well, that was battering. It was physical harm, deliberately inflicted; that was what it was.

But what we were observing was not just one thing or the

other. It had many manifestations. Neglect may not be abuse, but it *is* maltreatment. Similarly, neglect may not always be deliberate, but it *is* damaging. In our view, the failure-to-thrive cases seemed clearly linked to deliberate abuse. There was an indication of what might be called *active neglect.* The children did not thrive because—it seemed to us—they had been emotionally battered, they had been deprived of mothering, they had been starved of the substance necessary for their physical, spiritual or mental growth. Their bodies might not have been scarred but something in them had been damaged and sometimes beyond repair. In time, we noticed that apparently undamaged children were failing to come out of their lethargy. Whether this was due to malnutrition, psychic wounding, or some other circumstance, we could not tell.

My colleagues and I embarked on a research study of the children we saw in the course of our rounds. We saw cases of severe injury, of failure to thrive, of malnutrition, of poor skin hygiene, and other instances of neglect, of irritability, of repressed personality, of retardation possibly due either to malnutrition or previously unsuspected brain damage caused by whiplash shakings of the child as a very small baby. We came to realize that the battered-child or battered-baby syndrome was only part of the whole picture of child abuse, of the spectrum of maltreatment.

Our study began to take shape. Could there be a progression from one form of the disease to another? Could it be halted?

In our observation, a maltreated child often shows no signs of being battered, since battering is the last phase of the spectrum, but the child does show multiple, minor physical symptoms or evidence of emotional (at times nutritional) deprivation, neglect, and abuse. In cases of incipient or insidious maltreatment, we observed that the acute diagnosis acumen of the physician might very well permit early intervention and prevent the more severe injuries of inflicted trauma that are significant causes of childhood deaths. The willful neglect and abuse of children ranges from cases of mild deprivation or malnourishment through general neglect, accompanied by verbal abuse and a certain amount of cuffing around, to cases in which the child is the victim of premeditated trauma leading to permanent crippling or death. In our view, the awareness of physicians of the very early signs and symptoms of maltreament could save lives.

It might be suggested that insidious maltreatment is not necessarily the precursor of more serious abuse. But, we questioned, if an infant is neglected, malnourished, and slapped around, are his childhood years likely to be any better? We thought not. Parental habit has a way of hardening. Many of the little ones we observed to be in the very early stages of maltreatment had their counterparts outside our wards; they were the infants and small children who were seen in child-care centers and hospital emergency rooms and by private pediatricians. Seen only in a sense, many were not viewed as the victims of parental abuse and neglect in its initial stages. It occurred to us that children picked up and cared for at this time could be saved, but that children, whose plight was not fully observed and understood for what it was, would be back. We thought that if these children were not identified, the course of their disease halted, and their parents treated, there would come a time when the neglect, the indifference, the careless handling, might lead to minor abuse, such as a dislocation or a broken limb. This might escalate to a "fall" down a flight of stairs, which in turn, might lead to a severe beating. Eventually, it might lead to the child's arrival in the emergency room, battered and possibly dead. Or, that the budding abuse might take another turn, and the child might die of starvation or a neglect-induced illness permitted to rage unchecked.

Although we realized that it was useful, from the point of view of diagnosis and treatment, to be able to categorize physical abuse as one thing and neglect as another, we felt that such a distinction was really of little value to the child in need of help. What we were concerned with was the child who was maltreated in any way. Any treatment by which a child's potential development is retarded or completely suppressed, by mental, emotional or physical suffering, is *mal*treatment, whether it is negative (as in deprivation of emotional or material needs) or positive (as in verbal abuse or battering).

In coming to grips with the whole picture of neglect and abuse of children, we had to be able to see a situation varying from the deprivation of food, clothing, shelter, and parental love to incidents in which children were physically abused and mistreated by an adult, with resultant physical trauma and, perhaps, death. My colleagues and I, at both the Foundling Hospital and St. Vincent's Hospital and Medical Center of New York, began to be on the lookout for telltale signs of abuse. Previously, it might never have occurred to us that the child's condition could have been deliberately or, at least, parentally induced.

In the course of time, we noted that the child who is maltreated is often brought to the hospital or private physician with a history of failure to thrive, malnutrition (usually explained by "I don't know what to do with him, doctor, he just won't eat"), poor skin hygiene, irritability ("He's such a cranky baby, doesn't seem like one of us"), a repressed personality, and other signs of obvious or subtle neglect. Often the condition from which the child suffered on admission—"He won't eat"; "He bruises easily"; "His bones are very fragile and just keep breaking"—clears up magically in the hospital and returns only when the child returns home.

The more severely abused children are seen in hospital emergency rooms with external evidences of body trauma, such as multiple bruises, abrasions, cuts, lacerations, burns, soft tissue swelling, and hematomas. Inability to move certain extremities because of dislocations and fractures, associated with neurologic signs of intracranial damage, are additional signals that should arouse the suspicion of the attending physician. Children manifesting the battered-child syndrome give evidence of one or more of these complaints; the most severe cases arrive at the hospital or physician's office in convulsions or coma or dead on arrival. (It is perhaps difficult to comprehend why an abusing parent would take a moribund child to a physician, the murderer taking his victim for last-ditch medical care. Parental fear of legal entanglement often keeps the abusers from taking a battered child to a doctor or hospital until the child is in such acute, visible distress that even the neighbors begin to comment on it. Parental alarm, at the prospect of impending death and its possible consequences to them, finally overrides the initial fear. Then, too, there is the business of hospital-hopping. The terminal visit is likely to be just that: the last in a series of visits from one hospital to another and from one physician to another, in an attempt to forestall the suspicion of parental abuse that might arise after repeated visits to any single doctor.)

Thus the signs and symptoms indicating the maltreatment of children range from simple undernourishment in an infant who is reported as failing to thrive to the multiple fractures and inflicted trauma seen in the battered child. Injuries falling considerably short of the battered-child package of symptoms are not always easy to diagnose. But soft tissue lacerations, abrasions, burns, and hematomas involving any part of the body must be observed with suspicion and critically compared with the accompanying parental explanation. More enlightening is the presence of healed or scab-covered "old" abrasions or contusions of the skin. Also, the manifestations of multiple vitamin deficiencies are invariably evident in these children. Bites, too, are suspect, all kinds of bites. Sometimes small but angry-looking and infected swellings are earnestly described by the parents as insect bites; these often turn out to be inflicted wounds. Human bites, however, are never described as such (unless the parent shifts the blame to a sibling) but are frequent and unmistakable evidence of deliberate abuse. The Office of Chief Medical Examiner, City of New York, has reported that the largest percentage of human bite-marks encountered in the course of their forensic investigation has been found on battered-child homicide victims, most of whom exhibit multiple bite marks.

Subdural hematoma, with or without fracture of the skull, is frequently noted in maltreated children. Very often, though not always, the hematoma is, as Dr. Caffey was first to note, accompanied by fractures of the long bones. Nearly always this package of symptoms can be a dead giveaway to a physician, if not to the law.

Maltreatment of children by parents may occur at any age,

with a greater incidence in children under three years of age. The heaviest concentration of fatalities is in the newborn-to-12-months group. Obviously, an infant or very young child, even if he lives, cannot tell the story of how the trauma was inflicted; and many children old enough to speak will remain silent out of fear of their parents or, oddly enough, fear of what might happen to their parents. And the parents, naturally, seldom volunteer the truth and will only admit to something like it after being confronted with their guilt, and then only if the confrontation is handled with the greatest compassion and care. The history that is related by the parents is usually at extreme variance with the clinical picture and the physical findings noted on examination of the injured or otherwise mistreated child. Seeking out information involves precise detection of previous hospital admissions, something that is often very difficult and even impossible to do in the light of hospital-hopping.

In our early experience of interviewing parents and trying to obtain the background of the child, we found that, in many cases, we simply couldn't get at a medical history at all. Almost invariably, there was complete denial of knowledge of inflicted trauma to the child. Often the attitude of absolute innocence was so convincing that we nearly *were* convinced until we saw the X-rays. It was apparent to us that many, many physicians must have been fooled time and time again.

Lacking any type of history, we had to depend for our diagnosis on the physical examination, the X-ray findings, and our own high index of suspicion. Many of the parents gave the outward impression of being devoted, even overprotective parents, and maltreatment would have been only too easy to overlook if we had not become aware of the small, telltale signs. Ironically, if the abuse was minor, there was little we could do about it except treat it and tactfully refer the family to a social service worker; but if it was severe and repeated, we could obtain pictorial evidence and take very definite steps to salvage the child, though it was nearly too late. Sometimes, in the serious cases, we would see X-ray evidence of fractures in various stages of reparative change; sometimes we would see the subdural hematoma/long bone fracture combination; sometimes we would find no fractures or dislocations on first examination (that is, right after the fall from the crib or other supposed accident), since bone injury may remain obscure during the first few days after inflicted trauma, but then, upon reexamination, we would find evidence of bone repair. And not only would we see the fractures and the evidence of healing in various stages, we would also see unusual bone changes that assisted us in making very specific diagnoses. By the nature of the healing we could tell that the arm, for instance, had not been broken in a fall but had been twisted or yanked. In these cases, the story told by the X rays almost invariably contradicted the story told by the parents. When we found such a contradiction we would naturally pursue our investigation into the causes of the injuries and the means of preventing a recurrence.

For far too many years, before radiology came to the rescue and afterwards, the physically abused child was thought to be suffering from an unrecognized trauma, a strange, undiagnosed disease that weakened his bones and made him bruise easily and bleed a lot. Well, he was; the disease was child abuse, in one of its most virulent forms. But it was only one of many forms, as we soon discovered.

Again and again, though not always, we noted that physical abuse could be associated with maternal deprivation. We saw varying degrees and types of neglect unaccompanied by injury; sometimes we saw injury apparently unaccompanied by neglect. But, often, we saw cases in which physical abuse coexisted with neglect, or in which it was difficult to tell one from the other. We saw children in whom X-ray signs of retarded development coexisted with nutritional neglect; we saw children with lice as well as ruptured livers; we saw at least one child who was not only emaciated but dehydrated from having been deliberately deprived of water; we saw gaunt, hungry children who had been beaten within an inch of their lives; we saw children who had been locked in closets for days; we saw children who had been, carelessly or deliberately, dunked in tubs of scalding water; we saw children who had been left outside, half-naked, in freezing weather.

Where was the dividing line between neglect and abuse? Which was worse? Did it matter?

We kept coming back to that question of definition and decided that we were simply playing with words. Child abuse and child neglect are all part of the same package. Of course, there often is a difference between the neglectful parent and the abusive parent, and an understanding of this difference is vital to treating the parent and, ultimately, to saving the child, but, from the child's point of view, it is all maltreatment.

So we enlarged upon the "battered baby" concept and came up with the "maltreatment syndrome in children."

As our interest ripened, we found that the child-abuse phenomenon, which had seldom been reported before 1962, was now being observed and recorded in many parts of the country. Reports of maltreatment began coming our way from major cities, small towns, rural areas, and from overseas. It was not a disease confined to America. We found it was a disease that was present in almost every corner of the world, although possibly concentrated in ours. A substantial number of cases were now being reported from just about every so-called civilized country and from some of the uncivilized ones. We do not know yet whether the lack of reportage from some of the "uncivilized" countries is due to the nonpractice of child abuse or the total absence of a reportage system, but the observations of anthropologists would indicate that there are indeed some very primitive, gentle peoples among whom child abuse is unheard of and unthinkable. Unfortunately, not all primitive peoples are gentle nor their cultural patterns free from child maltreatment. Some tribes still practice infanticide. In others, the puberty rites are extremely cruel and painful. And there are individuals of various tribes and nations whose cultural heritage does not sanction the abuse of children but who then come in contact with us, for example, and something of us brushes off on them.

It does seem, on the whole, that the more modern, sophisticated, and technologically advanced the society, the greater the incidence of child abuse. Certainly we found that it was quite widespread in our democracy. We don't sacrifice our children to pagan gods, slaughter our firstborn or abandon our twins simply because they *are* our firstborn or our twins, calculatedly maim our youngsters so that they might be more effective beggars, or sell our children into slavery; but we do inflict deliberate, painful injuries and indignities upon our own children in our own homes; we do still subscribe unofficially to the doctrine of absolute parental authority; and we do treat our children just about the way we want to, from turning our hatred upon them to ignoring them completely.

It was my feeling that, perhaps, with the stresses and strains we were experiencing throughout the world because of various wars, poverty, insecurity, alcoholism, drug addiction, the murders of our public figures, the violence in the streets, and the other horrors that had become part of our lives, people had become frustrated beyond endurance. And, it seemed to me, the people who were most frustrated were those who were the most confined by the narrowness and tragedies of their own existence. These, I thought, were the people who would strike out at their children during a period of crisis.

In 1963, my colleagues and I published our paper, "The 'Maltreatment Syndrome' in Children," in the *New England Journal of Medicine* (*December 26, 1963*, pp. 1389-1394). In 1964, I followed it up with a book, *The Maltreated Child.* These publications were intended primarily for the medical profession, although I hoped that they would reach other people as well. It is tragic when a physician fails to recognize the symptoms of child abuse, but it is equally tragic when a neighbor ignores the plight of the beaten or neglected baby, and the cop on the corner never heard of such a thing in his life.

The medical profession accepted the maltreatment syndrome as an all-encompassing description of child abuse and neglect, and, in the main, agreed that the battered child phenomenon is in fact the last phase of the spectrum. In New York, if not throughout the country, we brought our findings to the attention of the public through various kinds of publicity, with emphasis on television and the press. I came in for some criticism because of this publicity. Physicians weren't supposed to indulge in that sort of thing. But I felt that even Kempe and his colleagues, with all the credit that was genuinely their due for the diagnosis of the battered child, were not getting enough of a hearing. It seemed to me that the battered-child syndrome in itself, if it were just going to remain a medical oddity, might very well get buried in the archives right along with many other medical syndromes that had been reported previously and filed away. In bringing our own findings to public attention, I felt, we were not only putting across the maltreated-child syndrome but helping to keep the plight of the battered baby visible.

Four years later, though, the situation, in terms of public and professional awareness of the maltreatment problem, seemed to be virtually unchanged. In a paper submitted to the *Medical Times* in October, 1967, Larry Silver, child psychiatrist at the Children's Hospital of the District of Columbia, reported that:

> In a recent survey by the Child Abuse Research Group of Children's Hospital of the District of Columbia, it was noted that many physicians in that metropolitan area were still not aware of the clinical, legal, and social aspects of the child-abuse syndrome (battered-child syndrome). Two reasons why this problem exists are that most of the investigative research has been done since 1962 and that much of the research in child abuse has been published in social work, legal and other specialized professional journals which the average practicing physician may not see. . . . Hopefully, the practicing physician will become alert to the child-abuse syndrome and to his role in working with his community in establishing an integrated program for prevention, protection, treatment, and assistance for the abused child and his family.

It was a plea that was to become increasingly familiar as the years rolled by: let the physician be aware, let him work with the community, let there be an integrated program for the handling of child abuse.

Interestingly, by this time, the emphasis on *battering* had begun to shift toward the more general term of *abuse*. Among the relatively few people who were deeply concerned over the problem of child maltreatment, there was a growing acceptance of the fact that there is more to abuse than battering alone. To return to Silver, "the child-abuse syndrome represents a spectrum of clinical conditions: at one end of the spectrum would be the malnourished, starving, or failure-to-thrive child; at the other end of the spectrum would be the child who has been severely traumatized physically. Some question whether psychological abuse should also be included." Parenthetically, there is no question in my mind that psychological abuse *must* be included.

Silver's opening comment raised another issue, one with which I had been wrestling for some time and haven't yet resolved: if practicing physicians were not then and are not yet aware of the child-abuse syndrome, what about our educators, what about our lawmakers, what about our law enforcers, what about the public?

The public has a need to know. In view of the lack of awareness, my colleagues and I have long felt that even if we are criticized for contributing to or participating in any publicity about the maltreated child in a news story or TV special or newscast about child abuse, the publicity is not only valuable but *necessary*. A disease that is kept hidden behind closed doors and shuttered windows, whose existence is ignored or denied, can never be cured. It seems to me that in order to get something done for a cause, we have to electrify the public and dramatically solicit its help. In the matter of child abuse, the public becomes electrified, literally galvanized with shock, even if only briefly, by some particularly unpleasant revelation or horror story. Then the shocked public demands that something be done, and it is done. Publicity happens to be one of the effective means of getting things done in our society.

After recovering from the shock we received from the initial burst of publicity (and criticism) over the concept of the maltreated child, my colleagues and I became increasingly interested in alerting the medical profession, social workers, and lay people. We did not, at that time, know very much about the abusing parents, but we were beginning to know quite a bit about the children and the maltreatment syndrome.

Following the publicity, I began to get letters from pediatricians who were, for the first time, noticing the syndrome for themselves, not because they hadn't seen it before, but because they had not allowed themselves to think that the parents might be responsible. I began to get calls and written requests from district attorneys who wanted to know what they could do to prove their cases. I got queries from teachers wanting to know what they could do about the child abuse and neglect cases they saw in their classrooms. I got letters from adults who had been maltreated as children and had either come out of it reasonably unscathed or hadn't. I got letters from mothers who were abusers and were hunting desperately for help for their children and themselves.

And yet, I was told again and again that I was exaggerating the problem. I was even told that maltreatment of children was a figment of my imagination, that its incidence was very low and certainly not responsible for a significant degree of mortality in children. I remember being on a podium in Washington, D.C., with the distinguished sociologist, Dr. David G. Gil, long before he embarked upon his well-known epidemiologic study of physical child abuse. He said to me, "Dr. Fontana, you just get too emotional about these cases."

Of course I did. As a pediatrician, I would get emotional over the death of any child, but I did feel particularly strongly about abuse as a cause of death.

At that time, we had no statistics; we only had our gut reactions to personal experiences. It was difficult for those of us who believed child maltreatment to be a major disease to convince those who did not.

But I think, in the course of the past ten years, we have had a measure of success.

When I first became interested in abuse, there was only one state, California, with a law applicable to the abuse of children. It did not specifically relate to children, but it was better than nothing; I had heard that, prompted by its existence, California legislators were preparing a law for reporting child abuse. It seemed to me that there was an urgent need for such a law in New York State.

In the fall of 1962, the Special Committee on Child Welfare

of the New York County Medical Society had become concerned enough by the abuse problem to spend five of its scheduled monthly meetings discussing it in considerable depth. Dr. Harold Jacobziner, a dedicated pediatrician, a pioneer in accident prevention, and a good friend, was chairman of the committee and became particularly interested in the problem. He was of great help in the search for a solution.

The committee studied the entire range of the problem. To its meetings came social workers, pediatricians, pathologists, judges, law enforcement officers, representatives of the legal profession and of various protective agencies, such as the Societies for the Prevention of Cruelty to Children. One of the most striking realizations to come out of these meetings was the fact that physicians were reluctant to look the problem in the eye and accept the responsibility for intervening on the child's behalf or at least reporting it. The mechanics of reportage were also discovered to be missing. How was the report to be made and to whom? Was the police department the proper agency? Would not an official child-protective agency be preferable? How would this be created? What safeguards could there be for parents and child? What about immunity from liability for the individual making the report? What could be done to create a comprehensive educational program to alert physicians and social workers, the lay public and public officials, to the need for awareness and action?

It was due in large part to Jacobziner's personal efforts that we were able to put the question of a child-abuse law on the agenda of the Special Committee on Child Welfare. We interviewed countless people and made a thorough study of existing legislation, such as it was. By 1963, other states also were beginning to move. We did everything we could to drum up interest in legislation in our own state. The special committee recommended that the New York County Medical Society support legislation making it mandatory for physicians and hospitals to report cases of abuse. The Citizens' Committee for Children became similarly concerned and pushed vigorously for legislation. The Interdepartmental Health Council of the City of New York made recommendations to the mayor stressing that legislation should not be so punitive of the offender as protective of the child. There was a growing interest, centered in the city of New York though not by any means confined to it, in getting a state child-abuse law passed.

The law was eventually passed and became effective July 1, 1964. In the meantime, there had been, and continued to be, a flurry of legislative action throughout the nation. The thrust of the legislation lay in mandatory reporting, with a view to protecting the child victims of abuse. In 1963, eighteen child-abuse bills were introduced, and eleven were passed. In 1964, ten additional states passed similar bills. In 1965, twenty-six states passed reporting laws, and several states began passing amendments to their earlier laws. Today there are child-abuse laws in all states.

One of the great pioneers in the field of child protection and, perhaps, the man most responsible for bringing professional and public attention to the urgent need for protective laws and services, is Dr. Vincent De Francis, director of the Children's Division of the American Humane Association. Due in large part to studies, papers, and reports issued by him or produced under his aegis and to his personal activism, responsible citizens throughout the country were alerted to the need for action and they began pressuring their legislatures to move ahead with unprecedented speed.

But, even after the passage of the New York state law, New York City had much to do. All available evidence, scant as it was, indicated that the disease of child abuse was particularly rampant in the city. Whether it was because of the large population, of the existing slums and ghettos, of the particular big-city stresses, or because the city is a melting pot of peoples, was not known. It was known that there was a problem of major proportions and that it was necessary to get city government officials committed to doing something about it. Fortunately, Dr. Howard J. Brown, then commissioner of Health Services in New York City, was very sympathetic toward these efforts. Dr. Brown approached Mayor John V. Lindsay and indicated that, "this might be something we might become interested in." As an immediate result, I became a special consultant to the mayor and to Dr. Brown in order to coordinate all related efforts. This was in mid-1967.

By early December 1968, Mayor Lindsay had formed a special task force to study the problem of child abuse and neglect in New York City. The timing of this move is, I feel, important, because it is often said that the task force was hastily formed after a horrifying, headlined case forced official recognition of the need to do something in a hurry. But, in fact, the task force was formed with considerable care and forethought months before the brutal murder. By the time the anguished public outcry arose, the special panel was already in full operation, making, as the mayor put it, "a thorough examination of the existing social, medical and legal community services involved in programs of child protection in New York City." Somebody *was* doing something. Task force investigators were conducting intensive studies and interviews in an attempt to identify the flaws in the social machinery so that we might come up with specific recommendations for the prevention of such dreadful incidents as the murder cases that made the headlines and the many other cases, equally as shocking, that did not so much as reach the newspapers. The task force was prepared, on receiving all the input, to make concrete proposals for the improvement of services to abused children and their families. It was to our own sorrow that we were unable to prevent the thousands of child-maltreatment cases that continued to come to our attention while we sought to find ways of changing our protective system, our fellow citizens, and ourselves.

In spite of the efforts of the task force and of the work of many eminent sociologists, pediatricians, psychologists, and other concerned individuals, the problem of child maltreatment does not assume its proper perspective in the public eye until individual cases appear in the newspapers. Even then, the perspective is often distorted because the news stories tend to make it seem that each case is just a hideous exception to the rule of happy families. Documented and publicized cases are not exceptions, though they may be extremes. Neglectful treatment of children, the beating and burning of children, sexual abuse of children, are not uncommon occurrences. They are daily occurrences, and, in fact, they have become so common that most maltreatment cases other than exceptionally brutal murders now appear in the back pages of our newspapers. Yet *they are there* and the number of them is staggering. It is a myth that we, in this nation, love our children.

The means to accurately pinpoint the incidence of abuse are not yet at our disposal. (A national central registry might be a help though not the complete answer.) It is difficult to estimate the number of children being physically abused or neglected in the course of a year. We do not even know how many cases of child maltreatment are *reported* across the nation; we do not know how many reported cases refer to neglect, how many to abandonment, how many to sexual abuse. We do not know how many cases go *unreported,* although we cannot help suspecting that what we see is only the tip of the iceberg. We do not know whether the figures reported for particular localities—such as the city of Denver, the state of California, metropolitan Miami, or greater New York—are typical of these localities only, or whether they reflect the figures for the nation at large.

But by sample, we can say that, in 1958, approximately 1,200 cases of children in need of care were referred to the public welfare departments in Denver for protective services. A 1964 study in California showed that about 20,000 children in that state needed protective services. In 1970, 1,343 cases of child abuse and neglect were reported to authorities in metropolitan Miami, 250 of which were described as, if not proved to be, battered-child cases. In 1971, the number of reported maltreatment cases in that area escalated to 3,396, including 253 alleged cases of battering. And in 1972, there were approximately 10,000 cases of child maltreatment reported in New York City.

These figures are certainly cause for deep concern, especially since a larger number of cases go unreported. In a recent survey in Rochester, New York, for example, it was estimated that ten percent of all traumas in children between infancy and the age of fourteen appearing in the emergency room of Rochester Central Hospital were due to abuse and another ten percent to neglect. That is, *twenty percent* of all traumas admitted to the children's emergency room fell into the category of maltreated children.

The United States Children's Bureau estimates that from 50,000 to 75,000 incidents of child abuse occur in this country each year. Dr. Vincent De Francis, of the Children's Division of the American Humane Association, estimates that 10,000 children are severely battered every year, at least 50,000 to 75,000 are sexually abused, 100,000 are emotionally neglected, and another 100,000 are physically, morally, and educationally neglected.

Dr. David G. Gil of Brandeis University conducted a two-year nationwide study of child abuse incidence for the United States Children's Bureau during the last five years of the 1960s with interesting, if ambiguous, results. He conceded a total of 5,993 cases of physically abused children in the states and territories of the United States for the year 1967 and 6,617 for 1968, arriving at his conclusions primarily through sifting registry reports and analyzing questionnaires. Dr. Gil concluded that the magnitude of the phenomenon had been exaggerated, "that the scope of physical abuse of children resulting in serious injury does not constitute a major social problem, at least in comparison with several more widespread and more serious social problems. . . . Even if allowance is made for underreporting, especially of fatalities, physical abuse cannot be considered a major cause of mortality and morbidity of children in the United States."

However, Gil himself suggests that, if one were to include the number of abuse cases *personally known* to a sample group queried, their unofficial reports, if extrapolated to the total population of the United States, would indicate an annual incidence of approximately 2,500,000 abused-child cases. (This reference is to physical abuse only, not the entire spectrum of maltreatment.) That figure of two-and-a-half million is a long, long way from the 5,993 of Gil's findings. Gil cautions us not to overinterpret the larger figure, since it is impossible to determine whether the unofficially reported cases refer to disciplinary slaps or something much more serious. But, granting such factors as vindictiveness or personal abhorrence for any form of corporal punishment, how many of the people questioned would have been likely to mistake an occasional outburst of parental indignation for abuse? The average layman, parent or other family member, surely knows the difference between a couple of whacks and unrestrained beatings. He slaps his children and has been slapped. Would he describe his own disciplinary blows as abuse? Hardly. Most parents, at some time or another in their lives, question their own disciplinary treatment of their children, and most know the difference between abuse and occasional overreaction to situations involving children. It is difficult to accept Gil's statement, in the light of his own extrapolation, that physical abuse of children "does not constitute a major social problem." No available figures agree with his assessment, least of all those available in New York City.

Conservatively, I would estimate that at least 150 children in New York City die each year as a result of maltreatment. In 1972, the New York Central Registry reported 51 deaths attributable to suspected parental maltreatment. This total did not include 24 additional cases known to the medical examiner or about 15 "fall" cases known to hospitals. I believe that a conservative estimate is that one or two children are being killed at the hands of their own parents in this country every day, at least 700 children are killed every year in the United States by their parents or guardians. And, based on increasingly reliable reports from individual communities throughout the country, we know that thousands of other children are permanently injured either physically or mentally.

I must agree with Dr. Gil that some of this horror is due to our national belief that physical force is a legitimate procedure in child rearing, and that "American culture encourages, in subtle ways, the use of a certain measure of physical force in rearing children"; but I must add that I feel that this force springs not so much from the desire to discipline as to show "who's boss around here" and the age-old concept that the child is the parent's property to do with as he pleases. I must also agree that the stresses and strains imposed by poverty precipitate incidents of child abuse, but incidents of child maltreatment occur on all socioeconomic levels. It is true that under conditions of poverty all problems are exacerbated, but it is also true that these problems tend to surface in families made visible by exposure to welfare services. Instances of child abuse in the more affluent families are not frequently exposed to public agencies and escape the public gaze, but they are nevertheless known to private practitioners, clergy, and neighbors.

I cannot help but feel that the soaring statistics, and they are soaring every year, are symptomatic of our violent, unhappy times; that they are not simply the result of better reportage or an influx of "the underprivileged" to our cities, but of the increased stresses that are confronting *all* society and the crest of violence that seems to be engulfing the world.

We must do all we can to eliminate poverty and change the value system that permits us to discipline our children by striking them, but let us not forget that discipline and poverty are not always the accompaniments of child maltreatment, and that we still have much to learn about ourselves and our reactions to stress and about the parents and other guardians who fail to relate to the children in their care.

Let no one think, because my focus happens to be my own experience in New York, that this is just another case of "Oh, well, but that's New York!" It isn't only this city. Dr. Howard Rusk, medical editor of the *New York Times,* has pointed out that New York City is not alone in this problem and that similar increases in the incidence of child maltreatment are being reported throughout the country. Other countries are no better off. Eustace Chesser of England's National Society for the Prevention of Cruelty to Children has said that between six and seven percent of all children in England are at one time or another in their lives "so neglected or ill-treated or become so maladjusted as to require the protection of community agencies."

No, this isn't happening in New York alone, or only in our major cities. It is happening, secretly, behind the facades of more homes than we will ever know. Our major cities present only the open wounds. In a sense, they *are* the open wounds. We see what is happening to our children in the great metropolises because society turns a spotlight on whatever is obvious and big. What about all the smaller cities, the country towns, and villages? What about the injuries we do not see, the cries we do not hear because someone doesn't care or doesn't want to get involved? We have to get involved. These are our own children.

Even at this late date, despite all the evidence that confronts us daily, I hear it said that those of us who are deeply interested in turning back the tide of child maltreatment are exaggerating or imagining the problem. But it is not an imagined problem to those who have, day after day, seen it face to face.

# CHAPTER THREE

# Behind Closed Doors

ONCE WE ACKNOWLEDGE that the picture of the abused child as invariably "battered" is an incomplete one, we open up a Pandora's box of maltreatment variations that stagger the imagination. We know they exist because we see the results in the pathologist's office and in the hospital beds and in the foundling homes, but, by the time we see them, we are usually too late to save the victim. I don't mean we're necessarily too late to save the life of the child, often we can do that. But we are too late to undo much of the damage that is already done. If we do not rescue the child when he is young, a year old, or two years at the most, it is too late. His future has been imprinted and inflicted on him. We cannot salvage a child when he is six, seven, or eight years old and has already been subjected to five, six, or seven years of beatings, maltreatment, and neglect. Such a child is beyond rescue.

The vast majority of child maltreatment cases are of the insidious variety in the sense that they are unseen or unrecognized at the time. Screams, broken bones, multiple bruises, and bloodied heads call public attention, but who knows what else is going on in the secrecy of the shuttered home? Furthemore, there is often a certain element of cunning involved in child abuse. Some of the most brutally abusive of parents do not actually batter the target child: they take care to hit him so that the bones don't break and the marks don't show, or they accidentally scald his buttocks or his feet in such a plausible manner that all they get by way of consequence is sympathy.

Then there are the even more silent and less visible types of abuse, the in-family sex crimes, the torture-by-deprivation cases, the various, subtle kinds of neglect and indifference; and the strange, often lethal accidents of very young infants and exploring toddlers.

We have often heard the mother's wail: "I took my eyes off him for a second." We sympathize; little children are very vulnerable. Things can happen to them in the blink of an eye. Children do fall often. They run into streets, get knocked down.

Accidents are the most common cause of death in children, and there is no doubt that most of these accidents are genuine. Up to the age of eighteen months the most frequent causes of death are burning, drowning, poisoning, and child abuse. From eighteen months to fourteen years, the predominant cause of injury or death is the automobile accident. In a recent study of a two-year period, over half of the accidental death cases in the one-to-fourteen category occurred to children under the age of five and, in eighty to ninety percent of cases, blunt-force injuries were noted.

In the very-young age group, infants from six weeks to six months old, an unexpected, mysterious, but not infrequent, phenomenon occurs: crib death or sudden, unexpected death in infants. It has been variously estimated that 10,000; 20,000; or 30,000 infants are found dead in their cribs each year. Generally, by exclusion of other causes, most of these deaths are labeled crib deaths, a loose diagnosis that is indicative of our medical ignorance but tacitly acknowledges the possibility of natural death due to accidental smothering, to a virus, or to anaphylactic reaction (an allergic reaction). It would be doing a great disservice to the many baffled and unhappy parents of crib death children to suggest that the mysterious, undiscovered cause, may be the parent. Most such deaths are exactly what they seem, medical mysteries and parental tragedies. However, some *apparent* crib deaths are caused by one parent or the other, for reasons that can only be guessed: postpartum depression in the mother, jealousy or impatience on the part of the father, or the desire to quietly dispose of an unwanted child who is now in the way.

Proof is hard to come by, but the more obvious cases of unnatural death tend to cast doubt on the acceptance of crib death as the only explanation.

*Tina.* Two weeks old. First described as crib-death baby, but hospital reports that death was due to drug withdrawal. Mother had been an addict prior to baby's death.

*Debbie.* Three months old. Mother rushes her to a hospital when she does not awaken after a nap. Baby is pronounced dead due to a skull fracture, contusions, and hemorrhage. Mother claims she was changing the child when Debbie accidentally fell to the floor. Afterwards, when placed in her crib, Debbie seemed perfectly all right to mother.

*David.* Six weeks old. Mother claims she found him on the floor after he had apparently rolled off the bed. Medical examination results in a report that causes of death are extensive multiple fractures of the skull, hemorrhage, and contusion of the brain.

*Susie.* Two months. Classified crib death. Cause of death not determined, but it is noted that the child was left unattended while the mother went shopping.

Perhaps none of these cases bears any resemblance to the classic crib death, but they do raise questions. If immediate and thorough examinations had not been made, and they are not always made in the case of tiny babies, would anyone have known that they were not just tragic cases of babies unaccountably found dead in their cribs? To what degree are these deaths to be considered accidental, or deliberate, or caused by negligence? And is the negligence that results in accidental death any less criminal than a deliberate push downstairs or out of a window? These questions take us away from the crib death and into other parts of the home.

*Jake.* One year old. Left momentarily unattended, fell down a flight of stairs. Died of head injury and intraabdominal bleeding.

*Jennie.* Nine years old. Fell out of a window. Medical examination shows that she had been strangled before the fall.

*Michael.* Four years old. Fell from a sixth-floor window. Who saw the accident? Apparently nobody.

*Antonio.* Three years old. Fell from a fifth-floor window.

In one recent ten-day period, twenty-two New York City children, ranging up to age fifteen, died in falls from windows, fire escapes, and roofs. In some cases, the children were old enough to be unattended and perhaps even to be permitted to play on the roof. In others, they were not old enough to be left unwatched near an open window. That is, if they *were* unwatched. Current case files show incident after incident of "falls from windows" that strongly suggest negligence or abuse.

Deaths by fire also raise suspicions. These, too, crop up repeatedly in the fatality files.

*Thomas.* Three-and-a-half years old. Burned to death in a fire at home. All other children saved. Heavy-drinking parents had reportedly left children alone for eighteen hours by the time the fire started.

*Rosemary.* Two years and ten months old; *Robert,* ten months old. Siblings died of smoke inhalation during fire. Mother charged with criminal neglect.

*Gerald.* One-and-a-half years old. Died in fire. Neglect complaint filed.

All of these sample cases have been selected at random from a bulging case file of recent incidents. They give only the barest outline of the picture of childhood accidents. There are other types of accidents. Children are drowned in bathtubs, scalded, asphyxiated; they fall from couches, fall from chairs, fall off bicycles; they suffocate in plastic bags, slip and strike themselves, strangulate while playing with cords, eat poison. Whether they fell or were burned or suffocated, most die. Once in a while a child survives the accident, but one almost wonders for what purpose, for what sort of future.

There is no question of accident in the true-life stories that follow. If it is any consolation to my fellow New Yorkers, they did not all occur in our city. They are the visible signs of a nationwide epidemic.

Gail, nine years old, habitually appeared at school shoeless and in tattered clothing. Time and time again she was issued shoes through a special school service for the needy, but she would come barefoot to school on the following day. The school guidance counselor finally referred Gail's case to a private protection agency. A caseworker visited the child's home and found a household of nine, unwashed, underclothed, and unfed, children. The father was employed but none too gainfully, and his own financial needs and wishes came first. He was irresponsible, immature and indifferent to his children. Their problems and needs were of no interest to him. The mother, who was of borderline intelligence and given to drink, virtually ignored the children until they produced something she could sell or pawn, something filched from a store or brought home from school, such as a pair of children's shoes.

The four children of Tom and Mary Lewis ranged in age from one to eight years. Left unattended for long periods of time, while their parents were at neighborhood bars or off on benders, the youngsters tried to look after each other and feed themselves. Understandably, they neglected to clean either themselves or their home. They did not know how to quiet the baby's cries. Their case was reported by a tenant in their building during one of the parents' more prolonged absences and the baby's most frantic crying spells. All four children, still unattended when a social worker arrived, were found to be dirty, undernourished, and scabby.

Thirteen-year-old Kathy Gaines was the oldest of three children in a well-to-do family. She and her two brothers were well-fed, well-clothed, packed off punctually to school but otherwise ignored by their parents, two educated, cultured people who enjoyed intellectual cocktail party conversation at other people's homes and vicious arguments in their own. They filled their children's material needs, but gave them the parental cold shoulder. The boys seemed not to care and were not noticeably affected at the time, but Kathy could not bear the family atmosphere. Constantly exposed to her parents' bitter quarrels and deprived of the affection she craved, Kathy developed severe anxiety attacks that included abdominal pains, headaches, choking sensations, and neurotic hair loss. Her parents remained uninterested even when the school psychiatrist intervened on her behalf. She has, therefore, shown no improvement.

Danny and Patrick Noble were five and seven, respectively, when they came to public attention. A neighbor reported to a social welfare agency that Mr. Noble, in her opinion, beat his children with excessive brutality, far beyond what was needed to keep such passive little boys, or any little boys, in line. She said she hated to make such a report because the Nobles seemed to be such wholesome, decent people, but she felt that someone ought to talk to them about the way they were handling their children. Mr. Noble, appearing at the agency without his wife, looked like a fine person. He was well-dressed, well-educated, well-spoken, self-assured, and gainfully employed in an executive position. There was nothing he wouldn't do for his family, he said. He admitted that he disciplined his children but explained that he was obliged to teach them obedience because his wife indulged them too much. Patient questioning elicited the fact that the last time he had disciplined Danny, the boy had ended up locked in the basement, lying at the bottom of the stairs with a broken leg.

Eight-year-old Mike Roberts was reported by the admitting physician at the county hospital to have been treated for lacerations, bruises, burn-like welts, and a broken arm. Investigation revealed that his injuries had been inflicted by his mother with a broomstick and the cord of an electric appliance, and that the attack was only the latest in a series. Mrs. Roberts could not understand why people were making such a fuss about it, Mike was *her* son and her business.

Three years in the life and death of the Green children: father drank excessively, worked only sporadically; mother was apathetic, personally filthy, terrorized by her husband. Parents and six children lived in cramped quarters under revolting, unsanitary conditions. Clothing was ragged, diet dangerously insufficient and unbalanced. The older children were given whiskey to drink. Two boys were hospitalized with broken bones, supposedly the result of accident; a girl for a knife wound in the arm; a baby for malnutrition and severe human bitewounds; another baby for ingesting kerosene. Two of the smaller children were dead on arrival at the emergency ward, both of them killed by what were vaguely described as accidents. All the children, the dead and the living, had bruises, scars, and bite marks on their bodies.

Sonya was seven months old when a policeman, chasing a mugger up a fire escape, heard her cries. He entered the shabby apartment and found her alone in a nearly bare bedroom, lying in a dresser drawer. Doctors at the Manhattan hospital where she was rushed found that she was starving and hadn't had any water for days. Today, over a year later, Sonya is blind, and her brain is permanently damaged. In all likelihood she will not suffer for very much longer; her prognosis is poor; she is expected to die soon.

Sharon is Sonya's older sister. She was discovered to have had two of her toes burned off. It is not clear how this happened, but it is hard to understand how such an injury could have been incurred by accident or neglect. Perhaps the perpetrator is the drug-addicted father or the slightly retarded mother. Sharon's prognosis, too, is poor. However, she will live.

Ten-year-old Delia was the oldest of six children, all of whom had previously been reported by welfare workers as being perpetually hungry, dirty, and begging for food in the streets. Delia took upon herself the responsibility of feeding her siblings and was often seen begging from the neighbors and the local shopkeepers. When the neglect petition was finally filed, it was too late; she had been lured to the room of a neighborhood drifter on the promise of food, and he had strangled her.

Wanda Kemp is nearly nine years old. She has an older sister and two stepsisters. Her father, John Kemp, had established himself as a successful, self-made and self-employed business- man before marrying a widow with two daughters. He settled his ready-made family into a comfortable middle-class home. Years passed, and the family grew. One day, when the young- est child, Wanda, was eight, Mrs. Kemp went to a family ser- vice agency with a reluctant report on a discovery she had made several months earlier. Upon investigating her story, the receiving agency was able to confirm what she had told them: Kemp had orally sodomized his own eight-year-old daughter, had full sexual intercourse with another natural daughter, had impregnated a stepdaughter, and had sexual intercourse with a second stepdaughter.

At the age of ten, Melissa Melendez was sexually assaulted by her mother's lover. The child complained to her mother. Mrs. Melendez casually dismissed the little girl's complaints even after the offense had been repeated several times and Me- lissa was clearly becoming extremely disturbed. Eventually, the child told her aunt, and the aunt went to the police. Mrs. Me- lendez was highly incensed over the interference of the aunt and the intrusion of the police, and steadfastly defended her lover at the expense of her child.

Eleven-year-old Jenny Morgan, examined at a county hos- pital after emergency admission for faintness and sever abdom- inal pains, was found to be twenty-six weeks pregnant. Inquiry revealed that her father, a hard-drinking, abusive man in his thirties, had browbeaten her into having intercourse with him on six occasions. "Your mother will never believe you," he had said, with some accuracy. Perhaps he should have said, "Your mother wouldn't care." Jenny was delivered of a stillborn child and sent to a home, where she appeared contented and docile for a while and then turned increasingly hostile and ob- streperous.

The parents of seven-month-old James Foreman were in- dicted by a grand jury and charged with criminally negligent homicide in the starvation death of the child. The dead boy's twin brother, Jerry, was admitted to a hospital also suffering severe malnutrition, and the two older children were removed immediately from their home and placed in a child center. (The welfare department had been in contact with this family for months. But, according to a preliminary report, there had been a breakdown of communications between the Foremans and their caseworker which resulted in the ending of home-maker service to the family.)

The little boy who was known to his foster parents as Scooter had lived with them from the time he was a few weeks old until a court order directed that he be returned to his natural parents. He was eighteen months old when he went home and nineteen months old when he died. His mother explained that she had flown into a rage because of his toilet habits and had kicked him, perhaps a bit too hard.

Baby Lorraine was four months old when neighbors heard a commotion and wailing from the Garcia apartment and called the police. When the patrolmen arrived they found Garcia, who had been minding the baby while the mother was out with the older child, holding little Lorraine wrapped in a blanket. He was sobbing hysterically. Bedroom furniture was smashed, and the apartment was splattered with blood. Garcia was crying, "My baby, my baby!" When the policeman pulled back the blanket they were appalled to see that most of the baby's head was missing. Garcia later admitted that he had beaten the child with his fists and then bashed her head against the wall when he became enraged by her crying.

Four-week-old Sandra was taken by patrolmen to the nearest medical center after they had been flagged down by her dis-traught mother and a neighbor. The baby's mother complained that her husband, Richard, had been mercilessly beating the baby with a stick because it would not stop crying. In the apartment, they found a heavy wooden stick which had ap-parently been used in the beating. They picked up the twenty-year-old father. He admitted to being a drug addict who would "use anything."

Ronald, two-and-a-half years old, lived briefly in a spotlessly clean and well-kept foster home with his younger brother Jeff (eighteen months), older sister Arlene (five), and their foster parents. One Saturday morning, the foster mother, Mrs. Maria

Rosario, woke her husband and said to him. "I think Ronnie is dead." Rosario looked at the child and called the police. They found that there were bruises and welts all over the infant's body, and that the other two children had bruises all over their bodies. The medical examiner found that Ronnie had died of malnutrition and severe multiple injuries. Arlene and Jeff, also bruised and close to starvation, appeared to have been beaten and neglected but were expected to survive. The foster mother was held without bail and sent for psychiatric observation.

One-year-old Rick was found by the coroner's investigator to have died of peritonitis and pleuritis caused by alcoholism. The young, divorced mother and her serviceman friend were accused of regularly feeding alcoholic beverages to the baby and were held without bail after being charged with murder.

Four-year-old Sylvie was picked up, hungry, cold, and terrified alongside the turnpike. Her parents had bundled her out of the car and left her there.

Danny was four years old when he was removed from his home and taken to hospital. He weighed fourteen pounds, eleven ounces, and his tiny limbs looked like knotted sticks. He had been found imprisoned in a playpen with a set of bedsprings lashed across the top. Juvenile officials charged his parents with neglect.

Seven small children in one family died tragically of parathion poisoning. The parents were held in jail when it became apparent that the father, if not both parents, "had guilty knowledge of the poisoning." Laboratory tests had shown that the children had received the parathion in their food and that there were traces of the poison on utensils found in the family kitchen. Neither parent had suffered any ill effects.

A twenty-seven-year-old mother was charged with murder after her three-year-old daughter was asphyxiated by a plastic bag pulled down over her head.

A young boxer, charged with the murder of his six-month-old daughter, told police that he had beaten the baby because "she would not stop crying." His eighteen-year-old wife said she had found the baby lying face down in her crib. "My husband was charged unfairly," she said. Autopsy showed the infant had died of brain hemorrhage caused by a severe beating.

Two-year-old Travis had two blackened eyes and a broken nose. "It was a compound fracture, a piece of the bone was sticking out," the police surgeon said. Christie, seven, had a badly battered face. "The entire front of her dress was full of blood." The third child, Ginger, had multiple bruises. "All of them had mosquito bites, and some of the bites were infected." Their seven-month-old baby sister, Karen, died after reportedly suffering injuries in a fall. She had "massive head injuries." Travis, Christie, and Ginger said that their parents had given them repeated beatings with open hand, fist, and belt.

From a report near the back of a suburban newspaper: "According to testimony, X, who had pleaded guilty to second-degree manslaughter, struck his child, T, twice for misbehaving. She hit her head on a baseboard the second time and died from brain hemorrhaging." Mr. X was sentenced to eight years in prison. "T's death was something of an embarrassment to Y County's Social Services Department because caseworkers twice warned their superiors, eighteen months before the two-year-old died, that the child should be removed from her family's environment under the state's children's rights law of 1969. The warnings, which were not acted upon, alleged that both of T's parents were addicts and had beaten her."

*Vernon.* Two years old. Death is due to fractures of the ribs and multiple tears of the liver, pancreas, and mesentery. The mother and her lover are on drugs. The mother says her lover beat the child.

*Sally.* Five years old. Second- and third-degree burns on her hands and palms. Mother says the child's father punished her for being naughty by holding her hands over the stove.

*Harold.* Nine years old. He is undernourished and inadequately clothed. His father works night and day, and his mother is said to be out of town. The boy is left alone to look after himself and often roams the streets at night. He goes to school once in a while.

*Luke.* One year old. First- and second-degree burns on face and chest. Mother claims the child, playing in the tub, turned on the hot water faucet and was burned before she could stop him.

*Anne.* Five years old. Dead on arrival when brought to hospital by mother and police. Death attributed to overdose of methadone. Mother admits to being an addict and says she left the drug "lying around."

*Matthew.* Seven months old. Hospital reports fracture of the right leg. X rays reveal an old fracture of the left arm. There are also scars on the child's shoulders and back. Mother says that five-year-old sibling, Ed, tried to take baby from crib and got his leg "entangled" in the bars of the crib.

*Connie and Rose.* Thirteen and ten years old, respectively. Brought to a police station-house by an older cousin to complain that their stepfather had repeatedly raped them. The mother denies their allegations, but police find other confirmation of their story.

*Vince.* Six years old. A school counselor reports that he is poorly dressed, always dirty and disheveled, apparently extremely undernourished, and virtually covered with untreated sores. The mother is an alcoholic who ignores school's suggestion that the child be given medical attention.

*Luis.* Four months old. Fracture of the left thigh bone. The mother's story is that he fell out of bed. At no time does she visit him during the several weeks he is in the hospital.

*Julio.* Seven years old. Admitted to hospital with welts, abrasions, and bruises all over his body and head, burn marks on his wrists. Mother reportedly tied his hands and beat him with a cord as punishment for disobedience.

*Diane and Marcia.* Eleven and nine years old, respectively. Found wandering around bus terminal late at night, begging for money to buy food. Told police that their mother didn't want them to come home because she had a visitor. They say their mother often has visitors.

*Adrienne.* Two years old. Brought to the hospital with lacerations and bruises. Mother reports the child fell downstairs. Several weeks later the mother brings the child back, this time with multiple bruises and a broken arm. The woman's story now is that the child's father is responsible.

Enough? More than enough? A seemingly endless recital of dreary happenings? But this is only a skimpy sampling, a skimming from the surface of a truly terrible reality which seems to be coldly trapped on the printed page instead of screaming for attention as it should. These are not just happenings; these are children, children chained in torture chambers from which they cannot free themselves. Is it possible to be clinically objective, not to think of the dreadful loneliness, the isolation, the helplessness, the terror, or the pain? Imagine the awful fear and anguish of a child whose parents are his enemies, of a child who has been burnt and beaten and knows that he will be burnt and beaten again. Whether it is worse to long for a loving touch and never receive it or cringe before a raised fist, I do not know. What must it be like to *be* the child, hurt again and again, cowering in a corner, waiting for the next time, listening for the tormentor's approach, trying to hide, failing, seeing pain come once again and then fleeing it, knowing nothing in life but hunger, helplessness, terror, and pain.

Unfortunately, it is not difficult to find an endless string of cases illustrative of physical abuse and neglect. The effects of maltreatment are visible on the child. What is difficult to pinpoint and describe is the more subtle maltreatment at which some parents are adept. In the upbringing of a child, there are countless sins of omission, as well as commission, that have their effect on the psyche. There are parental attitudes as damaging as a push down stairs or a command to stay "the hell out of the house" because mother's got company. There are the broken homes, the parade of "fathers," the constant moves and changes of school, the cold shouldering, the lack of guidance, the absence of standards, the excess of discipline or total lack of it, the verbal contempt, the hurtful language, the total inability to recognize a child as a human being with rights or to accept a child as a child. These are the insidious wounds with the invisible scars, scars that become visible as the child grows into adulthood. These victims, as children, may never see the inside of a hospital emergency room or a youth shelter; but these victims, as adults, have every good chance of winding up on the psychiatrist's couch, or in family court on neglect or abuse charges, or behind bars for a violent crime.

Such verbalizing attitudes as the following, for example, inflict emotional wounds:

"How can you expect me to love you when I know you're not doing your best?"

"I don't know why you have to be so stupid. All your brothers get good grades."

"Get away from me, you pest. Can't you see I'm busy?"

"Come to Mother, darling boy. Daddy's a beast, but Mummy loves you."

"So what if he doesn't want to go to school, who needs it? I dropped out and I'm making plenty of bread, so shut up."

"It was your father who wanted children, not me. You know something? Four lousy abortions I tried on your account, and I got stuck with you anyway."

"Who asked for your opinion?"

"Oh, what does it matter if the kid sees us? He's going to be doing it himself one of these days."

"If you don't stop that, I'm going to break your arm!"

The arm may never get broken, but the rage and hostility find their target. The simple lack of "parenting," of being protective and supportive, of touching the child with love, is a serious form of abuse that is not generally recognized as such. Why does the beautiful little four-year-old girl, who lives with her parents in their elegant duplex, kick out at adults, bite her playmates, and have hysterical tantrums? Because her handsome, successful parents both have important executive positions and busy social lives that leave no room for the child who is being brought up by a swinging French governess with outside interests of her own. Tough, you say. Well, yes; it is. This beautiful, physically healthy child is already an uncontrollable brat, a very unhappy little kid, an unloved, neglected kid.

Sufficient clinical evidence has been accumulated to show that the absence of sustained parental affection can produce, in an infant, a state of unhappiness, insecurity, and frustration which may lead to psychopathology. It is foolish to assume, as so many parents do, that the health and growth of a child depend only on nutrition, shelter, and the requisite visits to the pediatrician's office for the requisite shots. The growth, development, and health of a child depend much more on the attitudes of the parents toward him or her and the behavior resulting from such attitudes. Wholesome parental attitudes must encompass sustained parental affection, acceptance, and approval of the child. The cold-shouldered child is just as likely as the physically abused child to develop serious personality problems. If he is brought up in an emotional refrigerator in which there is little if any fondling and cuddling, he eventually comes to view the world as a cold and hostile place. He is likely to exhibit delinquent behavior, to retaliate against the world, and to inflict additional damage upon himself in the process of expressing his resentment. And then, of course, the world sees it as *his* fault.

On the other hand, he may not grow up at all. If a baby isn't fed and bathed with tenderness and played with regularly, if he isn't cuddled and petted, if he fails to receive tactile as well as emotional stimulation, he may fail to thrive and grow; he may get ill; he may show signs of retardation; he may eventually die from lack of love.

Not so long ago, the University of Wisconsin did an interesting study of rhesus monkeys growing up without love. The monkeys, as infants, were separated from their mothers and neither cuddled nor handled throughout their babyhood. Baby monkeys are not baby people, but the researchers found that the infant monkeys, when deprived of love, showed a "frightening comparability to children." Some of the baby monkeys were given a mother substitute in the form of a soft, cloth object suitable for hugging and cuddling. Hug and cuddle they did; they became strongly attached to the seemingly responsive, cloth mothers. Other monkeys were provided with mothers made of wire to which they could not respond with affection, even though they received their nourishment through the mother-objects. The monkeys with the cloth mothers developed more normally than those who had to make do with the wire mothers. (Monkeys provided with monkey playmates in their own age group also did relatively well.) The cloth, soft and pliable, gave a semblance of cuddling and love, but the wire was cold and unyielding. The monkeys receiving the least semblance of cuddling and affection grew up to be the most hostile monkeys. Denied normal affection, or even a facsimile of it in their early life, they refused to breast-feed or cuddle their own children, and, in many cases, *even abused them.*

Similarly, the indifference of a *human* parent can be shattering to a child, no matter whether it be the indifference of the drug-addicted parent, lost in his own nightmare-world, or the ambitious professional who simply hasn't time to bother with the baby.

In summary, what is the maltreated child? He is a child who is pushed around, thrown down stairs, dropped out of windows, burned with cigarette butts, fried on stove tops, scalded in boiling water, manhandled, beaten, tortured, a victim of bizarre accident, battered to death, found in a river or a rock-pile. He is ignored, to get into whatever trouble he may, hungry to the point of starvation, crawling with vermin, begging in the streets, arriving shoeless at school, sexually abused, a youthful drug addict, or the pawn of addict parents. He is life-starved and love-starved, insidiously neglected, growing up without a sense of self-esteem, a hater and potential killer, a future child abuser learning dreadful lessons in the art of handling his, or her, own children.

It is not only the immediate abuse that must concern us. It is the future. Because the child who survives maltreatment rarely recovers from it, he is permanently damaged in body, brain, or psyche, sometimes in all three.

# CHAPTER FOUR
# Problem Parents

IN THE AUGUST 5, 1893 ISSUE of the *Journal of the American Medical Association*, Professor I. N. Love's address to graduates of the Marion-Sims College of Medicine was published. Love remarked:

Time was when the only right seemingly granted to children was the right of being born, and, to this day, this right is granted them without their comfort or wishes being consulted. They are fully justified in asking the question, "What are we here for?" Surely in response to the selfish desires of the physical authors of their being. The changes have been rung for centuries in monotonous regularity upon the great obligation which children are under to their parents for bringing them into a world of suffering, care, worry, and death. There are many who still think that the only right of the child is to be born or, by those puritanically inclined, it may be granted the additional right of being "born again" or else be damned forever. . . . Truly a baby is a thing of beauty, and we have good authority for the statement that it is a joy forever; but are babies developed in the direction of being perpetual joys? Does their loveliness increase? Will they never pass into nothingness, cussedness? The statement has often been made, that the problem as to whether life is worth living depends much upon the liver; so we are safe in saying that the question as to whether a babe is worth the borning and all that the term implies depends upon those engaged in, and responsible for, the borning. . . .

It is the right of every child to have something more than the privilege of calling a man father. It is his right also to have that father realize that "filial affection, like patriotism, must be engrained also as an obligation, a thing to blush at if not possessed.". . .

The father calls the child into being. Having done so, he assumes a duty which he should not neglect. It is the right of every child to have something more in his father than a mere provider of food and raiment. If the father wants the honor, the respect, and the enjoyment of the sweetest part of life, he must needs make himself acquainted with the child from the day of its birth on. It is as much his duty to study the disposition, character, and general human nature of his child as it is the mother's; indeed he has no more right to shirk his part of the sentimental relations between parent and child than has the mother.

Professor Love, aptly named, not only made a number of points regarding parental responsibility for the development of a child as a perpetual joy (or otherwise), but also put his finger on an ill in social thinking that is just as apparent today as it was in 1893. He stressed the role of the father but his point is this: that we, adults, think of the child as having no rights or privileges other than that of being born, and, possibly, being fed and clothed.

Could not this viewpoint be in part responsible for the enormous, and steadily increasing, incidence of child abuse we see in the world around us? The parents who severely maltreat their children are not a race apart from the parents who do not; and, in fact, the parents or parental figures whom we glibly describe as "monsters" or "insane" are not the only parents who savage their own children in one way or another. Some really nice people do it, very ordinary-seeming people who could be your friends or neighbors and whose values, on the whole, are similar to yours. Men and women in every walk of life, in every economic circumstance, of every degree of education, and of many different types of background form the ranks of child abusers. The potential for child abuse is present in every stratum of our society. The people who maltreat their children seem to think that they, as parents, have all the family rights and privileges and that the children to whom they have given the pleasure of being born owe them all the duties and responsibilities. Why shouldn't they think that? Most of the rest of us do, too, to some degree or another.

We often hear, and some studies have shown, that abuse and neglect tend to occur most often in large families of low socioeconomic status and educational achievement. But there are several reasons for this overloading of reports from the lower socioeconomic stratum. Among the reasons are, first, children who are abused, battered, or otherwise maltreated by the more prosperous parents are likely to be taken for treatment by private physicians who, in their turn, are less likely to suspect the parents of culpability and also less inclined, if they do suspect, to "violate the confidence" of the parents. They overlook the fact that the parents are not the patients. Second, relatives, friends, and other associates of "respectable," "comfortably-off" abusers are far more eager to cover up this unfortunate "aberration," possibly while attempting to help the child privately at the same time, than they are to report it to authorities and expose the "nice" family to a public situation that is not nice at all. Third, lower-income families suffer more stresses and strains than higher-income families, exacerbating circumstances such as financial stress itself, overcrowding, and pressures relating to the breadwinner's inability to provide. These stresses and frustrations are triggers to acts of child abuse which might never otherwise have occurred.

Child maltreatment in families or by individuals who are already in contact with social agencies and, possibly, the law, are in a position to be easily spotted and swiftly reported. As the sociologist Serapio R. Zalba observed in an article which appeared in *Trans-action* (July-August 1971), "Lower-class parents find that their misconduct is everyone's business." More educated, upper-income, upper-class parents are less visible. They do have the means, and they use the means, to conceal their actions. Thus, while certain studies show that the majority of reported cases are found in socioeconomically deprived cases, the same studies show that cases are far from infrequent in the comfortable, ostensibly well-organized homes of the well-educated and professionally successful. Steele and

Pollock's Denver study of child-attacking parents, embracing a wide range of socioeconomic groups, observed no concentration of cases in any one group.

If all the people we studied were gathered together, they would not seem much different than a group picked by stopping the first several dozen people one would meet on a downtown street. . . a random cross-section sample of the general population. They were from all socioeconomic strata, laborers, farmers, blue-collar workers, white-collar workers, and top professional people. Some were in poverty, some were relatively wealthy, but most were in between. They lived in large metropolitan areas, small towns, and in rural communities (Ray E. Helfer and C. Henry Kempe, eds., *The Battered Child* [Chicago: The University of Chicago Press, 1968], ch. 6, "A Psychiatric Study of Parents Who Abuse Infants and Small Children," by Brandt F. Steele and Carl B. Pollock).

The poor are not the only multiproblem families. And parents who maltreat their children do not always look the part.

Doctors Brandt F. Steele and Carl B. Pollock, in the course of their study, came to feel that "in dealing with the abused child we are not observing an isolated, unique phenomenon, but only the extreme form of what we would call a pattern or style of child rearing quite prevalent in our culture."

If there is such a pattern of child rearing in our culture (and there is), it has its roots in our concept of children's rights. It cannot be denied that we do slap and strike our children in the name of discipline, though "irritation" might be the better word. There isn't any doubt in my mind that our casual acceptance of violence, coupled with the concept of parental omnipotence, is responsible for the prevalence of corporal punishment and for *some* child abuse. The rigidly authoritarian parent who feels justified in demanding and exacting absolute submission from his child and in beating him until he gets it, may be one abusive parent whose actions relate to our child-rearing philosophy; yet he has distorted the normal concepts of discipline and punishment for his own less-than-normal reasons. The parent who torments and beats a child in the name of punishment for a minor or nonexistent or irrelevant transgression is not, by any stretch of the imagination, punishing a crime. His action, often one of calculated cruelty, is completely unrelated to discipline and is rooted in his own perverse fascination with the act of abuse. In other words, he enjoys what he is doing. The parent who succumbs to a momentary fit of rage and lashes out at the child in an uncontrollable and hurtful outburst of hostility is neither disciplining nor punishing the child; he knows very well, whatever he might say, that he has been overwhelmed by angry impulses that have nothing to do with correcting the child. This parent is an uncomfortably familiar person. He comes close to being any parent. Many parents come very close to losing control. They slap out in anger, they yell and they shove, and, on occasion, they hit a little too hard, and then they take a deep breath, check their impulses, and stop before they go too far.

There is, I believe, a fairly clear-cut difference between discipline and abuse: the parent who disciplines has in mind the welfare and best interests of the child; the one who abuses is indulging himself. There is also a cutoff point, if not a precisely defined one, between the exasperation of the normal parent, who occasionally feels himself letting go and then puts on the brakes, and the unbridled rage of the abusing parent. That point is the imposition of control, the act of stopping before the hostile emotion gets out of hand.

Therefore, while there is, in our culture, a relationship between our child-rearing beliefs and acts of violence against children, it is extremely difficult to accept the possible implication that the deliberate and sometimes ingenious torture inflicted by many abusing parents is a natural extension of the bottom-slapping disciplinary practices of nonabusing parents. Parents who question themselves and their attitudes, who worry about their flashes of anger, who do not blame their children for their own abuse, who are concerned about their disciplinary modes and motivations, who wonder if their instinct to "retaliate" is normal, who pull themselves up short and count to ten before walloping and then restrain themselves instead, are not abusers.

We have yet to discover all the factors that contribute to parental inability to care for their children; we have yet to draw a composite picture of the cruel parent or come up with a behavioral profile of the abuser. In time, research studies on neglectful and abusive parents will no doubt come up with all the contributory factors, with the predictive clues that will help us prevent maltreatment. But I do not believe we will ever produce a composite picture of the abusing parent. He is not one type of person; he is *many*. His motives cannot be simply traced to poverty, to cruelty, to rage, to a mistaken concept of discipline, to our child-rearing philosophy, or to the violence in our society. They are rooted in the sociological, psychological, and even biological characteristics of the offender.

What kinds of parents can do the terrible things we know they do to their children? They are:

## EMOTIONALLY IMMATURE

In this large group we find those parents who are afraid to grow up. Some of them are literally little more than children themselves, having married before arriving at a suitable age to assume the responsibilities of partnership and child rearing. Many of them *never* grow up, never reach emotional maturity. Their own needs continue to come first.

And even these people, of course, are not all alike. Among them are those who resent the child for arriving and forcing them to assume the grown-up role which they are not yet, and may never be, ready. The child is a reminder of their presumed adulthood and adult duties, and gets in the way of their own childish wishes. He ties them down when they'd rather be about their own childish business.

Other parents, in their immaturity, are insecure; they try, therefore, for a sense of security, in part, by laying down the law to the underlings in the home. The child who does not conform to their standards of desirable child-behavior, who resists their parental authority in any way ("He's bad, he doesn't listen, he wets his pants, he won't stop crying, he won't go to sleep, he doesn't want to eat") is a threat to them. They become frightened. They attack.

Then again there are parents who assume that the child will fill their own needs for love and affection. They expect the child to behave like an adult, to assume the parental role, to take care of and help the child-parent, to be supportive, to fill the void in the parent's emotional life. Naturally, no child can do this, although sometimes the child tries pathetically to mother and comfort the emotionally barren parent. But certainly the very young child cannot begin to fulfill this role. He does not give, he demands. He does not smile and gurgle all the time; he yells for attention and he slops his food. He cannot nurture the parent, and when he fails to, as he must fail, the parent thinks, "He cries, he gives me nothing, the baby doesn't love me." As a result there is a turning away from the child, neglect, perhaps, abusive rage.

Also among this group are the untrusting, isolated people who have difficulty in relating to others and enormous difficulty in relating to their children. It may be that, to them, all people are strangers, or the child is a constant reminder of a hated parent or spouse, or even a hated child-self. "He's just like me. I was a bad child. My mother had to beat me; I have to beat this child."

It seems to me, that it is not a very large step from immaturity to imbalance. Some parents who maltreat their children are emotionally unstable.


## NEUROTIC OR PSYCHOTIC

These are the people with personality disorders ranging from relatively mild to severe. Very few in this category are so disturbed as to be completely out of touch with reality. They require intensive and, often, prolonged treatment.

The vast majority of the "disturbed" group, however, are parents whose own upbringing and background have distorted their personality, attitudes, and values and left them unprepared for parenthood. In this sense, they are much like the immature. They are incapable of mothering (or parenting) because they were not mothered themselves; their own emotions have been pummeled out of shape, and they cannot share themselves with others. In their frustration over being unable to care or share, they strike out at the nearest vulnerable being; they impute to their children characteristics and motives and attitudes that children simply do not have, qualities that would be malicious or calculating in an adult but are impossible in a child. "She's trying to destroy me. She's trying to wreck my marriage." A one-year-old obviously can have no such motive. Her existence may precipitate the destruction of her parents' marriage, but certainly she does not try to achieve this dubious advantage. "He likes to stir up trouble." At two years old, a child does not deliberately stir up trouble, particularly if he knows that he is going to get walloped for his troublemaking. In later years, perhaps, such a child might become a mischief-maker, at two, he is neither Machiavelli nor Sacher-Masoch.

"He hates me!" Not yet. He may in time, but at eighteen months he doesn't know what hatred is. "All the time he's trying to run things. He thinks he's the boss. I showed him who's in charge around here." At nine months old, the child in question was not ready to regard himself as "the boss," nor could his supposedly bossy behavior possibly have warranted the skullsplitting blow administered by his father. "Look at her give you the eye! That's how she picks up men; she's a regular sexpot!" This battered three-year-old, struck savagely and repeatedly by her mother, may very well have been seeking for affection from other people, but she did not have a need for sex nor the capacity to arrange a pickup.

It is characteristic, it is one of the main characteristics, of the emotionally undernourished or imbalanced parent that he or she assumes in the child an adult capacity for organized, purposeful behavior; behavior that is at odds with the parents' needs.

## MENTALLY DEFICIENT OR UNINFORMED

Mentally retarded individuals are not necessarily unloving parents nor necessarily unsuccessful parents. They are at a disadvantage in that they may not have been able to learn all they need to know about child rearing or develop the capacity to reason through domestic crises or other difficult life situations. But most, if they can be reached, are perfectly capable of learning how to give their children appropriate care and to put their learning into practice. It is usually when they cannot be reached and helped that they become overwhelmed by their own inadequacies, by the terrible difficulties of coping, and seek a way out through exaggerated carelessness or abandonment or abuse. They don't know what to do, and they don't know how to think. Their handicap is comparable to that of their emotionally retarded counterparts.

Some few are so seriously retarded that, with all the help and teaching in the world, they cannot learn to be effective parents; they cannot provide the organization, the care, or even the love. These parents are likely to be at such an extreme disadvantage in the arts of homemaking and parenting that the slightest additional difficulty makes their situation seem impossible to them, and they turn on the child, who not only happens to be even more helpless than they but is also contributing to their distress. They can't control their own impulses not simply because they don't know how to, but because they haven't the faintest idea that they should. These are uninformed parents at their extreme. The home situation in these cases can never be made satisfactory for the children.

The cases of borderline intelligence are, by definition, less clearcut: how much is the maltreatment due to the parents' intellectual shortcomings and how much to other factors? It is extremely difficult to say, and therefore extremely difficult to handle.

It is common though not constant in abuse situations that only one child in a family of several is singled out as the scapegoat. This is the child who is poorly clothed and has sores, who huddles in corners and gets burned by radiators; the child who is invisible to the parent when meals are served; the child who gets infections that are never treated; the child who falls down because she is too weak to stay on her feet; the child who is slow in learning to talk; the child who fails to thrive and, incidentally, always seems to be covered with bruises. Sometimes one parent or the other, or both, will actually encourage the child's siblings to torment and mock the scapegoat. When asked the reason for such treatment, the offending parent is likely to explain that the child is "different," "wicked," "an idiot," "crazy," "not like one of us"; and will try to give the impression that the child is an imbecilic changeling foisted off on a blameless family by a malign fate.

This attitude appears to be particularly common among parents of borderline intelligence. In all categories of maltreating parents we find that a "special kind of child" often triggers the maltreatment. He may be unlovable (because he is not cute), or difficult, or irritating, or finicky of appetite, or have a birth defect, or be a boy instead of a girl, or scowl instead of smile, or cry all the time, or have a particularly grating quality to his cry that drives his parents, or one of them, to distraction. But among the abusers of borderline intelligence, we are far more likely to hear the excuses that "there is something wrong with this child," "he doesn't belong to us," I don't know where he came from; he isn't one of us, he's different."

They really seem to believe this. They neglect or strike the unloved, unwanted, "different" one and get rid of him by degrees. In the case of a stepchild or foster child, of course, the offenders really have something going for them. The child is truly not their own, and they feel quite justified in imputing to it strange or monstrous qualities and treating it as an intruder. The child who is in the least bit difficult to handle, exposed to the potentially abusive parent of borderline intelligence who regards him as being unreasonably cranky or demanding or unchildlike, is in a precarious position indeed. He is "asking for trouble." Some studies have, in fact, found that the child *is* inexplicably irritating or difficult or unlovable, or all three, and if separated from the abusing parent is likely to be abused in a foster home with a previously untarnished record. Did the child bring it on himself or was he just a colicky kid who, maltreated from the start, developed into the impossible brat he was always thought to be?

Then there are parents of normal or near-normal intelligence who are so uninformed about child behavior and the parental role that they have no inkling of the child's normal developmental stages or how they should be dealt with. These people may be well-intentioned; but when the child deviates from what they think is the normal standard of behavior, that is, the behavior that they wish the child to exhibit, they tend to think the child is disobedient or deliberately obstructive. Often they react by punishing the recalcitrant one, not realizing for a minute that they are expecting ten-year-old behavior from their two-year-old. When their methods fail they do not think to change them; they become angry and frustrated and increase the punishment. If he messes his diapers, they "let him lie in his own dirt." They force the food down his throat until he vomits; then they hit him. If spanking doesn't work the first few times, they wallop him all the harder. And if the fist is not effective in making him pick up after himself and mind his manners, then perhaps the belt buckle will be. They just don't know that no child of his age can perform the miracles they expect of him. And so they punish him.


## DISCIPLINARIANS

Disciplinarians may have mixed motives, but their rationale for speaking roughly to their little boy and beating when he sneezes is the age-old one that to spare the rod is to spoil the child. Like their peers in some of the other categories, they are likely to explain their punitive actions by saying that this is the way they were brought up and this is the way they intend to bring up their children. And they *were* brought up that way, beaten themselves and taught to believe in the fist and the stick as necessary means of discipline. Superficially, they are only living out our national belief that physical punishment is a legitimate method of child rearing, possibly the most effective way of compelling obedience. If "normal" disciplinary practices include slaps, ear-tuggings and energetic spankings, how easy it is to justify severe beatings or chaining a child to a bedpost. "It's for his own good. How else will he ever learn to do as he is told?"

The adult who is reproached for this behavior is astonished or appears to be. First, it is his right to bring up his child as he pleases. Second, he is only trying to do the very best he can to "teach respect," "straighten the kid out," "wallop the non-sense out of him," "make him grow up to be a useful citizen." These individuals claim not to understand why severe physical punishment is not acceptable or effective. What was right for their parents was right for them. After all, look how well *they* turned out. In many cases, these are rigid people who do not consciously believe that they are doing anything wrong. Even if the punishment, which they tend to carry to extremes, results in the permanent maiming or death of the child, they may still see themselves as in the right. Some don't; they may be brought sharply to their senses by the tragedy they have caused. Others sorrow but shrug. They were "only doing their best." And some don't sorrow at all. "It was his own fault. If he had only listened. Anyway, that is the way we do things where we come from."

The latter may be a lie. And even when it is not, even when the maltreating parent has convinced himself that he is doing the right thing, there are factors other than the desire to bring up the child according to his own "standards." He may not know what they are himself, but the disciplinarian-parent frequently couples an I-am-god attitude with a terrible anger or a ferocious pleasure in what he is doing. In his own way he, like other abusers, is striking out against the child in anger and frustration, secure (if falsely) in the knowledge that corporal punishment is part of the American way of life.

## CRIMINAL/SADISTIC

There is a group or type of people, fortunately relatively small, who beat and torment and kill for what one can only regard as the sheer joy of it. Amoral, asocial, without conscience or remorse, with total callousness, incapable of normal human relationships, they go their way destroying whatever they touch. To them, the act of child abuse has no conceivable relation to any provocation or stress or precipitating factor or behavorial lapse on the part of the child. Their actions are perverse, bizarre, totally unrelated to anything the child might be or say or do. They are performed to satisfy the perpetrator's own appalling tastes.

Over the years we have read of, and been revolted by, a number of horror stories relating the abduction, murder, and mutilation of young children by strangers, individuals indulging their own disgusting predilections by seizing and mangling other people's children. These stories, these facts, are bad enough. But more recently, we have become aware of similar incidents in which not strangers but parents and stepparents are the perpetrators. They don't lure children anywhere; they have them right there at home.

A father, who first sodomized his baby daughter and then beat her to death, showed no remorse or even interest afterwards. It is difficult to understand the handsome young couple who admitted to the fatal beating of their four-year-old son and, by way of explanation, said they had done it for kicks and enjoyed it. It is no easier to grasp the mentality of the man who tortured the five-year-old son of his common-law wife, forced the child under an icy shower, threw him down on the living room floor and jumped up and down on his stomach, then settled down with a cold beer to watch television while the boy lay gasping and dying.

There is no point in dwelling on these cases at this stage. We will come to similar ones in later chapters. But these are the cases that sell newspapers. For anyone deeply concerned about the problem of child maltreatment they serve a dual and conflicting purpose: they bring sharp attention to the existence of child abuse, which is fine; but they overstress the criminal-sadistic element, leading readers to believe that child maltreatment is always equivalent to murder, that cases of it are so rare as to always wind up in the headlines, and that maltreatment is inevitably perpetrated by monstrously aberrant people. These *are* horrifying cases and compel action; but the greater problem is the submerged bulk of the iceberg, the insidious cases that lead to slow, unnoticed death, or maiming, or waste of potential, or generations of abuse.

Although I have made the statement that infanticide, physical abuse, abandonment, neglect, and various forms of maltreatment have existed throughout the ages, dependent to some degree on the particular stresses and strains of the times, I have to say again that this manifold disease appears to be steadily on the increase. How much this has directly to do with the strain of wars, with our emphasis on technological over human development—with what Dr. Milton Helpern, chief medical examiner of the city of New York, refers to as the "lack of decency" in the way people treat other people and children nowadays—I cannot really judge. But I do know that a relatively new element in our lives is contributing enormously to the number of children being maltreated today. The element is drug addiction.

## ADDICTS

Hard drugs are a relatively new arrival on the scene. Alcohol has been with us for a long time. So has alcoholism, a form of addiction. But, like the rest of our social ills, it seems to be on the increase. And with its increase has come an increase in child maltreatment.

Alcoholism is a lubricating agent in the inner machinery that produces abuse. A lot of alcoholics wouldn't dream of hurting their children, and their use of the lubricating agent may not result in obvious damage. Its influence may simply ooze its way through the home, subtly affecting all family relationships and distorting all attitudes. The alcoholic may be basically a good parent; but alcoholism in family life, even if it is not manifested in mother sleeping all day or father coming home to smash the furniture after losing his job, must have an insidiously detrimental effect on growing children. We cannot properly measure the uneasiness, the bewilderment, the insecurity they feel, and we are not surprised when they exhibit delinquent behavior.

Fortunately, many children of controlled alcoholics escape relatively unscathed. In other families and in other homes where there is less control, the damage may be overt and drastic. People who are preoccupied with drinking to the extent that they cannot function as employees or homemakers have little interest in their children's needs. They have to feed their habit. These are neglectful parents, mothers and fathers (or stepfathers or other surrogates), who leave their children alone for hours or even days on end, who don't care whether they go to school or not, who can't be bothered to keep them clean or take them to see a doctor, who can't afford to buy them clothes because their own habit consumes whatever money they may have. Equally harmful are those alcoholic parents who may or may not neglect their children but physically abuse them. They may be the most gentle of souls when sober, but the alcohol acts as a trigger, just as an accident in the kitchen or the cry of a child or some other provocation acts as a trigger for another type of parent, to a bout of abuse. This may be a regular occurrence or it may happen only occasionally, but even once may be too often.

What is true of alcoholics is even more true of drug addicts. I would estimate that about 7,000 of the child maltreatment cases seen in this city within the last year have involved drug-addicted parents. If the alcoholic is preoccupied with his habit to the neglect of his children or cannot afford to care for them while supporting his own needs, how much worse off is the drug addict and his family. Leaving aside for the moment the question of the addicted mother whose baby is born hooked and may die or be permanently damaged by the trauma of

infantile withdrawal, let us consider the family life of a child
in a drug-abusing household. It is bad enough when only one
parent is on drugs. (Often there *is* only one parent in the junkie
home, not infrequently a prostitute mother.) Suppose that
parent is the father. He will do anything for money—steal, rob,
mug, kill, anything but work. But where does the money go?
Not to the mother; not to the children; not to the home. It
goes into the junkie's veins. In the absence of money to provide the necessities of life, even the nonaddicted parent or
partner may become neglectful. But there may still be some
hope for the home and children so long as one parent is drug-
free. If both are addicted, the home becomes a "shooting gallery" and the neglect extreme. On a lovely high, who wants to
get up and warm the milk and feed a crying baby? And once
down from that high, who wants to do anything but get right
back up again? Who can be bothered to clean house? Change
the diapers? Wash the baby? Do something about his sores
and his rash? Take out the garbage? Buy *food?* Hock the furniture, maybe, to support the habit, but never to buy unnecessary stuff like food and clothes for the kids.

Situations of this sort often turn into murder, either by
starvation or disease or physical abuse or failure to notice that
the baby's crawling out the sixth-floor window. If they do
not, the child of such a couple stands a good chance of becoming an addict himself at a very early age. Not all the eight- and
nine- and ten-year-old addicts we see on our streets today
have been turned on by pushers or older children. More and
more of them become addicts because that is what their
parents are. This may be better than ending up dead in a sewer
at the age of three, dumped by addict parents; but I'm not at
all sure how much better.

In the area of drug and alcohol abuse, the lines between
categories blur. There are criminal-sadistic addicts and mentally defective alcoholics; there are drunks who are strict
disciplinarians according to their own lights, and mainliners
who are emotional disaster cases; there are drinkers and addicts
of all levels of intelligence and from all manner of environ-
ments; there are among them people who hate, people who

fear, people who have forgotten how to love, people who don't care what they are and don't want to change, and people who care terribly.

The disease of child maltreatment afflicts all kinds of parents, many, if not most, of whom do not recognize their behavior as misbehavior until it is pointed out to them. While it is true, as we will see in a moment, that the actions of some abusive mothers are in themselves a cry for help, the majority of maltreating parents are in no way ready to spare the rod, warm up the cold shoulder, subordinate their interests to the interests of the child, clean up the crib, doctor the sores, or admit wrongdoing in placing a child's hand over a gas flame to demonstrate what will happen to him if he plays around with the gas burners. They have little in common with the parents who, deep down, want to be spared from destroying their children; they have very little in common with each other. There are only a few factors that are more or less constant in the picture of parents who abuse, neglect, and batter their children; the most constant fact is that the parents themselves were nearly always abused or battered or neglected as children. Another near-constant is the inability of maltreating parents to identify with or relate to other people, including or especially their own children; and their lack of understanding of the needs and limitations of children. Battering parents, particularly, tend to share an inability to cope with stress; they require little provocation to lose control and give vent to their hostility. In David G. Gil's book, *Violence Against Children* (Cambridge: Harvard University Press, 1970) psychiatrist Irvin D. Milowe puts it this way: "The parent's childhood loads the gun, present life conflicts cause the parents to raise it; the child's phase-specific needs help pull the trigger. . . ."

We also find that child maltreatment occurs most frequently in broken or disintegrating homes, whether those homes be in the ghettos or in the more salubrious suburbs; and when it happens in a home that is apparently intact, the parents often interact like pieces in a jigsaw puzzle: a potentially abusive parent seems able to select a mate of somewhat similar if less pronounced proclivities, or one that is so passive that he or she is unable to interfere.

But apart from these general factors, the variations and gradations of difference between the many, many types of child abusers are virtually countless. What is cause for considerable concern is that one most constant factor: that the parents themselves were maltreated. This sometimes goes back for generations, and I am afraid it might go forward for many more. Today's abuse is not a healthy signpost for the future. As the twig is bent, if it doesn't break, so grows the tree; and in another generation we will have yet more trouble on our hands.

But our immediate concern is what is going on today. I have beside me a file from which I have pulled, with every intention of making a completely random selection, portraits of abusing parents. Interestingly, they don't look random at all. There is scarcely a horror story among them. Furthermore, the abuser in each case is the mother. In my experience the man/woman ratio is closer to fifty/fifty. But it should be remembered that in a broken home it is usually the mother who has charge of the children; and that in an intact home with an employed *or* unemployed father, it is still the mother who has to stay home tied to the children. It is, in short, usually the mother who is on the spot, often under conditions of domestic stress, and unable to get out for a break from the children.

The first thing that comes to hand from my "Parents" file is a letter sent from a small-to-middle-sized town in Central U.S.A. Its writer must remain anonymous.

I would like to tell you of my own case, to explain why I feel more strongly than most people that more effective laws to have cases of mistreated children reported are for the best interests of all concerned. I was (I suppose "battering parent" would be the best term) appalled to discover after the birth of my first child that I had spells of unprovoked viciousness toward the child. With the craftiness of a sick mind, I hid all evidence of scars or bruises or lied to explain them away. But something rational still operated enough to insist that my behavior was highly abnormal, and that I needed help. The horrible thing was that I did not know where to go for help, and when I finally forced myself to the offices of various social agencies, I was so afraid of having the child taken away and my behavior thus exposed to friends and relatives, that I could hardly speak of the problem. Even when I could, I found that social workers could not really help me.

At this time we were living in one of the states that did have a law on reporting the mistreatment of children. But to my confusion, the sick portion of my personality that willfully burned, beat, and terrorized the child covered its own tracks so well, that when I sat in someone's office, rational and calm, and explained what I had done, I was not taken seriously. I thoroughly wished that there was someone to stop me and help me.

Finally, I moved up through bureaus and agencies to a psychiatrist. Here I obtained help, but I might add that many people could not afford this. It remains my contention that parents who maliciously mistreat their children can be helped, but only by the most expert and advanced forms of treatment. The whole personality has to be remade to stop this one dangerous manifestation of mental illness, because that's what it is.

I know other parents with the same problem. I was somewhat primed to spot them, as the old saying goes, "It takes one to know one," and none of them showed enough change to indicate they were undergoing treatment. From my own experience, it took three years from the time the behavior began until I was finally getting competent help, and, at that, I was actively seeking help.

As for the statistics on such parents, some of them certainly fit. I spent my early years in welfare homes, acquired a stepfather at the age of five, and he beat me regularly until I left home at seventeen. I married, woefully immature and pregnant, at eighteen to a boy as young and inexperienced as myself. And undoubtedly the pressures of helping my husband work his way through five years of college, with two children before he graduated, added to the frustrations that erupted in violence against an innocent child. Incidentally, for a note on the other parent involved, since it is usually only one who abuses a child, my husband was unable to give me all the emotional support I needed, but he also felt helpless. He protected the child when he was there, but, of course, I only waited until he wasn't home. He did not want to take any action himself to report me, because that would involve breaking up his own family. He could not believe for a long time that my behavior could be so unbalanced, a hard thing to accept about someone you love and need.

I hope these details might be of some value or interest to you.

Competent help finally did solve the problem, although I am not yet able to feel as much warmth toward that child as the others. Somehow I hope I can make it up to her someday.

This may be one of the most honest and revealing self-portraits of an abusing mother that we are ever likely to see. The letter brings up a number of interesting questions and speculations, but to me the most salient feature is this: *This battering mother searched desperately for help and almost didn't find it.*

I can't help wondering how many other parents there are who are similarly searching but with less fortunate results.

## ELSA TOMASELLI

It was not too long ago that Mrs. Tomaselli and her problems came to our attention. Her three-and-a-half-year-old son, Rafael, was referred to the pediatric division because of dangerous physical abuse committed by his mother and reported by her. He was, in fact, hospitalized twice within a five-week period, and he was in extremely bad shape. The saving grace was that he had no skull fracture or brain damage. Mrs. Tomaselli voluntarily sought counseling at our psychiatric outpatient clinic because she said she was so "nervous and irritable" that she was unable to control herself around her small son. By her own admission, she was disciplining the boy for age-appropriate behavior. Even in the presence of social work and medical professionals, she beat Rafael and threatened to throw him down the stairs, out the window, and so on. She admitted to beating the child severely with a hand, a belt, or any other convenient implement and described how, in outbursts of rage, she would throw him across the room and against the wall, or down on the floor, or punch him black and blue. She was afraid of what she might eventually do to the child even though her husband and other children had gotten into the habit of intervening protectively.

Mr. and Mrs. Tomaselli have been married for twenty-five

years. There are nine children out of fifteen pregnancies, some of which are suspected to have been terminated by criminal abortions. Six of the children live at home with their parents. Rafael is the youngest child. (His oldest sibling is twenty-six.)

Mrs. Tomaselli's own background is a miserable one. She was raised in a home in which bickering and fighting were constant, the comforts very few. Her four older siblings left home as soon as they could find somewhere else to go, and she moved out with her out-of-wedlock pregnancy when she was eighteen.

Mr. Tomaselli's past was even more unfortunate. At the age of four he witnessed the murder of his own father by another man. He grew up in a child-care institution, which he left at age sixteen. Some twenty years ago he had a nervous breakdown and spent a year or two under treatment at a state hospital. Apart from this hiatus, he worked steadily throughout the years and took pride in being able to support his family on his modest pay. His wife, however, complained that, steadily employed though he might be, he was not so steady around the house and didn't take much interest in the children.

The Tomaselli marriage has been a stormy one, and, until a few years ago, Mr. Tomaselli used to beat his wife until she turned black and blue, fracturing several ribs in the process. She went around for years with black eyes and broken fingers and bruises. But by the time the Tomasellis came to our attention, he had given up physical beatings and only beat her verbally.

What we saw in Elsa Tomaselli was a depressed and distraught middle-aged woman who had been "nervous" and "irritable" for a number of years. Her story of her marriage, calmly told, sounded like a tale of jungle warfare. She expressed deep remorse and guilt over her uncontrollable anger and violence toward her little son, but she didn't know how to stop herself. It seemed to us that she was a woman overwhelmed by many real and mostly inescapable problems, a miserable marriage, poverty, too many pregnancies, too many people in too few rooms, no beauty or pleasure in her world, and nothing to look forward to.

Mr. Tomaselli was of very little help to her or to the social service agency in seeking a solution. He was, in fact, part of the problem. That he was actually "supporting" his large family out of his small earnings was self-delusion; his take-home pay did not stretch to meet the family's needs. His attitude toward his wife swung wildly from brief moments of sympathetic care to furious bursts of rage in which he would belittle and insult her. He seemed to have no idea of the extent of Mrs. Tomaselli's problem in regard to Rafael, even though he once called the police to their home to report that she was abusing the boy. It was our impression that he had done this not so much to save either Rafael or the mother as to spite his wife. Certainly at no time did he appear to realize how dangerous the situation was nor come near to understanding the depth of her despair. It did seem that her life was insupportable. It was not surprising that she had been driven to strike out. Too bad the target had to be her little boy.

## AUDREY BRANDON

Mrs. Brandon is an attractive, poised woman of about thirty, articulate and spontaneous of speech. She entered our file when her seven-year-old boy, Alec, was admitted to the hospital from the emergency clinic, having been brought in by ambulance from his home accompanied by his mother and several policemen.

A divorcee, Mrs. Brandon had been having mounting problems with Alec since he was about four, when he had started having temper tantrums and showing jealousy of his mother's occasional male visitors. As time wore on, Alec, who was a quick and bright boy, increasingly provoked his mother with what she considered to be rather subtle, sneakily clever forms of disobedience. After an escalating series of incidents that irritated and outraged her, capped by an instance of almost frightening defiance, she lost her head and began beating him hysterically. They were in the bathroom at the time, preparing for his bath; she yanked him from his feet and thrust him into the tub and held him underwater. He fought back savagely, came up for air, smashed his head against a soap-dish, started to bleed profusely. The sight of the blood suddenly shocked her out of her hysteria. She had a terrible feeling that she had come close to killing him, and that she would have killed him if the blood hadn't brought her to her senses.

She called the police to notify them that she had beaten her child and may have hurt him very seriously. He was admitted to the hospital with multiple abrasions and contusions, and his left shoulder appeared to be dislocated. Mrs. Brandon was once again in an hysterical state, appalled by what she had done and afraid of what she might do in the future. She was quite badly bruised since Alec had kicked and pummeled her in his struggle for life.

Audrey Brandon's own parents had been divorced when she was one year old. She, her sister, and her mother had moved in with the maternal grandparents, who were comfortably off but lacking affection and constantly on the move because of the demands of their business. When Audrey was nine her mother remarried. The stepfather was well-intentioned but always busy. There was a great deal of moving about from one part of the country to another and no place to call home.

As a girl, Mrs. Brandon had been an excellent student who breezed through her courses. She also had the makings of a fine professional dancer as well as a flair for creative writing. When she married, she entered into a business partnership with her husband Paul and was largely responsible for the success of their joint enterprise. Paul was not the most mature of men. When the baby was born he became childishly jealous of the child; he refused to hold him or play with him, complained about his crying, and finally left home. That was when Alec was eight months old.

After the divorce, Mrs. Brandon went into business for herself. She rapidly made a success of it and was soon operating a very lucrative public relations consultancy from her home. She raised Alec with the help of a series of housekeepers who were perhaps more mother to him than she was herself. Husband Paul rarely visited, and when he did he talked only about his own problems and showed no interest in Alec. Mrs. Brandon tried to build a satisfactory home and life without him; she made sure that Alec always had the best of everything. Although she worked long hours, she managed to entertain at home once in a while.

And then Alec began to bother her. He didn't do the typical naughty-boy things. He was "calculating," he was "sly," he "deliberately needled" his mother. She described him as a provocateur, a sneak, a kid who said one thing to the housekeeper behind her back and something else to her, who denied having said anything to the housekeeper at all, who was hostile to men who called at the house, who broke his promises, who did the opposite of everything she asked of him, talked back to her, and generally drove her to distraction. On occasion, when she became exasperated and spoke sharply to him he would shout back defiantly and accuse her of hating him. He was yelling at her and making an obscene gesture when her control snapped, and she came close to killing him.

Mrs. Brandon welcomed all the help she could get from the Society for the Prevention of Cruelty to Children, from the court, from the appointed psychiatrist, and she was cooperative in every respect. She was frightened by her poorly controlled anger and acutely aware of the seriousness of her problem. It was perfectly apparent to her that, if left to her own devices and without any change in herself or the boy, she was entirely capable of losing control again and not regaining it before beating Alec to death. She had the brains to understand what was happening to her, even if not *why* it was happening; her intellect was superior, she was highly creative, she had plenty of business savvy, and she had a strong personality. In some respects, life had not shortchanged her. But her childhood was rootless and loveless. Out of her own emotional deprivation, she had picked a weak and immature husband and then failed to come to grips with her own role as mother. She demanded too much of Alec; he was incapable of giving her the adult love and care and understanding that she craved and, of course, incapable of the mature behavior and perception she expected. And she in turn could not provide the selfless love he needed. Without realizing it, she was neglecting his deepest needs just as her own had been neglected and was providing him with a home life just as unstable and sterile as hers had been. And he, a goodlooking, healthy, intelligent boy, was well on his way to becoming very much like his mother. With all her intelligence, she insisted that he understood everything she said to him and could master his behavior if he wanted to. But Alec, at seven, could do no such thing; and she, at thirty, couldn't either. Not until she sought help and received it.

## JULIA GOMEZ

This woman, twenty-seven years old when she came before the court on a neglect petition, was married to a passive, dependent man of her own age. In the seven years of their marriage, they had had five children. Mrs. Gomez had been brought to court by the Society for the Prevention of Cruelty to Children, which had been keeping voluminous hospital and case records on the Gomez family over a period of years. On the strength of these records and caseworker observations, the society alleged that Mrs. Gomez beat her children so severely that one little girl had probably died of beatings at the age of two; that another in the hospital, aged one-and-a-half, had been beaten with extreme severity and was not yet out of danger; and that in all likelihood the other children had also been beaten even though not hospitalized.

Mrs. Gomez denied the allegations. What precipitated Mrs. Gomez's arrival in court at this time, trailed unwillingly by her husband Efram, was the condition of her ten-month-old baby, Juanita. The child was in the hospital with fractures of the radius and ulna, multiple swellings and bruises, and damage to internal organs. Checking her history, we found that she had previously been hospitalized only a few weeks earlier on a diagnosis of malnutrition, and that she had, two months earlier, been a patient at another hospital with a fracture of the right ulna and abscess of the right temple.

Juanita's older sister, Carmelita, deceased, had been admitted five times to various hospitals with fractures. On a sixth occasion, she had been taken to Bellevue Hospital emergency room where she was pronounced dead on arrival from internal hemorrhages.

No action had been taken at that time. Mrs. Gomez had vaguely ascribed the death of Carmelita to prematurity. Now, on being reinterviewed, she said that the had awakened early one morning to find the child having a convulsion in her crib. Mrs. Gomez had panicked, she said, picked Carmelita up out of her crib, suddenly had a dizzy spell, fell downstairs, and landed on top of the child whom she still held in her arms.

The child, as noted, was dead on arrival at Bellevue. Mrs. Gomez was totally without mark or injury.

The Gomez family lived in a housing project which had been in a state of deterioration for a number of years. Efram Gomez, employed in a menial and poorly-paying job, had no relatives in this country. Julia Gomez had unemployed parents and several siblings living in another borough, whom she saw only on very rare occasions. She was lonely, she said, and would like to have seen them more often, but she could not afford the transportation and she did not get along at all well with her parents.

Julia Gomez said that she, like her husband, was of the Pentecostal faith and neither drank nor smoked. She seemed to be tense and nervous when interviewed and denied almost everything that was asked of her even when no accusation was implicit in the question. Even more passive than her husband, she appeared "very dull and cowlike" to those who interviewed her. She had dropped out of public school in the eighth grade at the age of fifteen, having achieved a very poor school record; and she gave the impression of being of borderline intelligence at best and possibly mentally defective.

Mrs. Gomez was not only nervous of manner to the observers but repeatedly, in interviews with social workers, described

herself as very nervous, not of the interview situation in particular, but of everything. She said that she got terribly nervous and started screaming whenever anything happened to
the children. Since the children were constantly "falling out of
bed" and otherwise managing to hurt themselves, she must
have done considerable screaming. Her various accounts of
how one child had nearly fallen out of a window, why another
had strange "tumors" or "blisters" (her words) on his head,
and whether she had or had not had convulsions as a child or
epileptic seizures as an adult were conflicting and confusing.

When asked whether she had many friends or acquaintances,
she shrugged and said that she talked to very few people. Her
social contacts were extremely limited. She never got out
except to shop because she was tied down with the children
all day. She didn't know her neighbors in the project and didn't
intend to get to know them because she disapproved of them.
But she was a meticulous housekeeper. Her home was very
neat and clean. So were her surviving children: compulsively
neat and clean, suitably dressed, underweight, and very quiet.

This mother, after her initial resistance, was most cooperative
in attitude. She agreed to everything; she would do just exactly
whatever she was advised to do, and she would most certainly
accept any suggestions or plans involving further investigation
into past history or her care of the children still at home. But
even while she was saying all this, her vague, nervous, flat,
not-quite-with-it manner did not change; and it hasn't changed
yet. Maybe it never will.

## DOROTHY CLARK

This mother of two little boys is not married to their father.
He does not live with the family nor does he wish to marry
Dorothy "yet." He explains that he is on public assistance and
would be ashamed not to be able to support his family as a
husband and father should.

When Dorothy Clark first brought three-month-old Eddie

to the emergency room, she seemed to be doing it out of genuine concern for him. He cried terribly, she said, whenever he moved or tried to move his left leg. She thought he might have hurt himself falling out of the plastic baby seat in his crib, even though he only landed on the mattress and did not fall to the floor.

When X-rays showed a fracture of the left femur, this story began to sound more than a little unlikely. While Eddie was in the hospital for treatment of that fracture, routine X-rays were made of the long bones and skull. X-rays of the ribs and upper extremities were somewhat ambiguous (revealing areas of periosteal elevation), but there was no doubt about the three fractures revealed by the skull X-rays.

Dorothy Clark denied neglect or abuse of her child and seemed very concerned about him. Eddie was treated and released as a well baby.

Six months later, he was readmitted with additional leg fractures. It was now very difficult to accept the accident theory.

Eddie was a year old when his brother William was born. William was eleven days old when he was admitted to the hospital with gangrene of both feet. His mother had noticed that the baby's feet were cold and turning blue, and she had anxiously rushed him in to the emergency room. Because of Dorothy Clark's history with Eddie, who was actually awaiting placement as a result of court action against his mother, abuse was strongly suspected. Again, it was difficult to prove or disprove. It was possible that a virus had caused the baby's condition. Sad to say, amputation of both feet was necessary. Dorothy Clark appeared to be most distressed.

While William was being treated, Eddie was placed in a foster home. Dorothy Clark seemed to be quite relieved that he had been removed from her care, even while insisting that she wanted to have both children with her. Similarly, when it was suggested to her that baby, William, now a seriously handicapped child, needed long-term rehabilitative care in a hospital setting, she at first demurred and then quite gladly acceded to his placement in an appropriate institution.

By now it was obvious that the coincidental happenings could not be accidental. Either abuse or extreme negligence was surely indicated. An investigation got under way.

Dorothy, in her midtwenties at the time of these mishaps, was born in a southern state. She was the only child of battering parents. Her parents separated when she was three years old, and she was raised by her mother and maternal grandparents in a home that met all essential material needs. A bright girl, she graduated from high school with good grades and entered the state college to study nursing at her own expense. After completing two years of the course, she interrupted her studies and came to New York to earn the money to carry her through the rest of her training so that she would not have to continue working part-time while studying. She had worked part-time during those first two years, and, though her grades had not suffered, she had had to work extremely long hours and had become exhausted. Her mother, though employed herself, had been unable to help her financially. No assistance had come from the father throughout the years.

Dorothy Clark worked in New York for a year. For whatever reason, the strangeness of the lonely city or her own inability to reach out, she made no friends. With her usual diligence, she worked very hard and did manage to save money. Unfortunately, her mother became very ill, lost her own job, and needed both Dorothy's presence and her savings. Dorothy went home and spent a year looking after her ailing mother. Then she returned to New York without finishing her nursing course and went to work in a factory. The city still seemed strange and inimical, and she had virtually no social life. The first person to show friendship to her in New York became the father of her children, a man "too proud" to marry her until he could find a job, which he seemed to have great difficulty in doing.

When interviewed, Dorothy Clark was still very much alone; a confused, unhappy young woman entrapped by loneliness into an emotional involvement with a young man no more secure than she. In regard to her children, she presented a conflicting picture of guilt, bewilderment, and irritation. She resented the questions and their implications, but she was a bright enough young woman to realize that her inability to explain what happened to Eddie and William inevitably cast suspicion on her. She said that she missed her children and was very lonely without them, yet at the same time she was glad that she no longer had the responsibility for them. It had been very hard for her, working and trying to look after them at the same time, without a steady man to help her.

As for her lover, he had not been supportive during her pregnancies and was with another woman during both of her confinements. When the babies arrived, he was very critical of her handling of them without being in any way helpful, and, after the accidents occurred, he wondered aloud in public and at great length how they could possibly have happened. As the investigation progressed, he gradually withdrew from her, and though to the end he swore he fully intended to marry her some day, she was virtually abandoned.

Perhaps he did so because Dorothy Clark finally confessed. She was adamant in her insistence that she had nothing to do with Eddie's injuries, but William had irritated her with his little-baby demands and his everlasting crying, and she had bound a rope around both his legs and hung him upside down. Then, when his feet turned blue and cold, she cut him down and brought him in for help.

These are the guilty parents, with revealing glimpses of the spouse or lover, the silent partner in crime.

The preceding parental portraits are typical of the majority or at least of a very large number of problem parents, but bear little resemblance to the popularly accepted picture of the maltreating parent as a fiend in human form. Granted, these people have done some appalling things and one or two of them may be beyond rehabilitation; granted, too, that there are appreciable numbers of maltreating parents who do seem to us depraved beyond recognition as human beings, and with whom we find it impossible to identify. There are many cases on record of calculated mistreatment, of prolonged torture, of brutal beating culminating in a little body being packed into a suitcase or buried in the woods or weighted down in a river. But

there are many more cases of parents who are not conspic-
uously different from you or me, or what we might have been,
who are, in a sense, striking back at their own past or their
own unbearable present; who are, in effect, in the very act of
abuse, crying out "Help me! Where am I going to turn?"

# CHAPTER FIVE

# Sick Families and the Violence Cycle

IT IS VERY DIFFICULT for the most remorseful and guilt-ridden of maltreating parents to seek help, and even more difficult for help to seek them out. Our sympathies lie with the children, but it is not only the children who cry. Parents cry, too, for the pain they cause and the pain they feel themselves. There is often a look of bewilderment and despair on a young parent's face. Swift denials are followed by sudden, terrible remorse. There are sobs of recollection mingled with those of relief.

A young woman brought her baby son to my office not long ago. He was the picture of happiness and health. His visit was routine. Hers was less so. She seemed to be a serene, contented woman. She had heard about my crusade for children, my anger over our national do-nothingness in the face of the problem, and about my public statements which maintained that stiffer penalties were necessary in some child-abuse cases to make hard-core abusive parents realize that they cannot go on hurting their children and getting away with it.

She began calmly enough, telling me she was particularly interested in my viewpoints and what I was trying to do because she abused her first two children when they were very small. She had been very careful to do it only when alone with them, she said, and she did it in little, mean ways (and now her voice started to break), holding each child, in its turn, just a little too tightly, pinching where the marks would not show, placing a hand over the small, crying mouth and keeping it there until the child could scarcely breathe, and biting the fingertips in spite of the screams.

Even while doing these things she had hated herself. But she couldn't tell anyone, least of all her husband. She couldn't understand why she was doing it; she wanted desperately to stop. "I was frightened. And I was terribly ashamed. I didn't want anybody to know. I couldn't talk to a psychiatrist or a social worker or anyone like that. I couldn't tell a stranger, or a friend, or my mother, or my sister. I couldn't bring myself to go to one of those public agencies. But I was desperate. I bought books. I went to the library, and I read, and I studied, and I began to understand a little bit more about my kids and myself. Now I've stopped. I'm all right now. But it was hell. It was absolute hell."

She didn't tell me what books she had read that she had found so helpful. I wish she had, because other parents might find them helpful too. But I was glad that she had found them and impressed that she had tried so hard to help herself and that she had succeeded. Soon afterwards she left my office, gently hugging her baby. Exactly how she made it I don't suppose she'll ever be able to tell me. But I think she must be a young woman of unusual inner resources. She made it, and I am proud of her.

Yet I am haunted by the shadow image of her story. It is heartening that she was able to help herself, and disheartening that she was unable to reach out to other people in her need. Was this because, like many other child abusers, she simply could not share her emotions or her fears, that she did not have sufficient trust in other people to seek their help, that she had not learned to "use" others legitimately in time of trouble, as most of the rest of us have? Or had we, those of us who had cried out the longest and loudest against the monstrosity of child abuse, branded her so deeply with her sense of stigma that we had crowded her into her corner to be alone with her excessive shame? The latter is a sobering thought. And there is something else that bothers me here. "Public agencies," be-

lieve it or not, exist to serve the public. Perhaps if their image
were a little more wholesome and their record more reputable,
she might have felt differently about turning to one to seek the
help it was established to provide. The trouble is, I suppose,
that we as a people have come to rely on our institutions to
think and act for us; and our institutions—not just our buildings
and organizations and public bodies but our principles, concepts, laws, ideals, and systems—are badly administered. We
have come to rely on them to let us down. And they do.

In spite of these agencies, and once in a while because of
them, maltreated parents who earnestly seek help can actually
be helped. Sometimes when the system works at all it works
reasonably well. Treatment, though not a miracle cure, is available. But unfortunately our institutions may fall down on the
job, and the seekers of help may fail in their search. The parent
who has to wait for months before a psychiatrist can give her
an appointment, the parent whose caseworker never seems to
have the time to come and visit her, is standing in line for help
but getting nowhere.

Then there are the many people who do not seek help. Deep
inside, the majority of these people are probably hoping that
help of some kind will seek them out, which it is likely to do
only after they have severely maltreated their children. Deep
inside a fair-sized minority is the hope that they will be able to
go on doing what they are doing without ever being discovered.

It is when the maltreatment is not discovered, exposed, and
stopped that the violence cycle begins.

Maltreatment is not a clear-cut matter of interaction between
abusing parent and target child. It is a family affair, involving
the active abuser/neglecter, the passively cooperative or un-
seeing mate, and the other children in the family, who may or
may not be active participants but are certainly observers. And
while it is true that maltreatment, particularly physical abuse,
is often directed primarily at one child, it has happened time
and time again that the child who is removed from the abusing
household by death or by the intervention of a social agency
has been replaced as scapegoat by a second child and sometimes by a third. It can hardly be imagined what the environ-

ment of ugliness and terror must do to the child who is part of it, who sees what is happening to one or more of his siblings, who perhaps wonders whether he may be next. Prime target or not, he stands very little chance of growing up whole. The survivors are not necessarily the lucky ones, nor is society likely to be much enriched by their survival.

## THE RIVERA FAMILY

At the time this case broke, none of the children had been fortunate enough to have been removed from the family home. They were all being maltreated, some more badly then others. It is difficult to see a bright future for any of them.

This family made news, though not a major news story, when police found seven-year-old Jimmy Rivera wandering the streets with both his hands severely burned. When they took him back to his home they found seven siblings ranging in age from 18 months to 12 years, all of whom were, to one degree or another, bruised, burned, and scarred from beatings. The parents were not at home. The youngest child was found tied up in a bedroom. Older children explained that their mother often did that, whether she was going out or not, so that the baby wouldn't be a nuisance. The patrolmen afterwards described the home as unbelievably filthy and the bedroom as a torture chamber, not just because it had been used to imprison a fettered child but because there were objects in it, hurtful objects, that were sinisterly out of place in a child's room.

Upon being picked up and charged with child abuse, Mr. and Mrs. Rivera (thirty-five and twenty-seven years old) expressed surprise at the police attitude. But of course children must be made to behave! Who else was to keep them in line if not the parents, and how else could it be done but by using the greatest firmness and showing who was in charge? "This is the way we bring up our children where we come from," they explained. "Everybody does it." (Perhaps this was true of the environment from which they came, a subculture within a culture that is not notable for condemning this type of child rearing.) Part of discipline, apparently, was to keep them hungrv as well as whipped, because all the children were thin to the point of emaciation. The twelve-year-old was already a school dropout said to be adept with his switchblade. And the two little girls who did go to school on occasion were not particularly welcome there because they sometimes dug their fingers into other children's eyes and pulled their hair; and they had even been known to kick their teachers in the shins. Of course, the other kids and their teachers had done little to deserve this; but somebody had. Who exactly? One is not quite sure.

Through some quirk of fate or court this family has, to date, been permitted to remain intact. The parents have cleaned up the place and made a number of promises regarding the future treatment of their children. An overloaded caseworker from a private protective agency makes spot checks as he can. But the core of the problem has not been reached, and the family situation has not been essentially changed. The children have already been hurt and are growing up in a hurtful environment, probably hungry, possibly in terror, certainly to some extent patterning themselves after the parents; each in his own way being molded and becoming hardened by precept and circumstance.

What can we say of families like the Riveras and the reasons why they make maltreatment a life-style? What hope is there for their rehabilitation and, ultimately, their salvation? There is little hope, under our present system of dealing with the multiply deprived. The Riveras of today and tomorrow are the result of generations of poverty and ignorance and distorted values. Where and why and how the cycle started, we don't know.

## THE NEWTON FAMILY

The Newtons, by contrast, were financially stable, "respectable," middle-class people. Due to the diligence of the father, James Newton, in his younger days, they lived in an apparently pleasant home on a good street in a large but neighborly town. Mrs. Alma Newton kept the house spotlessly clean. The four teenagers always presented a nice appearance and seemed to be very well cared for. Of the four, the boy was the most lively, but the girls also made a good impression by virtue of their good manners. For some reason they were not doing very well in school in spite of their intelligence. The oldest daughter had, in fact, dropped out with less than a year of high school to go. There was some talk of her "trying to make up her mind what to do with her life" and, perhaps, coming back to graduate, so nobody found it necessary to put any pressure on her. As for the two other girls, their scholastic performance was no major problem even if disappointing, and the Newtons were never called in for parent-teacher discussions.

The only thing that seemed at all unusual about the Newtons was that they kept very much to themselves. The children rarely had friends to the house. Only the boy had an occasional visitor. The parents never had any company, nor did they have any social life outside the home. Mr. Newton worked a nine-to-five job and always came home promptly, never lingering for a drink with his colleagues on the way, although some evenings he was seen at the delicatessen picking up a six-pack of beer. Even during the day when Mrs. Newton went shopping, an errand she more often saved for Saturdays when her husband or one of the children could come with her, she didn't pause to chat with her neighbors. She would exchange a short greeting but nothing more than that.

One day Barbie, by that time seventeen, went to the police. She told the police that she had a child at home, that her own father was the father of her baby, and that he had been having sexual relations with her for more than four years. To make matters even worse, she said, he was doing the same thing with her two sisters, and she didn't want to see them ruined as she had been. The police found it hard to believe her story. She looked like such a nice girl and not from one of the lower-class families that was usually associated with this type of behavior. But, soliciting the help of a protective agency, they investigated.

They discovered that Carol, fourteen, had been only nine years old when her father had first forced intercourse with her and that he continued to do so. Susan, thirteen, said that she had been eight years old when he had begun molesting her, and she couldn't make him stay away from her, either. And Mrs. Newton, after her initial shock of being discovered in what amounted to complicity, admitted that she had known about the situation for some time but had not reported it for fear of losing her husband. Unfortunately, this is a typical reaction in many incest cases. In my observation, the wives are usually passive, weak, afraid of their husbands yet equally afraid of losing the man's "love" and of breaking up the tightly-knit family. Sometimes, unpleasant though the thought may be, the wife of an incestuous father is secretly glad of the man's attentions to the daughters because she is freed from sexual intercourse with him.

In the Newton family, only James Jr., the son, had not known for sure what had been going on. On a couple of occasions, he had tried to intervene on the mistaken assumption that his father was beating one of the girls. He had been belted for his pains and harshly ordered to mind his own business. He was not too surprised when he learned the truth.

How will these children grow? And what will become of Barbie's baby? I would hate to predict, not because I am afraid my predictions will not be accurate, but because I am very much afraid they will.

The pattern of the Newton family had been cut out in a previous generation, if not before that. As a child, Mrs. Newton had been sexually molested by a friend of the family. She married James Newton when she was sixteen and already pregnant by him. Mr. Newton was the offspring of an illegitimate and possibly incestuous union between his mother and her brother, although no one knew for certain. As an infant, he had been severely and repeatedly beaten by the man who presumed to be, but wasn't, the father. At the age of eight, he was a sturdy and rapidly growing boy despite the beatings. Jim Newton started having sexual relations with his aunt, who was then about twenty, and he continued through his early adolescence.

At the same time, his brother was sexually involved with their sister. It was the Newton way of life. And then James Newton married, had children, and raped his daughters.

The incest taboo may very well have been overdone. Certain cultural attitudes and styles accept such a situation as a norm, or at least not something to get terribly excited about. But the Newtons happened to be living just off Main Street, USA, where it is not really understood, and the Newton daughters are growing up in a culture that can't accept and can't understand what happened to them and is likely to hurt them further.

James Newton was labeled "psychopath" and institutionalized. He leaves behind him a confused and friendless wife, four troubled youngsters, and a grandson who is his own child.

We do not know nearly enough about the sexual abuse of children and its causes and effects; we know little more than the nature of the crimes committed and some of the circumstances surrounding them. Without getting into precise, legal terminology, which varies slightly from state to state, we can list them as forced rape (sometimes culminating in murder); consensual rape; sexual misconduct; sexual abuse or fondling of intimate parts; forced and consensual sodomy; public lewdness or indecent exposure, endangering the child's welfare in terms of morals, health, and safety; and incest, here defined as complete sexual intercourse between close blood relations, that is, between persons so closely related that marriage between them would be illegal. Sexual victimization of a child by an adult member of the immediate family may not necessarily constitute incest, but parent-child sodomy isn't wholesome, either.

Dr. Vincent De Francis, director of the Children's Division of the American Humane Association, has estimated that 100,000 children throughout the country are subjected to sexual abuse each year. By no means all of this is perpetrated by parents; but much, perhaps most of it, is permitted by the negligence or negative complicity of one or both parents.

As yet, no attempt has been made by any public agency, or any private one that I know of, to compile information on the nationwide incidence and seriousness of sex offenses against children. Nowhere in the FBI's annual *Uniform Crime Reports* do we find *any* breakdown of crimes against children or so much as a mention of child sex abuse. Police statistics and the FBI figures reflecting them are adult-oriented and offender-oriented. Interestingly, the professional literature on sex offenses is predominantly offender-oriented, and amazingly little of it deals with the probable incidence of sex crimes against children or the effects of such abuse upon the child-victims in terms of their psychosexual development. In the course of working with patients, especially as a psychiatrist or a prison doctor, the effect upon certain individuals may be observed. But the studies in this area have been few and limited.

Of course, it will be recognized that one of the difficulties in gathering data on child molestation is that like most incidents of physical abuse and neglect, though not for exactly the same reasons, incidents of sexual victimization of children are frequently not reported to any record-keeping agency. Often, even if the perpetrator is a stranger, they are not mentioned to anyone beyond the family circle. Sexual abuse is a very "hush-hush" crime.

Nevertheless, we do know a little something about it, largely because some of the older victims have turned in desperation to a school counselor or the police or a Society for the Prevention of Cruelty to Children for help. An outraged aunt or, very occasionally, a mother, has reported to the police or some other agency.

Dr. Vincent De Francis initiated and directed a three-year study of sexual abuse in children, using New York City as the site. The study was funded by the United States Children's Bureau and assisted by the Brooklyn Society for the Prevention of Cruelty to Children, which has recorded thousands of sex-abuse cases over the years. De Francis's findings, reported in 1969, suggested a probable annual incidence of at least 3,000 and possibly over 4,000 cases in the five boroughs of the city of New York. (David Gil's 1967 study indicated a nationwide incidence of 12,000. It is hard to believe that New York could account for 25 percent or more of the nation's sex offenses against children. Surely the most conservative of estimates must be between 50,000 to 70,000.)

Analysis of the cases in the De Francis study showed that twenty-seven percent of the offenders were members of the child's own household: parent, stepparent, or paramour of the mother. Another eleven percent did not live in the household but were closely related to the child by blood or marriage. In total, thirty-eight percent could be said to be members of the family. An additional thirty-seven percent of the offenders were friends or acquaintances: neighbors, visitors, father's buddies, casual neighborhood contacts of the children themselves, such as the man at the candy store. The remaining twenty-five percent were allegedly strangers, though there is a strong possibility that in some cases the child deliberately failed to identify the perpetrator either out of fear or affection or a mixture of both.

According to this study, then, at least 75 percent and possibly up to 80 percent of the offenders were individuals known to the children, people whom the children had some reason to believe they could trust. Furthermore, a large proportion of the cases occurred in or near the child's own home or in the home of the offender. A minority of the offenses took place in public areas, and only a minuscule proportion occurred in such traditional lurking grounds of the stranger-molester as the schoolyard, empty lot, movie theatre, or automobile. One is forced to assume from this, and other aspects of the lengthy study support the assumption, that the parents were at least partly responsible in the vast majority of cases. Where they were not themselves the perpetrators, they contributed to the likelihood of occurrence through apathy, negligence, a deliberate rejection of the facts, or cooperated by indifference toward the offender.

In the incest cases, the principal offender was the father, traditionally the protector of the child. In the majority of these cases, many of which extended over a period of time and involved more than one child, the mother knew very well what was happening but either encouraged the deviant behavior for her own reasons or could not bring herself to do anything about it. Interestingly, although I suppose not surprisingly, neglect—physical, moral, medical, emotional, and educational—was also found in seventy-nine percent of the cases and physical abuse in eleven percent of the families. Two-thirds of the sexually exploited children showed signs of emotional disturbance, which might have existed before the sexual abuse took place. The median age of the victims was eleven-and-a-half years. The oldest children were just under sixteen, and the youngest were infants.

If these children are now being treated with supportive loving care and understanding, they may grow up to be normal. But who is looking after them, and how are they being cared for?

## THE CROSSMAN AND CORELLI FAMILIES

Two-and-a-half-year old Joseph Crossman, an energetic and attractive little boy, is the product of an interracial marriage. The paternal grandparents had strongly disapproved of the union and had done everything they could to prevent it; the maternal grandparents, like the rest of Mary Baker Crossman's family, had long since vanished from the young woman's life. Daniel Crossman, a New Yorker, is the scion of a wealthy family. He has his M.A. and is heading for a Ph.D. while working part-time at an interesting and creative job for good pay. His wife Mary, born somewhere in the South, is reluctant to talk about her early years. She is the child of a mother and father who "gave away" their children to various people in the community. Mary wound up with elderly guardians who gave her physical care, an education, but not emotional warmth. She was a brilliant student and obtained an excellent job after high school graduation. It was through a work contract that she met her husband-to-be, by whom she became pregnant before marriage.

Daniel and Mary Crossman are both afraid that one or the other will kill little Joseph if he remains at home. When Joe was nearly two-and-a-half he was taken to hospital for a checkup. His mother said that he was hyperactive, perpetually in motion, always jumping from high places, and terrifying her husband and herself; that he fell often, had dreadful temper tantrums, and was constantly demanding. His father agreed, and added that Joe not only liked to stir up trouble but actually provoked them to anger because he *enjoyed* physical abuse. In support of the latter statement, Mary said that he wouldn't go to sleep until he had been spanked, and that he was always doing things he knew she would have to spank him for. He was "a little monster." He "plagued" them both deliberately and unmercifully, but especially his mother because Daniel could spend a good deal of time at the university or his office. So what were they to do with their overactive, hysterical, thoroughly irritating little boy?

Joe was given a thorough examination during his hospital stay. He proved to be a healthy, normal youngster, as energetic as described but not at all the impossible child reported by his parents. A social worker turned up the information that Joe had a nice, quiet, conforming older brother at home, Mrs. Crossman's son by a previous relationship, who was always being hassled and annoyed by Joe. Joe would hit him, steal his toys, and destroy what he had built, and five-year-old David, even though frequently upset, would not fight back.

The stated reason for Joe's presence in the hospital at this time was that he had fallen or jumped out of their apartment window *again*, as his mother commented irritably, and the Crossmans were afraid that he might have hurt his shoulder or suffered some internal injury.

His shoulder was perfectly fine and he had no internal injuries, but the Crossmans didn't seem to want to take him home. Further investigation turned up the fact that they had once requested that the child be separated from them. Then little Joe's history began to unravel. He had become a problem baby at the age of three months when, for some obscure reason, he had started to cry constantly. Nothing would shut him up. He wasn't ill and his appetite was good. His father, in desperation, started giving him doses of Scotch so that he could rest in the little time that he had off from his work and studies. But the purpose of the Scotch was not to make the baby sleep, Daniel Crossman admitted; it was to *burn* him. Burning, like spanking, made the child conform.

During the next three months, Joe periodically ran high temperatures which eventually resulted in his being taken to a local hospital for a thorough medical examination. All tests were satisfactory; Joe had left his temperature at home. And he found it there when he got back. A second and third trip to the hospital produced the same unrevealing results. There was absolutely nothing wrong with Joe. Finally, physicians told the Crossmans to take him home and never bring him back; they were just wasting everybody's time.

At the age of one-and-a-half, Joe fell or was dropped out of a window at a height equivalent to a story-and-a-half. Again he was taken to hospital. Again, physical examination and X rays were negative. Joe was completely unscathed.

Nothing much happened to Joe for almost a year except for some small falls, his tantrums, and his one-sided battles with quiet David, who was always rescued by one of the parents before any real damage could be done. However, his excessive energy and the memory of his fall from the window so disturbed his mother and father that Mrs. Crossman couldn't stand to have him around the house, and she actually sent him away on two occasions. Mr. Crossman often fed him heavy doses of tranquilizers or alcohol to quiet him down. After all, they couldn't have him constantly disturbing the peace of the home.

When two-and-a-half-year-old Joe was brought to the hospital after his second recorded fall from a window, he was restless, but not hyperactive. He had no injuries. He was not particularly demanding and hadn't had a temper tantrum. There was nothing deviant about his behavior except that he seldom smiled and his speech was perhaps a little more garbled than that of other two-year-olds. According to his parents, he had become increasingly hostile, disobedient, and self-abusive; but he didn't exhibit this behavior to his examiners. Two interesting things, however, were noted: he seemed to have an elevated threshold to pain; and his mother, present throughout his various physical tests and verbal examinations, did not say a word to him nor reach out a comforting hand. Neither did he turn to her. It was as if they had nothing to do with each other.

Thus, Joe Crossman has been repeatedly hospitalized by his parents though there has never been anything physically wrong with him.

Although the boy's physical condition at this time was good, as usual, hospital authorities were uneasy about him and notified the Child Protective Agency. Suddenly the Crossmans became very concerned about what might happen to them if authorities investigated Joe's previous home life, and they tried to kidnap Joe from the hospital before the court hearing. They need not have worried. Joe remained in the hospital pending the decision of the court; but the judge decided in favor of the Crossmans and returned Joe to his home.

So far as the adult Crossmans were concerned, the decision was in their favor, not because they wanted Joe home but because they didn't want the disgrace of having him taken away from them by the law. The way it turned out is a pity. They were, in their own strange way, making some sort of effort to solve their problem.

But now Joe is home again, still unwanted, with parents who are completely incapable of handling him, and a too-quiet older brother who is in scarcely a better position than Joe.

The Corellis, on the surface, are in no way like the Crossmans. Their background is different, they live in a very much smaller city, theirs is not a mixed marriage; and they are not even the same type of family. But they do have something in common. They, too, are quite well-educated, very intelligent people, with no major material problems.

Janet and Paul Corelli became the parents of a handsome baby boy five months after their marriage. Seven weeks later, he was dead. This is a small family with a short history.

Janet was a shy, retiring person. People who knew her at all described her as introverted. She had been an excellent student throughout her elementary and high school years and a very good student during her first two years of college, but she could not cope with the pressures of college life and dropped out in her junior year. She might have been able to make it had it not been for her parents, both of whom were brilliant people with many degrees, who demanded nothing short of perfection from her. Janet simply gave up under the strain of their excessive demands.

She worked for two years and then married Paul, a tremendously outgoing young man who taught part time at the state university and was studying for an advanced degree that would give him a full-time and much better job. Their first home was modest but very pleasant and comfortable, and there was every reason to suppose that within a couple of years they would be taking a step upward. Furthermore, parents on both sides were quite well off and could help out in an emergency. But they couldn't do much about the kind of emergencies that did occur.

When the baby was about four weeks old, he was taken to the hospital with multiple bruises and a subdural hematoma. He remained there for treatment for a week and was released in good condition.

A little more than two weeks later, he was back. This time he was even more badly bruised than before. He also had sores on his body, discolorations on both feet, and another subdural hematoma. Treatment kept him alive for a little while but not for long. The family life of the young Corellis came to an abrupt end.

The autopsy that was clearly indicated showed that every one of the baby's ribs was fractured, some of them in two or three places. Furthermore, not all the fractures were in the same stage of healing, making it obvious that some had been inflicted prior to the instance resulting in the baby's death. The pathologist concluded that death was the result of severe trauma consistent with a beating. He was viewing a fatal case of the battered-baby syndrome.

The young husband, who appeared to make all the decisions, also did all the talking. Mrs. Corelli said only that she did not kill her baby. She showed little emotional reaction when interrogated. Paul Corelli claimed to have no idea what had happened. He said that he had never dropped the baby and did not know of any time that the baby had been dropped. He couldn't imagine how the little one could have become so severely battered.

The problem for investigators was to build a case against

their suspect, the person considered most likely to have committed the act by reasons of circumstance. Had any single person had exclusive opportunity to commit the assaults against the child? Neither of the Corellis could be ruled out. Was there anything in the background of either parent that might point more to one than to the other? Anything in the individual that might be revealed by psychological testing? The burden of proof was on the state to show that one specific person committed the act beyond a reasonable doubt, and this wasn't going to be easy.

Whatever the judgment in this case, no one has to worry about the baby's future. He had his seven weeks of life, and that was that. But questions remain. Could anyone possibly have predicted what was to happen? Could it have been prevented? Is this a "typical" case? No case is really typical. But this one is by no means singular.

## THE X FAMILIES

These are the families without known number, without identity, without name, without reality as families. They are so amorphous, so drifting, so disorganized, so unfamily that they seem intangible. These are the families who live in the nightmare world of drugs.

Much of the time they do not form a unit that is even remotely recognizable as a family. But once in a while they do, presenting an ugly travesty of the real thing. One such family consisted of a married couple and three children. The parents were a pair of drug addicts who abused all of their children and murdered one of them. At one stage in this family's life, after the mother had been arrested for the third time on a prostitution charge, the children were taken away from their parents and placed in a children's center. No matter how overcrowded and uncongenial the center, it would have been better if they had all stayed there, and better yet if they had been placed in foster homes. But several social agencies, in their wisdom, decided that the parents were suitable guardians after all, and the two older children were returned to them.

The four-year-old boy was beaten to death by the father, according to the mother, because he sucked his thumb. His disappearance from the family scene came to light when the woman took the five-year-old girl to the hospital to have her treated for head injuries, cigarette burns, and various cuts and bruises that appeared to have been inflicted by ropes and a belt buckle. The child remained in a semicoma for three months. The parents refused to talk about their absent boy, although on one occasion they did borrow a neighbor's son to stand in for him when a caseworker visited their squalid home. But eventually the small skeleton was discovered and, through the clothing, traced to them.

The little girl remained in the hospital and the younger boy in the children's center. The parents went on trial, their damage done.

## OTHER FAMILIES

One family consists of a junkie mother and nine children ranging in age from three to twelve. There is no husband in this family, although a number of men spend varying amounts of time in the rat-infested basement apartment. One or more of the men may be the father of one or more of the children, but they are probably all customers. The mother is using the place as a drug factory and earns good money, little of which is spent on the children. The twelve-year-old boy is on drugs, and the eleven-year-old-girl is prostituting to help out with the family budget. It is only to be expected that the next oldest boy and the next oldest girl might soon follow in the footsteps of their siblings.

In a cold, unfurnished apartment, there are four children living alone. No one knows what happened to the mother and father. These children range in age from six to twelve years old.

The twelve-year-old girl is on drugs and is prostituting to support her habit and to buy sparse food supplies for the younger children. This is a family of children abandoned by junkie parents.

A woman, who has already had three out-of-wedlock children by three different men, signs herself out of the hospital two days after the premature birth of her fourth child, leaving an address that proves to be false. On the third day, the infant suffers serious withdrawal symptoms. It twitches convulsively, utters high-pitched screams, claws at its face, clenches and unclenches its tiny hands repeatedly, doesn't want to eat and vomits when it does, suffers disturbances of respiratory and central nervous systems. It suffers from neonatal drug addiction. It is very small and very ill, this baby junkie, but with care and medication it recovers. That is, it survives.

Three weeks later, the mother makes a surprise return to the hospital and demands her baby. A check is done on her. She has a record of several arrests for using and selling drugs, for prostitution, for shoplifting; her third child died at the age of six months from a gastrointestinal disorder caused by improper feeding; her other two children are home with a severe contagious disease. The woman begs, pleads, threatens, yells, finally promises; she will take the sick children to hospital if she can take her infant home. (She is in no position to make deals; she has no understanding of her own situation.) A caseworker makes a home visit with the mother and finds that the two sick children are very seriously ill, extremely undernourished, and very poorly cared for. The apartment is shabby and is as ill-cared for as the children. The woman lives with her addict-paramour, who is not home for the visit. The two of them sell drugs and use the place as a shooting gallery. Following the caseworker's report, the two sick children are promptly placed in a hospital, and the infant discharged to a foster home. The mother agrees to enter a special hospital detoxification program. She does not show up. She and her paramour move out of the apartment and temporarily disappear from public view. They will be surfacing again one of these days.

Not all babies born to addict mothers are addicted babies.

The acquisition of the baby's habit depends on the mother's usage; the frequency and size of her dosage, how long she has been on drugs, and the time she last took the drug before delivery. But in two-thirds of the addict-birth cases, the infants go through withdrawal symptoms; and roughly two-thirds of the withdrawal babies endure great discomfort and pain. Their ordeal might start within two or three hours of birth or within two or three days. Cold turkey is as agonizing for an infant as it is for an adult. The newborn infant does not have the strength necessary to cope with it. The tremors, the grasping, the coughing, the sneezing, and the clawing can go on, even with treatment, for many days. Without treatment, the symptoms are naturally worse and are likely to lead to death through severe convulsions or dehydration.

But even if the treatment of withdrawal symptoms, which is also the treatment of the addiction, is successful, the battle isn't over. More than half of the babies may be premature or underweight, and nearly all of them evidence lack of prenatal care. Most do not grow as well as normal children during the first years of life even if they do receive good care, which they seldom do in their own homes. There is research to show that, after discharge from the hospital and for some time afterwards, they experience a recurrence of withdrawal symptoms, such as hyperactivity or agitation, tremulousness, appetite disorders, and the like. They seem to be very hungry, or thirsty, and tend to drink too much milk and then they throw up. They are frequently colicky. Their mothers complain about their irritability and sleeplessness. Dr. Carl Zelson, Harlem Metropolitan Hospital's director of nurseries, has found that recovered baby addicts are nearly all hard to handle, cry a lot, are very restless, and that their sleep patterns are disorganized, a possible indication of brain damage. As they grow they tend to exhibit a number of behavioral disorders. However, the extent of their dysfunction is difficult to determine because follow-up studies are lacking.

Possibly even more severe postnatal withdrawal symptoms have been noted in infants delivered by methadone-maintained addicts. There is also some indication that sudden infant death, within about three months after birth, is more common among children of methadone-maintained mothers than children of mothers on heroin. One has to consider the possibility that there may be something more to these deaths than the neglect common to the addict's way of life; that the methadone taken during pregnancy might have caused subtle detrimental changes in the infant, leading to sudden death. It is too early to do anything more than speculate. But the possibility cannot be excluded.

Addicted infants are, by law in New York, regarded as abused from birth, and attempts are made to turn them over to foster homes or institutions or the homes of nonaddicted relatives. But many of them, for want of anywhere else to go, are taken to the mother's home, to the same environment in which the mother or both parents became addicts themselves. And children who are returned to such an environment are almost invariably abused, neglected, or abandoned.

We have, today, an epidemic of infantile addiction; and we also have an epidemic of juvenile maltreatment resulting from parental addiction.

What actually happens to these kids when they get home? They vanish for a while into the parental environment; they go back to mothers who, at best, do not know how to mother, to love, or even to care for themselves; or to parents who, at worst, wilfully mistreat and then destroy them. Seldom are they given what we would consider the basic necessities of life: adequate food, a bed, clothes, education, and affection. As we have already seen, many of these children become addicts themselves at a very early age. They grow up in shooting-gallery homes, acquire the habit, hustle to pay for it, and eventually breed more addicts. Others don't last that long.

Some of the latter show up early in hospitals and morgues. Many of them arrive with needle punctures, bitemarks, knife wounds, burns, massive bruises, and even bullet wounds. Some have been starved to death; others are strangulated, suffocated, decapitated, scalded to death, drowned, dumped in incinerators, thrown out with the garbage, or left in alleyways to die. These are the results of deliberate abuse by addict parents, or by the customers or lovers of prostitute mothers, or by addicted friends of the addicted parents.

Other fatalities of addicted households are the results of negligence. Addict parents, even when they try to be good parents, are no more capable of looking after their children than they are of looking after themselves. But most of them don't even try. Addicts are too wrapped up in hustling or peddling to give their children any attention, unless they get in the way, and, least of all, any care. These children, the ultimate in neglected children, are left in filth, without food, without clothing, without any medical attention, totally without supervision. Death by malnutrition or disease is not the worst fate that may befall them. Left alone, they play childishly with matches and burn themselves to death. They toddle onto the fire escape and fall to the sidewalk below, not necessarily to die. They shiver themselves to death, virtually die of exposure, in broken-windowed, unheated apartments. They try to look after each other, clumsily, and fail: a six-year-old, trying to do his best, may accidentally drown the baby in the bathtub or scald him to death or drop him on his head. They wander out into the streets and beg for food in the middle of the night. Some of them never come back.

And of those who survive this hell, a few, miraculously, make it to a better life. In New York today, we know of addict family cycles that are entering their third, fourth, and even fifth generation. And our crime rate is climbing as the children grow.

Not your children? But you or your children may very well be hurt or maimed or killed by one of them.

This disease of child abuse and neglect, if not properly managed—and it is scarcely being managed at all—leads to critical consequences. One out of two battered or severely neglected children dies after being returned to its parents. In these specific instances, the violence cycle is brought to an abrupt end. But in addition to these needless tragedies, a large percentage of surviving abused children, whether they were starved as infants or beaten as toddlers, become lame, mentally retarded, blind, physically damaged beyond repair, or psychologically crippled.

Just as the majority of yesterday's maltreated children are the maltreating parents of today, so the maltreated children of today will become the maltreating parents of tomorrow. We see this acted out from generation to generation: abuse breeds abuse, and violence breeds violence, and one horror breeds another. If we are subjected to abuse, we either disintegrate under pressure or learn from our aggressors to become aggressors ourselves.

What is true of the battering and neglect cycles is true also of the sexual-abuse cycle. This is not something that can be proved by a massive display of figures because there aren't any, but a study of available case histories shows that the pattern of sexual abuse in the family is very similar to that of physical abuse. Sexual abuse carries its curse from generation to generation. The pattern shifts and rearranges itself, but unless there is effective outside intervention it continues. The sexually abused little girl grows up to marry or cohabit with a man who sexually abuses their children; the incestuous father begets an incestuous or promiscuous son or daughter; the adult sexual-psychopath frequently turns out to have been the product of an undesirable sexual union or the victim of childhood seduction.

But the pattern does not confine itself to the family because even secret sins have a way of spilling over into society. We have good reason to expect that out of the ranks of today's maltreated children will not only emerge tomorrow's maltreating parents but also tomorrow's hard-core criminals. That is why we *are* all involved, whether we want to know it or not and whatever we think of platitudes regarding noninvolvement. Karl Menninger believed that every criminal was unloved and maltreated as a child. There is increasing evidence today that he was right. The probable, future tendency of abused children is to become the murderers, robbers, rapists, and perpetrators of violence in our society. To put it crudely: if they don't beat up on their own kids, they'll beat up on someone else. And they may do both!

Psychiatrists see this; judges see this; often the police see this. At a December 1971 hearing of the New York State Legislature's Select Committee on Child Abuse and Neglect, this point was brought home dramatically. Dr. Shervert H. Frazier, Jr., a psychiatrist with the State Department of Mental Health and also clinical psychiatrist at Columbia College of Physicians and Surgeons, reported that his study of ninety murderers revealed that as children they had been "victims of remorseless brutality." Dr. Frazier's study, which focused not on New York but the rural areas of Texas and Minnesota, revealed that his convicted-killer subjects had been, in their youth, stripped and beaten, choked, put outside to lie naked in the snow, thrown through glass doors, or mishandled in a number of ways by alcoholic parents. He also found that there had been emphasis on guns in the killers' early years, and he cited a photograph he had seen which showed a budding murderer at the age of three proudly clutching a rifle that was taller than he.

Dr. Arthur H. Green, an assistant professor of psychiatry at Downstate Medical Center in Brooklyn, reported on his findings. His child-oriented study of the Brooklyn area, a site quite different from rural Minnesota or Texas, strongly indicated that child abuse points directly toward adolescent and adult criminality.

Family Court Judge Nanette Dembitz, who had seen the troubled parents and children filing through her courtroom and had heard endless agonizing cases, made this impassioned observation before the Committee of the New York State Legislature on Child Abuse and Neglect (December 7, 1971):

Maltreatment of children is a hurt to all citizens, not only because of their compassion for the young and weak but also from the standpoint of their own self-interest. "Crime in the streets" is a central concern, and the root of crime in the streets is the neglect of children. . . . A child growing up in a situation of indifference to his well-being and of violence, cannot respect himself or others. It is as natural for a maltreated child to grow up to carry a knife as it is for a loved and cared-for child to carry a pen or pencil.

She spoke of children growing up with an alcoholic mother and a violent man in the house; or spending their formative years with a paranoic parent; or being shuttled off to the home of a neighbor for makeshift day-care while the mother is in jail or being detoxified, a neighbor who is a narcotics pusher; or left in a hotel room with drug addicts not related to the family. "Crime in the streets from these roots is to be expected—it is not surprising."

A police spokesman contributed the comment that, of over 66,000 robberies reported in a single month, a large proportion were street crimes committed by youngsters who were raised in families where some form of child abuse had been practiced.

Our trouble to date has been that we have seen the results too late. We have not stepped in to break the violence cycle. We bolt our doors and isolate ourselves for our own safety. But in doing so we are not promoting safety for ourselves or anyone else. We are closing our eyes to the present and refusing to look into the future.

Very well, let us look into the past:

*Arthur Bremer.* "My future was small, my past an insult to any human being," he wrote in his strange diary. On May 15, 1972, this young man attempted to assassinate Governor George Wallace of Alabama. He did not succeed in his purpose, but his several shots inflicted terrible damage. The second youngest of five children, Arthur Herman Bremer was raised in a shabby working-class section of Milwaukee's south side. According to court records and files of various social service agencies, the Bremers were a problem family in which neglect and parental quarreling were the order of the day. From the diary: "My mother must have thought I was a canoe, she paddled me so much." Alternately abused and totally neglected, living in a violent and vitriolic atmosphere, Arthur grew up a lonely misfit with his own weird dreams, which he eventually acted out.

*Sirhan B. Sirhan.* On June 6, 1968, this assassin successfully gunned down Robert Kennedy. Diligent reporters, digging into the Sirhan family background in Palestine, learned from neighbors that the senior Sirhan allegedly had been in the hab-

it of beating his six children with sticks and fists when they diso-
beyed him. Once, the neighbors recalled, he had held a hot iron
to Sirhan Bishara's heel. When things became difficult and
decisions had to be made, the mother dominated the family,
but apparently she did not interfere with her husband's abuse
of the children. After the Arab-Israeli War, she brought the
family to the United States and kept the children together
when the father abandoned them and returned to Palestine.
The mother loved her children, yet her love seems to have
been a limited love. She has been described as rigid, harsh,
narrow-minded, and unyielding.

*James Earl Ray.* The Ray family of Mississippi, like the Sirhan
family of Palestine and California, found it difficult to handle
the everyday problems of living and impossible to handle the
difficult ones. James, the oldest of nine children, was born on
March 10, 1928. On April 4, 1968, he shot and killed Dr. Martin
Luther King. As James was growing up, the family, indigent
and apparently shiftless, drifted from one shabby home to another, caring so little about themselves that even the family
name drifted from Ray to Rayns to Raines and back again to
Ray. The children drifted too; they wandered off and wound
up in various foster homes. Those who stayed home did so under conditions of unspeakable poverty and neglect. James,
though the oldest and biggest, always seemed to wear second-
hand clothes. Presumably the father, a chronic alcoholic, could
afford none of his children's needs. They did, however, manage
to get some schooling. It didn't help most of them much, least
of all James. From an early age, he was regarded by his teachers as dishonest, discourteous, a rule-breaker, a thief, and a
vicious bully. Now the world knows him as a killer.

*Lee Harvey Oswald.* Here is another pathetic individual. On
November 22, 1963, Lee Harvey Oswald killed the president
of the United States, John F. Kennedy, and the Dallas police
patrolman, J. D. Tippit. Oswald had grown up in a fatherless
home; his father died two months before he was born. His
mother remarried when he was five, but the marriage was a

failure and ended three years later in divorce. Mother and son were virtual strangers. While in public school in New York, the boy was diagnosed as an "emotionally disturbed youngster." He was such a problem to his parent, that he was admitted into children's center, a special training institution that houses some of the most deprived children in New York. As one of the staff said later, "We let Lee Harvey Oswald go down the drain when he was a student here. I tell you, any child who doesn't have a problem when he comes here will have one when he leaves."

*Guiseppe Zangara.* Here we skip back over thirty years to an almost forgotten name but a well-remembered case. On February 15, 1933, Zangara attempted to assassinate President-elect Franklin D. Roosevelt while he was delivering a speech in Miami, Florida. Zangara, only five feet tall, stood on a chair and fired several shots. He missed Roosevelt but fatally wounded Mayor Anton Cermak of Chicago. Guiseppe Zangara had been born in Italy. His mother died in 1902, when he was two years old, and his father remarried soon afterwards. The boy started school when he was six, but two months later his father called an abrupt halt to his education, yanked him out of school, and put him to work. So Guiseppe grew up a child laborer, unmothered, and unschooled.

*John N. Schrank.* Chances are we'd remember if his well-aimed shot had been fatal. (Perhaps 50-odd years from now our great-grandchildren will have difficulty in recalling the names and deeds of Oswald, Sirhan, Ray, and Bremer.) On October 14, 1921, John Schrank shot Theodore Roosevelt in the chest from a distance of about six feet. Fortunately, the bullet plowed into a very thick speech folded double in Roosevelt's pocket. Schrank had been born in Bavaria. His father died shortly after his birth and his mother wasted little time in remarrying. The boy was turned over to his aunt and uncle for his upbringing. The arrangement turned out to be permanent. When John was thirteen, he and his surrogate parents emigrated to the United States. The boy went to work for his uncle, spending his adolescence and young manhood as a bartender in his uncle's New York saloon. Like our other more recent assassins, Schrank was a loner. He did not find out how to relate to other people, in spite of his supposedly congenial work. Once he said, "I never had a friend in my life."

*John Wilkes Booth.* Yes, this John we will remember. He was not like our other killers. He wasn't burned with a hot iron or sent to work at the age of six or dragged from one hovel to another. Nor was he a loner. He was handsome, talented, admired, if unbalanced; he had a great many acquaintances and some accomplices. But there were important elements missing in his family life when he was a boy. He was the ninth of ten children born to his unmarried parents. His father, an Englishman, was already married to another woman when, in romantic storybook fashion, he fell in love with a flower girl. He got her pregnant and ran away with her to the United States, where they produced child after child. John was thirteen when his parents finally married. His mother was almost solely responsible for rearing him; his father and older brother were frequently away for weeks and months at a time on theatrical tours. John dropped out of school, where he was considered undisciplined, to cool his heels at home, where his mother found him disobedient and unruly. In his young manhood he was a successful actor, but of course his best-known role was that of the assassin of Abraham Lincoln.

These are a few of history's famous criminals; famous because they struck out at famous people. If they had chosen everyday targets such as you, your neighbor, a farmer, a ghetto storekeeper, or a housewife, the odds are that we would never have heard of them or learned anything about their backgrounds. But as things are, we do know something about them, enough to suggest, though not to prove, that a cold or callous or savage childhood environment produces the cold or callous or savage adult; it leads to a violent future.

An interesting study could be done of the growing-up years of criminals such as John Dillinger and other young men who have rampaged through murder sprees, of the outwardly calm people who suddenly go beserk and spray bullets indiscriminately into groups of passing strangers. I am sure that childhood abuse will be found: not necessarily of the whiplash or belt-buckle variety but in the shape of a family environment that is unnatural, uncomfortable, unstable, unwarming, unprotective, unnourishing, unloving, and hostile to the development of a whole human being.

# CHAPTER SIX

# Annemarie Thanks You

IT WAS THE SHORTEST OF NOTES, mailed from Menlo Park, N.Y., on April 7, 1969, and all it said was "Annemarie thanks you." The note was unsigned, but the envelope bore a name and return address. It was from Iris and Anthony Riccio, the foster parents of Annemarie Lombardo, and it was written after her funeral. It caught me offguard. My eyes blurred. I felt myself shaking.

It wasn't as if nobody had cared, that nobody was doing anything. Our city administrators are busy. They are not omniscient. They can't know everything that is happening, or isn't happening, without being thoroughly briefed. Few people were aware, back in 1967, of the extent of child abuse throughout the nation or our city. Mayor John V. Lindsay of New York was deeply concerned when child abuse was called to his attention and took immediate preliminary steps to combat it. On December 11, 1968, he wrote to me:

The realization that child abuse is a major health and social problem in our city has prompted me to create a special Task Force on Child Abuse.
The task force will have the responsibility to make a thorough examination of the existing social, medical, and legal community services involved in the program of child protection in New York

City. A very specific purpose will be to evaluate the effectiveness of the 1964 New York State Child-Abuse Law and the administrative machinery set up to carry out its mandate. I expect that the task force in its report to me will make specific recommendations for the prevention of child abuse and the improvement of services to abused children and their families.

I know you are intensely interested in the problem of child abuse and I feel that you are uniquely qualified to help us with this problem. For these reasons I would be most grateful if you would assume chairmanship of the task force.

This letter was a preview of many letters I was to receive in the years to come, a few of them of the "Annemarie thanks you" variety, a few more requesting advice, consultancy or committee membership, more of them saying, "for God's sake, somebody do something," and many more demanding to know why nothing was ever done. The letter writers, even the most demanding, were sincere. They could not know how hard we were trying and how hard it was to make an impact and achieve results.

The formation of the special task force was announced on January 23, 1969. In a report to the mayor, Dr. Bernard Bucove, successor to Dr. Howard J. Brown as city health services commissioner, had pointed out that getting child-abuse cases reported quickly to the authorities was a major aspect of the problem. He observed that the number actually reported represented only a small proportion of the children who were abused and neglected. Mayor Lindsay, in announcing the formation of the task force, noted that since the passage of the New York Child-Abuse Law of 1964, the number of reported cases had risen from about 300 a year to 956 in 1968. We wondered how much a more effective reporting system would change that figure. It has, in fact, ballooned it to almost incredible proportions, but we still don't know how many cases go unreported. Perhaps worse is the fact that we still don't know how to follow up the known cases effectively so as to save the children and rehabilitate the families.

The task force, as originally formed, consisted of myself as chairman; Assemblyman (later Borough President) Robert

Abrams of the Bronx; Thomas T. Becker of the New York Society for the Prevention of Cruelty to Children; Dr. Matthew Brody, representing the coordinating council of the five New York county medical societies; Dr. John V. Connorton of the Greater New York Hospital Association; Dr. Elinor Downs, Columbia University School of Public Health and Administrative Medicine; Judge Harold A. Felix, Family Court of Brooklyn; Dr. David Harris, assistant city commissioner for maternal and child health services; the late Sherwood Norman, National Council on Crime and Delinquency; Mrs. Harry N. Pratt, Citizens Committee for Children; Robert D. Steefel of the law firm of Stroock, Stroock and Lavan; and State Senator William C. Thompson of Brooklyn. As principal investigator, we chose Theo Solomon, assisted by research assistants Deborah Berger and Gloria Pessirilo. In all our efforts, we were immeasurably aided and encouraged by Human Resources Administrator Jule Sugarman, chairman of the Interagency Council on Child Welfare, and Mrs. Barbara Blum, staff director of the Interagency Council and deputy commissioner of Mental Health and Retardation Services.

Though the task force roster changed slightly as time went by, I want to mention these names not only because they represent a roll call of truly caring people but because, together, they constitute the first group of its kind in this country. These people dedicated themselves to a difficult and often heartbreaking task. As a task force, we have had our blind spots, we have made our mistakes, and we still have our problems, but, in balance, we have been effective and productive. If nothing else, the task force has turned the spotlight sharply on all the abuses within the prevention-protection system that is supposed to deal with child abuse; and it serves as a model to all communities throughout the country that care to profit by our errors and achievements. For this, special credit is due to Mayor Lindsay and Barbara Blum.

We rolled up our sleeves and, without waiting for the funds, threw ourselves into our work. But within a matter of weeks it suddenly seemed as if it were all mockery.

At two o'clock in the morning of March 22, 1969, three-

year-old Annemarie Lombardo was reported missing from her
home by her mother, Helene, and her stepfather, Joseph
Coplin. The mother said that she had left the little girl alone
for just a few minutes outside the Coplin tenement home on
Avenue C in New York, and, when she had returned to pick
her up, the child had disappeared.

New York City's police machinery swung into action. The
report had come in on Saturday morning. The search was fruitless through the weekend. Detectives investigating the disappearance were told by tenants of the Avenue C building that
the child was frequently beaten, supposedly because she wet
her bed. No clues to the child's whereabouts turned up.

Police divers eventually turned their attention to the rivers
flanking Manhattan. On Tuesday, March 25, after hours of
searching the East River, they found the child's body. It was
a little thing, slightly over three feet tall and weighing about
forty-five pounds, but it weighed heavy because the pockets
of the child's clothes were weighted down with rocks.

According to the assistant chief medical examiner, the body
showed "extensive fresh and recent contusions of the scalp
and face and multiple contusions of the lower extremities."
His conclusion was that she had been beaten to death.

The stepfather was charged with killing her with his fists,
and the mother was held as a material witness. Several days
later, a grand jury indicted Joseph Coplin on a two-count
charge of murder and first-degree manslaughter.

As the investigation proceeded, more and more of the
neighbors and visitors to the Coplin home began to talk.
One woman tenant in the building told detectives that she
had seen Annemarie looking so ill, with her face swollen
like a big balloon, that she had given Helene Coplin ten
dollars to take the child to a doctor. The mother herself admitted to investigating officers that her husband had instructed her to get penicillin tablets for the little girl. She said
she had done so and administered to the child nine adult-
sized tablets. Visitors to the Coplin apartment confirmed early
stories that Annemarie had frequently been severely punished
for wetting the bed. It seemed as if she had not only been

brutally disposed of but had suffered for weeks before her death.

Among the first people to tell their story after the terrible news broke were Mr. and Mrs. Anthony Riccio, Annemarie's former foster-parents.

Initial press reports quoted them as saying that they had become the little girl's foster parents through the New York Foundling Hospital when she was ten months old. Then, in mid-December, 1968, the family court had permitted the natural mother to take her home. The Riccios had protested this move. Annemarie was perfectly happy with them in their comfortable home; they loved her and were anxious for her welfare. Helene Coplin, they said, had a criminal record and was scarcely a fit mother for the child. (She had been convicted of felonius assault in the knifing of another woman.) But the Foundling Hospital had raised no objection to the child's return to the mother, under the impression that Helene and her husband, Joseph, were now capable of properly caring for her.

On January 1, 1969, the story continued. Mrs. Riccio picked up Annemarie at the Coplin home to take her to see the Christmas tree at Rockefeller Center. She observed that the child had a black eye. On taking her home that evening and bathing her before bedtime (Annemarie was to spend the night), she saw bruises on the little girl's back. The next day the Riccios took Annemarie to the New York Foundling Hospital for examination. She was found to be bruised over the left eye and on the side of the head; and she also had sixteen small bruises on the lower part of the body. The day after that, January 3, the Riccios appeared with Annemarie at a family court hearing, charging that she was being physically abused.

Annemarie had originally come to the attention of the family court in 1966 because of a neglect proceeding instituted by the Society for the Prevention of Cruelty to Children. It had been decided that the mother, no longer living with Annemarie's father and not yet married to Joseph Coplin, was unfit to take care of her. Now, in this second neglect proceeding, attended by Mrs. Riccio, the natural mother, a Foundling Hospital representative, a law guardian (a legal-aid attorney to represent the interests of the child), and a probation officer, it was observed by the court that the child was bruised as described. Mrs. Riccio testified that Annemarie told her, "Joey did it." When asked by the judge how she got the bruises, the child would only say she "fell." In answer to the judge's questions she replied that her mother didn't spank her, her stepfather, Joey, sometimes did, and she didn't like him. But the bruises? She said she fell.

The judge said that she did not believe the child could have received "all those bruises just from falling," but could elicit no other answer from the mother or the child. Joseph Coplin was not present to be questioned, and the medical report was not produced. The judge adjourned the matter until January 27. On that day, neither the child nor the mother appeared in court. The case was once again adjourned, this time until February 24. Mrs. Coplin had again failed to appear. The court issued a warrant for her arrest and the production of the child.

The warrant was never served, and the child was never produced. When her body was discovered and the various family court proceedings were described in the newspapers, a furor broke. The papers, in reporting what was presumably the news, made such comments as these:

Here was a case of a child being taken away on a family court order from foster parents who were giving her their love and a good home. She was returned to her mother, now married to a Joseph Coplin. On February 27 [sic], the former foster-parents [Mr. and Mrs. Anthony Riccio] got Mrs. Coplin and the child into family court and showed the presiding judge a mass of welts on the poor thing's body. But the judge refused to send Annemarie back to the Riccios.

And:

Although the judge saw signs of the beatings and Annemarie told her that "mommy's husband" had inflicted them, the judge refused to take her out of the Coplin family custody.

And:

When the Riccios saw the youngster after two weeks with the Coplin couple, her body showed signs of beating. The Foundling Hospital then joined the Riccios in asking the family court judge to take her away from Coplin and his wife.

Unfortunately, it was not true that the Foundling Hospital "had joined the Riccios in asking" as this report would have it. Neither was it true, as another story insisted, that "the New York Foundling Hospital had vigorously opposed the transfer of Annemarie, in a plea to family court, to her mother and stepfather from the safety of a foster home."

But at the time I believed it *was* true. The physician who had examined her when she was brought in by the Riccios on January 2 had recorded his findings in detail. Ater reviewing the medical records, I was convinced that she had been abused. I had specifically instructed the examining physician to include our findings in a full report and bring that report to the attention of the family court judge. When I heard that the child had been dumped into the river I was outraged and upset. The idea of the judge refusing to take the child away from the custody of Coplin and his wife, despite the strong recommendations of doctors and social workers that she must be removed for her own safety, was appalling. I said so publicly.

So now there was a controversy. We were all working toward the same essential goal, child protection; but now we were at cross-purposes.

It might be wondered if it is not pointless to rehash this situation. Yes, it is. But the fact that it did occur, that it could occur, lies at the very heart of the matter. It shows the recriminations after a tragedy due to a lack of communications.

Immediately after the story of Annemarie began to emerge, two special investigations got under way. The task force convened an emergency meeting to probe the circumstances of the case and prepare a report; and the Judiciary Relations Committee of the Appellate Division's First Department undertook, at the Mayor's behest, an examination of the roles of all individuals and agencies involved. Judge Harold Stevens was to head this inquiry. The Manhattan District Attorney's Office, at the same time, was conducting its own investigation of not only the Annemarie case but other instances of child abuse and murder.

The public was at last aware of the problem of child abuse, and, if the investigations were effective, we might find some of the solutions.

Let me reconstruct the case as I came to see it during my own personal inquiry, not as chairman of the task force, which of course was also occupying me at the time, but as medical director of the New York Foundling Hospital.

Helene Bache, later Coplin, had been known to welfare services for some years. In 1959, she had been committed to Bellevue Hospital. Examination there showed her to be of borderline intelligence (I.Q. 67), and that her mental development was uneven, primitive, and disorganized. Doctors found her to have self-destructive impulses and diagnosed her as schizophrenic reactive with depressive features. She had made several attempts at suicide and was on drugs. From Bellevue, she went to Creedmoor State Hospital, from which she was signed out by her mother after three months. Still periodically on drugs, she formed a relationship with Robert Lombardo.

Annemarie Lombardo was born on August 3, 1965, the out-of-wedlock daughter of Helene Bache and Robert Lombardo. On September 10, 1965, Annemarie was admitted to New York Foundling Hospital through the department of welfare and, shortly afterwards, placed in a temporary boarding home. Later she was placed with Mr. and Mrs. Anthony Riccio, foster parents of excellent record in whose home she was, by all accounts, very happy and much loved. She was too young, even by the end of her stay with them, to comprehend her status as a foster child or why she had two mothers. She did realize, though, that some day she might eventually be going home with her "other mother," Helene. In the meantime, she was reportedly improving her relationship with that other mother, who visited her quite frequently and was enjoying her visits with her half siblings, Alan and Josephine, who lived with her maternal grandmother.

Things had begun to look up for Helene. After the birth of Annemarie and the placement of the child in a happy home, Helene apparently stopped taking drugs and seemed to become more stable in her personal life. She married Joseph Coplin on September 25, 1967 and began to show an interest in retrieving Annemarie. When Coplin was employed, she said, they would be able to provide for her in her own home. As for herself, she told the Foundling caseworker, she was straightened out and longed for her child.

On November 26, 1968, she appeared in Manhattan Family Court to say that she wanted her child back. On that date, the judge granted, pending a further hearing, a request by the Foundling Hospital for a one-year extension of placement, and adjourned the matter to December 12 for a hearing on the mother's application for discharge.

On December 12, Helene and Joseph Coplin appeared together in court to ask for the return of the child. Two representatives of the Foundling Hospital were also in attendance: a social worker and her supervisor, both of whom were familiar with the case and with Helene's apparently changed attitude and life-style, although neither had visited the home nor met Joseph Coplin. Mr. Coplin, presenting a good appearance, testified that he was willing and ready to assume responsibility for Annemarie, that he was now regularly employed and able to support her, and that he was in full agreement with his wife Helene's wish that the child be discharged to them. Based on the testimony of the social worker, who had talked to Helene and been convinced of her sincerity, and on the testimony and attitude of the Coplin couple, the judge awarded custody of Annemarie, without any supervision, to the natural mother and her husband. The Riccios were most distressed.

Thus, on December 16, 1968, the placement office of the New York Foundling Hospital made the notation on their files that "Annemarie Lombardo was discharged to her natural mother today."

But it seemed that both family court and the Foundling's social workers had been conned by the Coplins' happy-family attitude and their expressed determination to look after little

Annemarie together. According to welfare department records, we later discovered, Joseph Coplin was not working and was not supporting his wife and stepdaughter. Supposedly, Coplin told a welfare investigator that "everything I said in court was a lie. I only did it because she wanted the kid back." I have not been able to pin this story down to its source. But the fact of the matter is that the welfare department had been supporting Helene and Coplin for many months because Joseph Coplin was not employed and had virtually abandoned his wife, Helene, and his older daughter, Josephine. It was only when Helene insisted that she wanted Annemarie back that he returned to play the role of husband. Coplin's unemployment and desertion were not known to the court at the time of Annemarie's discharge from placement, because there had been no communication between court and welfare department. Similarly, the welfare department did not know that Annemarie had been returned to her mother until it received notification from the Foundling Hospital early in January.

It was not early enough. On New Year's day the Riccios took Annemarie out for her holiday treat and found her covered with black and blue marks. On January 2, they took the child to the Foundling Hospital, as duly recorded in the newspapers, where the examining doctor found about sixteen black and blue marks and ventured the opinion that the child had been pinched in those places. The foster mother told the social work supervisor that Annemarie had said, "Joey hit me because I had a big mouth." The supervisor tried to reach Helene Coplin by telephone, failed, and sent her a telegram telling her to contact the Foundling the following day. She also notified the court immediately and was advised by the judge that the foster parents who were understandably reluctant to return the child to the Coplins, should file a Petition of Neglect, and that a hearing would be held on the following morning.

Helene Coplin telephoned the following day, by which time the foster parents and the child were already at the court. She showed up several hours later and immediately initiated a shouting match with the Riccios. She screamed that the Riccios were taking her child away from her, and Anthony Riccio answered that they were all there for the child's sake. The case was not called until late in the afternoon. Joseph Coplin did not appear. Others present, in addition to the main parties, were the Foundling's social work supervisor, who spent some time discussing Annemarie's changed behavior with Mrs. Riccio and the law guardian. The child had become restless, nervous, aggressive, and foulmouthed during her two weeks with the Coplins.

When quetioned by the court, Helene Coplin insisted that Annemarie had sustained her injuries by falling off a swing and off a bicycle. Annemarie, tired and cranky at the end of a long day of waiting around, also said several times that she had fallen but did indicate that the injury to her eye had been caused by her stepfather.

When queried by the judge as to the position and interest of the Foundling, the Hospital's representative explained that, since the decision of the court at the previous (December) hearing had been an out-an-out discharge, the Foundling no longer had any official obligation in the matter. However, the supervisor added, she could vouch for the foster mother's good character and faithful service to the Foundling. There was a moral obligation to bring the new evidence to court. Should it become necessary, the Foundling would be willing to take the child back. The judge examined the child and further tried to elicit answers from her and, after some deliberation, made the disposition that the mother could continue caring for the child. No medical testimony was asked for or produced. The judge made a number of suggestions regarding the handling of the child by the natural mother, and said that Helene needed counseling and should receive it from someone in her own area. The court further suggested that Helene consider day care for the child.

The judge adjourned the case until January 27, requesting that in the meantime Helene Coplin receive counseling from the Catholic Charities center in her district. At the judge's request the Foundling Hospital's social work supervisor accompanied Helene Coplin to the court social worker so that he could make the referral.

On January 7, the supervisor received a call from the court

social worker claiming that the judge had made an unauthorized referral because Mrs. Coplin did not really want counseling. However, he thought that she would probably go along with it anyway. The supervisor told him that her understanding was that placement of the child with her natural mother was contingent upon Mrs. Coplin's receiving counseling from her local Catholic Charities, and that if the court social worker had any questions he should go back to the judge. He said that he was writing to the Foundling for further material on the case; she said that she would be glad to forward it to him upon receiving his letter.

On the following day, the supervisor came to see me at my request to clarify what had been done to date in the Annemarie Lombardo case. She described in detail the activities of her department. I requested that her report be made out to protective services with an addendum mentioning the fact that I particularly wanted to bring this case to their attention. I was especially interested in knowing if the judge had seen the child's bruises, and was answered in the affirmative.

But on January 2, a doctor on my staff had examined the child and written a "suspicion of abuse" report immediately, yet that report was not received by the department of social services protective unit until January 9. Where had it been lying during those intervening days? I don't know.

I do know that on the adjourned date, January 27, the only people in court were the judge, the former foster parents, the Foundling Hospital representative, the probation officer, the law guardian, and a representative from Catholic Charities. The court reporting officer said that the mother was too ill to be in court. Coplin's condition was not referred to. No doctor from my staff was present, nor had the welfare department had any communication with the court that I know of. Under the circumstances, I suppose these last two points were academic; without the mother and the child, there could be no hearing.

Again, an adjournment. The presiding judge directed that the mother be notified to appear in court on February 24 and asked the representative from the Catholic Charities to follow up the case with home visits in the interim.

At the adjourned hearing on February 24, presided ovei by a different judge, Helene Coplin again failed to appear. Annemarie, of course, was not there either. A warrant was ordered for the arrest of the mother and the production of the child.

The warrant squad sent a letter to the mother advising her of the court's action. Helene Coplin did not respond. On March 12, two warrant squad officers designated to serve in juvenile cases went to the Coplin home and attempted to gain entrance by knocking on the door. There was no answer. They left and made no further attempt to serve the warrant.

At 2:00 A.M., March 22, Helene Coplin reported to the police that her daughter had disappeared. On March 25, Annemarie was dredged up from the bottom of the East River.

The city reeled with shock, a reaction that combined fascinated horror, revulsion, pity, loathing for the monstrous killer whoever it might be, and a need to know how such a thing could have happened in New York when the little girl could have been safe with her loving foster parents.

The one fact that emerged immediately was that, over the protests of those foster parents, Annemarie had been returned by family court to a mother and stepfather under whose care she had been murdered. It was then that I launched into my attack against family court. As it later developed, not all the material had been brought to the judge's attention, or judges, I should say, since four actually figured in the Annemarie case. I, too, had been the victim of certain misinformation and mistaken assumptions. The haphazard division of responsibilities, the faulty coordination, the gaps and flaws in the chain of information, the human weaknesses and errors, these were the things that destroyed Annemarie. At first it seemed obvious that a family court judge was to blame. But gradually it emerged that one social worker had not done *this* and the other social worker had not done *that;* that information in the possession of one agency had not been shared with other agencies; that reports that were to have been sent posthaste were around for days; that investigations that should have been pursued never were begun; that statements that should have been verified by a personal check were accepted at face value; that testimony that should have been produced in court was not produced, either in the person of the individual possessing the knowledge or in the form of a report; that *this* person thought that *that* person was taking care of something that *that* person was not. It was a case of all-round mishandling; it was a matter of no one really knowing what the next one was doing and, in some cases, not caring enough to try to find out.

This has been the problem not only in the Annemarie case but in every case that has similarly been lost. There has been no communication between the various disciplines: the doctor doesn't speak to the social worker, the social worker doesn't speak to the public agency, and nobody talks to the judge, who does not always request pertinent information. Nobody has been accountable.

I opened up a beehive with public criticism of family court. The fact that much of what I said was exaggerated and mis-quoted didn't help the situation. I don't believe there was a family court judge at that time who didn't sincerely wish that I would just quietly disappear.

However, quite coincidentally, I did them a favor. There were a good many people who were genuinely indignant over *my* indignation and nevertheless conducted themselves with dignity and decency; but there were also some who, for their own reasons, seemed to dedicate themselves to discrediting me. Approaches were made to His Eminence Terence Cardinal Cooke, archbishop of New York, and to the administrator of the New York Foundling Hospital, and other people in more or less comparable positions, with a view to having me rep-rimanded, disavowed or put out of a job, or all three. My telephone and doorbell began to ring without letup. In between calls from friends, from people with mild complaints or dis-interested parties trying to get at the facts, I got calls from a number of individuals who seemed to have serious designs on my general wellbeing including my career. Some left vitriolic, abusive messages; and some told me quite plainly that they intended to destroy me. The mail from these people wasn't very much more pleasant.

The case of Annemarie would be the greater tragedy if it

could not be put to some constructive use, if it did not bring accurate information to light and shock the public into *informed*, not simply emotional, awareness; if it did not bring about needed reforms in the social machinery designed to deal with the abused child and the abusing family.

The first visible result of the new concern was a new law, to be effective in the state of New York on June 1, 1969, mandating reforms in the family court system. The governor's approval memorandum, filed with the bill when he signed it into law on April 28, read:

The bill establishes in the family court a "child-abuse part," to be held separate from all other proceedings of the court. The child-abuse part is given jurisdiction of all proceedings relating to abused children, and is charged with the immediate protection of such children. The family court would be required to maintain a special staff to expedite proceedings in the child-abuse part. In New York City, an abused child would be represented during all stages of the proceedings by a police attorney, and in counties outside New York City by the district attorney or an assistant district attorney.

The bill establishes a simplified procedure for the issuance of a summons in a "Child-Abuse Case" and for obtaining records, photographs, or other evidence from hospitals, social services districts or other public or private agencies.

Detailed provisions in the bill require a medical examination by a physician appointed or designated by the court, and the taking of colored photographs of the areas of trauma visible on the abused child for evidentiary purposes. The bill also provides that any physician treating an abused child under sixteen years of age shall have the right to keep such child in his custody until the child has been transferred to the appropriate police authorities. Provision is also made in the legislation for the medical and psychiatric examination of persons charged with child abuse.

This was enthusiastically hailed in some quarters as a great piece of legislation, as a "bill of rights for battered children." Hopes ran high that it would give "countless other children . . . a better chance for healthy, happy lives."

But the Committee on the Family Court and Family Law did not share these hopes:

It is the opinion of this committee that there is no basis for a claim that the new law. . . will be the cause of countless other children having a better chance for happy and healthy lives. The law was hastily drafted in response to newspaper sensationalism arising from the Lombardo case and has all the defects which may be expected of a headlong plunge into a complicated problem. . . .

The committee upon its study of the law finds it bad because it suffers from numerous defects in draftmanship, because parts of it raise constitutional problems, because it unduly interferes with the judiciary by imposing through statutory mandate a special part of the family court, because without providing the necessary additional funds it imposes burdens on the family court and its staff, on the police commissioner of the city of New York, because of its interjection of the police and the district attorneys into what should be civil proceedings in a civil court, and because of its unwise repudiation of the use of law guardians to represent children.

Nevertheless there was reason to hope that the new law would help to streamline procedures and speed up action in child maltreatment cases. The cry was, "We must try to avoid another Annemarie!" And the first bright hope was that the new law, instantly labeled the Child's Bill of Rights, would serve that purpose.

The mayor's task force, in the meantime, had made its own recommendations to the city. These were:

1. That at the state level, an individual experienced in the problem of child abuse and neglect be appointed to supervise and coordinate the three separate disciplines of reporting, investigative and legal involved in the protection of these children under the regulation set up by the present statutes.

2. That this supervisor be assigned a physician experienced in the care and welfare of children in order to advise him on the medical and psychological problems as they affect the child and his family, with psychiatric assistance available on a consulting basis.

3. That the staff of the investigative agency be immediately increased with experienced social workers oriented in the problem of child abuse and neglect, since the very lives of innocent children may be at stake. Only experienced social workers

should be employed in this branch of the department of social services.

4. A pediatrician experienced in the care of children should be assigned to the investigative office on a consultative basis and should review all reported cases of child abuse and neglect with the agency to determine whether or not the case is to be presented to the family court.

5. That the reporting agency, whether individual or corporate, be advised of all progress and be involved in the outcome of the case.

6. That a sufficient number of judges be appointed *immediately* to handle the large number of child abuse and neglect cases specifically.

7. That a special panel of judges be appointed by the administrative judge of the family court to hear cases of child maltreatment.

8. That the judges' determination or decision to return the child to the home must be made after personal consultation with social worker and physician involved in the case.

9. That one judge follow through on a specific case of child maltreatment in order to insure proper management and preservation of the family and child.

10. That a careful review of the accomplishments of the overall function of the family court be carried out each year to evaluate the true effectiveness of these recommendations.

Of course, it was not enough to recommend. We had to work very hard to implement our recommendations. In some cases, we succeeded up to a point.

Almost lost in the shuffle of all the frenzied effort to make it up to Annemarie (as if we ever could), to make her death "meaningful," bury our own shame, and rebuild the system that had let her die, was little Teresa Rodriguez. She had been beaten up on March 22, the day Annemarie was reported missing.

In an affidavit to the Bronx Criminal Court, Mrs. Isabella Rodriguez charged that on March 22 her paramour, Juan Ortiz, had kicked and beaten her in the presence of 18-month-old

Teresa. The frightened child had cried throughout her mother's ordeal. Enraged by her cries, Ortiz had turned on her and strung her up by her wrists in the bathroom. While she hung suspended from the shower curtain bar he lashed her repeatedly with a belt that was thirty inches wide, a quarter-of-an-inch thick, studded with metal eyelets, and finished with a heavy metal buckle. The eyelets, it was said, punctured her skin from her head to her toes. "You can match the metal eyelets of the belt to the wounds on Teresa's body," a detective said. What wounds the heavy buckle inflicted were not specified.

The affidavit further alleged that, when Ortiz was through beating the child, he cut her loose from the rod and let her drop heavily to the floor. The fall broke her left arm. Mrs. Rodriguez tried to go to her child, to pick her up, to treat her wounds, to comfort her. Ortiz wouldn't let her get near, wouldn't let her touch Teresa. The child lay on the bathroom floor for almost two days. Mrs. Rodriguez was finally able to take her to Fordham hospital when Ortiz went to work. Little Teresa was admitted in critical condition. Ortiz was arrested at his place of work. Although Teresa was declared out of danger within a few days, she was expected to have to remain in the hospital for another two months.

That was a bad time, a dreadful time. Within the space of little more than a week, a four-year-old died of malnutrition, a sixteen-month-old baby was thrown by his father from a thirteenth-floor bedroom window; a little boy was beaten to death by his mother's boyfriend; Annemarie was left in the East River with rocks in her pockets; and Teresa Rodriguez had lain on a bathroom floor for nearly two days with a broken arm.

Each new episode was a further goad, another painful sting, driving us all to find some way of seeing to it that these things would not happen to other children.

The Judiciary Relations Committee of the Appellate Division, First Department, released its report on June 24, 1969. It was a thorough document, based on the sworn testimony of seventeen witnesses and an examination of the role and performance of every participant, "of each public officer and social agency representative and the manner in which they have all worked together within the family court settings." The committee concluded that nearly every individual and agency connected with the case, both inside and outside family court, had fumbled in some way, either through negligence, poor judgment, or ineptitude. "It cannot overlook the conclusion that if the family court and the complex of public and private agencies operating within it had functioned more effectively, (Annemarie Lombardo) would probably not have met her tragic death."

Under the heading of *The Processing of Neglect Cases in Family Court,* the report observes that:

It is quite apparent from even a brief examination of the family court that its daily operation is marked by heavy caseloads and inadequate resources to deal with individual cases. With thirty to forty cases on the calendar each day, sufficient time is not available to deal with some of the most complex problems presented within the entire court system.

The auxiliary services available to the court are inadequate and underfinanced, and suitable treatment programs are not available for all juveniles found neglected, delinquent, or in need of supervision. The rehabilitative alternatives open to the court are often inappropriate and family court judges are compelled to make dispositions which they know may not have constructive results. Removing a neglected child from his home does not ensure that the child will receive the love and care necessary for proper development.

Two of the four judges in the Lombardo case came in for criticism by the committee, although the report stressed that both were handicapped by inadequate assistance in obtaining all the relevant facts. The Foundling Hospital received a healthy dose of criticism for failing to provide the court with information about Joseph Coplin and living conditions in the Coplin home, although "an abundance of evidence actually existed in the community which would have demonstrated the necessity of removing the child." The report observed that "no attempt to obtain that information had ever been made by the social agencies and consequently it was not made known to [the] judge. . . ." There was also comment about the Foundling representative's recommendation, in the December hearing, to return the child to her mother; and about her lack, in the January hearing, of recommendation to remove the child from the custody of the mother in spite of a medical report showing that the child had "approximately sixteen small bruises on her buttocks, a bruise over her left eye, and a bruise on the side of her head." In sworn testimony to the committee, the Foundling Hospital's representative had said: "I didn't take the position that this was an abused child." There was misjudgment upon misjudgment, mistake upon mistake.

What of the law guardian, who was assigned to represent Annemarie under a contract agreement beween the appellate division and the Legal Aid Society? What had he done for her? Nothing. Yet he was known as a competent lawyer. The role of law guardian is ill-defined and, in this particular case, seems not to have been acted out at all. As the child's "counsel," he was at a disadvantage because he did not have adequate investigative services at his disposal; he was not aware of all the data. But, the committee's report noted, he should nevertheless have "forcefully requested that there be only a short adjournment on January 3, 1969," instead of permitting an adjournment of four weeks. Further, he should have demanded the production of the medical report, as well as the presence of the child's stepfather, and "he should have been prepared during the December and January hearings to discuss that portion of the unfavorable background of (Helene Coplin) which was available to him in his files." And, particularly on January 27, when neither the mother nor the child was in court, he should have raised the question of temporary remand or contacted Child Protective Unit by telephone when the bruises were found on Annemarie Lombardo.

He should have; they should have; we should have. We all should have done what we didn't. By law, the Foundling Hospital should immediately have notified the Bureau of Child Welfare by telephone when the bruises were found on Annemarie's body on January 2 and followed it up with a written report within forty-eight hours. But the telephone call was apparently not made, and the report was not mailed until

January 8. Ordinarily the bureau, on receipt of such a report, would have been obligated to investigate, but the bureau did not investigate on the grounds that the case was already in court.

Nevertheless, if the bureau had investigated, it could have performed a valuable service. When the bureau received the Foundling's report on January 9, it was "still two months before the child died," and information obtained through investigation by the bureau "would have been of great assistance to the court on January 27 . . . or even February 24."

In New York City, the Bureau of Child Welfare is part of the city's Department of Social Services. In another part of that department, a caseworker had information about the Coplin family that was unknown to either the bureau or the court or any other agency. The left hand didn't know what the right hand was doing.

And as for the Warrant Squad: No attempt was made to serve the January 24 warrant on Helene Coplin until March 12, and then the attempt was abandoned after the initial futile attempt. Why? Because no priority had been given to the execution of the warrant, and without a priority notification it was not uncommon for several months to pass before attempts were made to serve a warrant. Some warrants were never executed. Why not? Because of the enormous backlog of warrants, and because the Warrant Squad of New York County Family Court (Juvenile Term) consisted at that time of only two men. These two officers had a workload of 3,500 warrants to service per year. How could they possibly serve them all? They couldn't.

The committee report also commented on the failure of the Catholic Charities representative to follow up the case, to visit the Coplin home, or to provide counseling for Helene, as requested by the judge. Something had gone wrong here too.

We are all to blame. From one agency to another, lacking communication not only between agencies but within agencies, we had shuffled our faulty assumptions and our mistakes; and along the line we had lost and sacrificed Annemarie.

She slipped down into a communication gap. It sounds

horribly facetious, putting it that way, but that is what happened.

As the committee summed it up: "The committee's study of this case reveals clearly that error of judgment prevailed outside of the family court setting as well as within it. A fair appraisal of blame for this tragedy, however, must focus on the lack of resources within the family court complex and the lack of coordination among the various agencies and disciplines . . . To avoid tragedies of this kind in the future, attention must be devoted to the weaknesses of the underfinanced and uncoordinated family court complex."

The committee's recommendations included the immediate expansion of the New York County Family Court Warrant Squad; the marking of warrants in child-abuse cases to identify them as such in order to give them priority, or "rush" status; provision of attorneys for petitioners in abuse and neglect cases; a reexamination of the role of the law guardian in such cases; the immediate establishment of a central registry of child-abuse information, to be maintained by the Office of Probation; a sharing of reports and investigation results between the Bureau of Child Welfare and the Office of Probation; more funds for the family court, Bureau of Child Welfare, and Office of Probation; an immediate change in the policy of the Bureau of Child Welfare which precluded initiation of an investigation after a matter reached family court; elimination of short-term rotation of judges to permit a judge to follow through on a case; the review by a public agency, such as the Office of Probation or the Bureau of Child Welfare, of the casework material, and recommendations of private placement agencies; and the restructuring of family court with a view to establishing "all-purpose" parts or terms which process different kinds of family cases in order to avoid fragmentation of a family's problems among several judges.

The next step was to develop and spell out all the steps in this major program of overhaul. Then they had to be implemented.

Joseph Coplin went on trial in late November for the murder of Annemarie.

Witness after witness came to the stand to describe how they had visited the apartment of Joseph and Helene Coplin within the ten days preceding Annemarie's death and seen the child with her head so swollen that she could hardly see out of her eyes. Several of these visitors were addicts who had come to the apartment to use it as a shooting gallery. Both Joseph and Helene had been on heroin, they said, and Joseph would let them use the place to get high in exchange for a snort for himself.

One witness (an addict friend of Helene's) testified: "I saw Annemarie huddled by the toilet, just sitting there. I put my hands out to her and said, 'Annemarie, come here, baby.' She backed away like she was frightened. . . One eye was black, all black and blue. She was black and blue down her back from the top all the way down to her legs. Her head was twice the normal size, all out of proportion."

Some days later this witness again visited Helene and saw that Annemarie was very much worse. "The child's mouth was all busted open. The whole face was swollen. It was almost twice the size I last saw it."

She saw Annemarie again on the last day of the little girl's life: "I saw Annemarie laying on the bed, covered up to her forehead. I only saw the top of her head, but it was enormous." And the witness added that she thought Annemarie "was scared to death."

Other addict witnesses, who had gone several times to the apartment during the last week to ten days of Annemarie's life, confirmed this story and added details to it: "Her head was swollen two feet wide," "Her face was black," "She was cowering in the bathroom," "She was staring at the wall," "She was in another world."

The neighbor who had given Helene money to take the child to see a doctor (which Helene did not do) also testified that she had seen Annemarie with her head and face badly swollen. Her daughter's boyfriend saw Annemarie, too, and was concerned enough by her condition to later call upon the Coplins to find out how Annemarie was doing. Annemarie was doing fine, he was told.

One witness testified that she had inquired after Annemarie and had been told that the little girl was "lying on the floor in the bedroom, because she wet the bed." The witness said she tried to get into the bedroom to see her but Coplin seemed to be blocking her way. She did manage to approach a few feet but could not get close to the child. As she approached, she testified, Coplin "threw a blanket over the baby; only one hand was sticking out. It moved a little." This must have been just about the end.

At least eight people saw Annemarie and recoiled in horror during her dying days. Not one of them, neither visiting addict or friendly neighbor, made any attempt to notify the police or call a doctor or the Society for the Prevention of Cruelty to Children or find out from any public or private agency what they could reasonably and decently be expected to do. Maybe they felt somebody else was doing it. Nobody was.

Joseph Coplin, convicted of murder "under depraved circumstances," was sentenced to twenty years in prison.

Various shakeups and overhauls were under way in both public and private agencies. A number of structural changes were instituted in family court. We were all very much more aware, now; more alert; more concerned; better equipped to deal with the whole tangled, tragic problem of our neglected and battered children. I hadn't done much to deserve Annemarie's thanks though I had tried. But now perhaps, something effective and concrete could be done for children like her.

We had been shocked into action. At least little Annemarie's death, cruel, wasteful, and inexcusable as it was, had served some purpose. Or had it?

# CHAPTER SEVEN

# The Mayor's Task Force on Child Abuse and Neglect

WHEN THE MAYOR'S Task Force on Child Abuse and Neglect started work early in 1969, it did so against the backdrop of the New York State legislature's 1964 child-abuse law. Among other provisions, that law mandated the reporting of suspected child-abuse cases by physicians and other professionals in a position to observe them. The first registry of child-abuse, though not neglect, cases in the eastern United States was promptly established in New York City. In the first year of its operation, it was the recipient of more than 300 abuse reports. The number rose to 416 in 1966, 706 in 1967, and 956 in 1968, and to over 10,000 in 1972.

Most of us in the field of child health and welfare felt that even these growing figures represented only a fraction of the total number of New York City's physically abused children, quite apart from the number of children otherwise maltreated. As it developed, we were right; and, as the years passed and the reporting system was revised to include neglect cases as well as additional sources of reports, we saw the figures climbing to reach a very much closer approximation of the true annual toal.

But in the beginning of 1969, we were only making primitive guesses as to the scope of the disease and how effectively it was being combated. In the opinion of Health Services Administrator Bernard Bucove and Mayor John Lindsay, it was time to evaluate whether the law and the administrative machinery for carrying out its purposes had been effective during those five years since its passage. It was recognized that the reporting and identification of abused children was only a first step, and that a thorough examination of the existing social, medical, and legal community services involved in the vital business of child protection was needed to determine whether or not these services were equal to their task and what to do if they were not. The task force was to study the effectiveness of existing programs for the reporting and follow-up of abused *and* neglected children; the availability of foster homes and other custodial facilities in the community to provide care for the child whose home situation was hazardous to his welfare; the availability of psychiatric care and other services for the rehabilitation of the emotionally disturbed parents of maltreated children; and the adequacy of educational programs to enable health professionals, social workers, and legal authorities to deal with the problems of child abuse and neglect. Upon concluding our study we were expected to make specific recommendations toward the prevention of child abuse and the improvement of services to abused children and their families.

We were given the funds to do the job, and we picked a research team to do it with. For two years, our research staff made notes, studied, drafted interim reports, and drew up preliminary recommendations. The task force team met regularly to discuss progress and problems, and sift through the vast amount of data that was coming in. We were, at the same time, playing a dreadful kind of numbers game. . . more than 10,000 cases one year, close to 15,000 the next, and how many more will we have per year before we know what to do about it? And we were grimly aware that each one of those cases, those hundreds and thousands of cases, represented a helpless, frightened child, not just a statistic.

Inevitably, there were some rumblings in the watchdog press about the time it was taking us to complete the research and the report. This didn't hurt; it was indicative of healthy interest. But the problem was complex, the machinery intricate, and the required information of enormous range. We used structured questionnaires and also did both structured and unstructured interviews. Our research group went into the family courts, the hospitals, the child-protective units, the Societies for the Prevention of Cruelty to Children, and the social agencies; and they interviewed social workers, field investigators, bureau heads, hospital directors, pediatricians, interns, radiologists, nurses, psychiatrists, judges, probation officers, teachers, lawyers, people representing virtually all agencies and professions having any contact with the problem of child abuse and neglect.

In the first week of January, 1971, Mayor Lindsay was presented with a complete if not polished draft of our final report and recommendations. At the same time I offered a quick verbal rundown of what was really happening in our city; of the scope and horror of child abuse, of the bureaucratic tangle, of the need to act quickly but not with careless haste. I emphasized to the mayor that this was a far more important issue than many of the other things we tend to get excited about, such as sanitation, pollution, subway service and fares, and city traffic, and that we had to give the highest priority to child abuse if we were going to save children's lives in New York City.

We had tried, in our lengthy report, to cover as much as possible. Certainly we covered, exhaustively, the four main areas that we had been specifically requested to study. In our recommendations, we stressed the need for disseminating information about child abuse and neglect to the medical, social, and legal professions; for a full-time central registry to receive and computerize all reports of neglect as well as abuse; an agency of prime responsibility to coordinate all efforts; and for streamlining preventive, protective, and rehabilitative services so that there would be less wasteful duplication of effort, more personal follow-up, and fewer gaps that would allow a child like Annemarie to pass unnoticed. These were all very concrete and detailed recommendations, most of which we knew would require considerable planning, time, and a certain amount of funding to be made workable.

After the initial presentation, Mayor Lindsay asked what was thought to be the most important recommendation. On behalf of the task force, and on the strength of my own convictions, I replied that the most urgent priority was a computerized central registry of all child-abuse and neglect cases in the city. True, we already had *a* central registry, operated by the Bureau of Child Welfare. But it operated on a five-day-a-week, nine-to-five basis, shorter hours than those kept by child abusers, and functioned only as a recipient of reports and primary investigative service. Thus, mandated sources had the means of getting information but often could not.

This was a nearly useless procedure from the point of view of practical child-protection. What we needed was a completely centralized service, working on a round-the-clock basis, that would receive reports of suspected child abuse and neglect cases from both mandated reporting sources and interested members of the public, investigate the reports, and not only institute the necessary action but maintain information files for the use of authorized institutions and individuals. Then, for example, if a doctor in an emergency room, a social worker on a home visit, a principal in school, or a pediatrician in his office were to be confronted with what he considered to be a likely case of abuse, he would be able to call up the central registry and find out whether or not the child in question had previously been reported as a suspicious case. If he had, if the child had been reported before as a possible maltreatment case or had been to other hospitals with similar abuse-type symptoms, there would be good reason to take action and file a new report with a view to a complete investigation. Without this pool of information, our hands had been at least half-tied. With it, we would have detailed records available for cross-checking suspected cases. It would offer a hope of saving many young lives; and it would also, in time, provide us with data for statistical analysis of what we were looking for, where we were likely to find it, how better to recognize it, and what we were accomplishing.

The mayor listened. Very soon afterwards, he acted. On March 7, 1971, he announced the establishment of a new, centralized Emergency Children's Service to receive all reports of suspected child abuse and neglect. The service would operate twenty-four hours a day, seven days a week, and would cover all parts of the city. It had one emergency telephone number, in operation at the time of the announcement, to receive calls from anybody in any borough. This new consolidated service had been developed and was to be operated by the Interagency Council on Child Welfare and the welfare department, and was, in effect, taking over the less centralized service previously performed by the welfare department's Bureau of Child Welfare. The creation of such a one-office service was a major step toward the coordination, cooperation, and streamlining that we of the task force had been urging; and we could begin to hope that now we had a truly centralized system that would serve both as hot line and information pool.

There was the number—431-4680: the save-a-child number. But who would use it? Even now, although this number has been widely publicized and circulated, only a small minority of my fellow New Yorkers are aware of its existence. Exactly who, in New York, is under mandate to report? Physicians, dentists, osteopaths, podiatrists, optometrists, chiropractors, residents, interns, registered nurses, hospital personnel, school officials, social service personnel, medical examiners, coroners, and Christian Science practitioners are *if* they have reasonable cause to suspect that a child is abused or neglected. Private citizens are not mandated to report. Yet they have as much human responsibility as the professionals. The number in New York is for their use as well. More people, friends, neighbors, relatives of suspected abusers, might dial it if they realized, first, that they are not "squealing" on anyone when they report and, second, they are extremely unlikely to "get involved." The honest wish not to tell tales out of school and get a fellow human being into trouble must be over-ridden by the realization that he is probably already in trouble, that he may be desperate for help, and that a child may be in danger. *Calling this number, or the save-a-child number in the community, is in the best interests of all concerned.* As to becoming involved in an unpleasant situation, once the report is made, the whole matter is out of the caller's hands. The investigative process gets quietly under way without further assistance from the person calling in. Contrary to popular belief, it can be, and usually is, conducted with tact and discretion. If suspicions prove correct, the caller has performed a valuable service. If not, no harm is done. Yes, there are such things as crank calls and malicious accusations. These do not pay off in any satisfaction for the callers.

I have digressed because I think the central emergency service is of enormous value to any community in the United States, but it will not achieve its purpose until people stop making unconstructive complaints about "the system" and start helping to make it work. Certainly it still has its faults, but these will not be corrected by inaction.

In early June of 1971, the Task Force on Child Abuse and Neglect submitted its final, formal report to Mayor Lindsay. Ordinarily upon completion of the job for which it was primarily created, a task force is disbanded. It has become old and stale. Its members have tired and tend to become lax about attendance. They are only too glad to turn in their report and go their separate ways, happy to have completed their task. But, though the mayor's Task Force on Child Abuse and Neglect had fulfilled its directives with energy and enthusiasm, its members did not feel that the job was done. We had met very frequently, for long hours, and usually with 100 percent attendance. We felt that we had accomplished much. But we also felt that our task force was neither old nor tired, and that its usefulness was by no means over. Our recommendations could neither be permitted to gather dust on a shelf nor could they be considered the final answer. We knew that as time went by we would, as individuals, become aware of more problem areas, and we would need an open channel in order to deal flexibly with the continuing challenge and to offer new and even more concrete plans for meeting it. To our great gratification, Mayor Lindsay and Health Resources Commissioner Jule Sugarman decided that the task force must not be disbanded, but must remain in existence as a vital force and given the staff and monies to find ways to implement our recommendations. And so, even while our "final" report was being made public, we were setting new goals.

The full-time emergency service and computerized registry were already proving their worth in keeping track of maltreated children. The save-a-child number, 431-4680, was handling twenty to thirty calls a day. About half of these calls were being entered in the registry.

The *New York Times* of June 5, 1971, concluded a brief story on the task force report:

> The task force's report also made such recommendations as the designation of one agency to be the central reporting receiver of all abuse and neglect cases, that such an agency have investigating capacity at short notice, and that information be shared by all concerned agencies.
>
> Meanwhile, in the Bronx, Mr. and Mrs. Bob Wilkens of 598 East 138th Street were indicted on a charge of criminally negligent homicide in the death of their two-month-old baby, Willie. Bronx District Attorney Burton B. Roberts said the indictment charged that the child died because he had allegedly not been given food or water for three days.

Efforts and hopes are not enough. Nothing ever seems to be enough. The story was an ironic and tragic commentary on what we were trying to do. And it wasn't the only one.

Shortly after midnight on June 26, 1971, thirteen-month-old Laura Butera was found in her parents' apartment beaten almost to the point of death. She died on her way to the hospital.

In bringing the case before the grand jury, Bronx District Attorney Burton Roberts alleged that the little girl had died as a result of beatings, burning, malnutrition, and lack of medical treatment. The parents, Tom Butera and Ligia Campo, were subsequently indicted on charges of murder, criminally negligent homicide, and second-degree manslaughter.

When the police had found Laura dying in her home, they also found her seven brothers and sisters in only slightly better condition. All appeared to be suffering from beatings and malnutrition. Charlene, age three, weighed only fifteen pounds. The seven surviving children, ranging in age from two to twelve, were taken to children's emergency shelters. A child welfare spokesman commented that all of them were "sorely neglected."

And the stories began again: "Child Dies While Court Wheels Turn." "The child died despite the fact that the family problem was known to several city agencies including family court." "She might be alive today except for red tape and inaction by family court." "Family court was aware of the case of the Butera children but took only paper action." "The court issued a warrant but did not serve it." (The court does not serve warrants; it is not geared to. A warrant squad does.)

An inquiring reporter, one assumes, was on the job again. Almost three weeks after the death of the child, it became known that the police had actually taken Ligia Campo and her eight bruised and malnourished children to Bronx Family Court on May 5, more than seven weeks before Laura died. One of the pair of patrolmen described the Butera apartment as a hellhole. "The apartment was burnt out and looked like a bomb went off in it," he said. "There were some bunk beds for the children to sleep in, but it was filthy, with junk all over the place. The children looked awful, hungry, dirty, beaten, and bruised."

Why had the police picked up the family at that time? They had been acting on a warrant from family court. Why had family court issued the warrant? Apparently because a Bureau of Child Welfare caseworker had been concerned about the neglect conditions in the Butera family and Mr. Butera's rejection of all offers of help. And what had happened at family court that day? The judge saw the mother but not the children who were in the court nursery with a nurse who examined them and gave them milk and something to eat. The father, who was supposed to be there, was not. There is another report, however, that the father *was* there, that he was picked up separately and did appear in court while the children were down in the nursery, but the Bureau of Child Welfare worker wasn't there. Who actually was there? This is something to look into.

Another newspaper reported: "Despite the fact that the Butera children, all then showing signs of beating and malnutrition, were in family court only seven weeks before the baby's death, and Tom Butera was arrested for assaulting one of his older children's teachers only five weeks before Laura's death, the children were never removed from the parents' custody." It was true, they were not. At the May 5 hearing, at which Tom Butera and/or the caseworker may or may not have been present, the children were returned to the mother's custody and the case was adjourned until May 25. According to a spokesman for the Department of Social Services (of which the Bureau of Child Welfare is a part), no one, including the judge, knew about the condition of the children downstairs. No one? No one but the nurse on duty; no one but the patrolmen who had brought them in; no one but the caseworker who had been kept by Butera from seeing them recently but had a fair idea of how they had been neglected earlier. No one but the mother was available to the court to describe the condition of the children. The hearing, therefore, was adjourned. Ligia Campo went home with her eight hungry, dirty, beaten, and bruised children and, presumably, with Tom Butera.

Here is the crux of the stories:

The case of Laura Butera and her seven brothers and sisters was known to the welfare department's Bureau of Child Welfare for a year before her death and to the Bronx Family Court more than six months. Last December, after six months of investigation, the bureau asked the family court for a neglect petition against the parents. The court issued a warrant to bring the parents into court so that the judge could decide whether to issue a removal order. What followed was a series of adjournments, missed court appearances, and failure to serve warrants on the parents.

It was not by any means a clear picture, but its very lack of clarity indicated that the procedural changes in family court, the supposedly improved liaison between all agencies, and the changes in the warrant squad had not had the desired effect.

And, in fact, the warrant squad had *not* changed. This is about the only truth to emerge immediately from the midst of all the confusion. Not one single officer had been added to the overburdened warrant squad since the murder of Annemarie Lombardo two years before.

On June 22, after that series of adjournments and missed court appearances, the judge ordered a warrant executed. Ac-

cording to the Department of Social Services, it was the concerned caseworker who had precipitated the issuance of this
warrant, too. She had not, for some time, been able to enter
the Butera apartment to find out what was going on, and she
had become anxious for the children.

The warrant was not served, for the usual reason: a backlog
of other unserved warrants. Four days later, Laura Butera was
dead.

The ball of blame started bouncing around. Almost automatically it landed first in family court but got batted back
promptly to the police department's warrant squad for not
serving the warrant and to the Bureau of Child Welfare for
not following up the case and making it clear that swift action
had been needed. The warrant squad had no answer at all; it
was supposed to have been enlarged to a minimum of ten and
never had been. On behalf of the Bureau of Child Welfare, a
spokesman for the Department of Social Services agreed that
no evidence had been presented to family court to show that
Laura Butera was in imminent danger, but pointed out that
the caseworker had been kept out of the Butera home, and
that it had been anxiety on the caseworker's part that had led
to the ordering of the warrant.

Thus we were left with many of the same old questions.
What had really happened? Exactly what had gone wrong?
The task force met in emergency session to try to get to the
bottom of the case. Only too obviously, there were still great
gaps in our protective system. But in this case, it was not obvious what the gaps were, apart from the mix-up at the May
5 hearing and the nonserving of the warrant.

The facts, as we were able to put them together, formed a
long and dreary tale, still perhaps an incomplete one, yet one
that is particularly revealing of the very real human problems
involved in protecting children from their parents.

The Butera family first came to the attention of the Bronx
Office of the Bureau of Child Welfare back in April, 1969,
when the Morrisania Hospital called to report that a Mrs. Butera (Ligia Campo) had given birth to a baby, Marina, in
March, but had been discharged without the child. The wo-

man had told them she could not take the baby home because she had no clothing for it, even though the hospital would have supplied it. She said she would call for Marina when she had everything ready for her at home. Nine days later the child was still in the hospital. Mr. Butera, in response to a telegram from the hospital, phoned in and said that the Veterans Social Service Center had given them $100 for a layette, and that he would be picking up the baby in a few days. In spite of repeated reminders by the hospital, the parents failed to call for Marina.

The Bureau of Child Welfare caseworker attempted to visit the Buteras but was only able to get as far as her own telephone. Tom Buteras refused to let her visit the home and indicated that her concern for the baby and her interest in the family circumstances were not appreciated.

Butera did pick up the baby a few days later. In the meantime the caseworker compared notes with the Veterans Social Service Center and asked for their cooperation. Veterans Service, already active with the Butera family, were considering court action because of what they felt to be evidence of neglect. The Bureau of Child Welfare sent them a memo outlining available facts, and advised that they were withdrawing because the family was rejecting their services. They requested that Veterans Service stay with the case and follow up.

In June of 1970, the Bureau of Child Welfare received another telephone call from Morrisania Hospital. This time the news was that Mrs. Butera had given birth to another baby girl, Laura, on May 18 and had again gone off without her child. The Bureau of Child Welfare renewed its active interest, and this time the caseworker was able to visit the mother at home. Living conditions, she noted, were extremely poor, and the mother held a strap with which she threatened the children. But Ligia did not strike her children in the worker's presence, and the worker saw no signs of physical abuse. She did find, however, that the children had received no preventive medical-care and presented a neglected appearance. Two days later, the worker visited the school at which the three oldest children were registered and which they presumably attended. She learned that their attendance record was extremely poor. According to teachers and school officials, the children's clothing and physical condition when they did show up indicated that they were given less than minimal care, that they were neglected. They also evidenced not only intellectual but emotional problems that required professional attention, which they were not receiving.

This information was supplemented by the case record from the Veterans Social Service Center, which had been supplying the family with public assistance for some years. That record noted both general and medical neglect of the children's needs as well as the poor living conditions of the household.

On June 28, the caseworker again visited the Butera home. Present were Tom and Ligia and seven children. Laura, six weeks old, had not yet been picked up from the hospital. The caseworker suggested that placement be considered for Laura, and, in addition, offered both homemaker service and assistance in obtaining medical care for all the children. Tom Butera was interested in the offer of homemaker service but refused placement for the baby. As for medical care, it wasn't needed. The Butera children, he said, were perfectly healthy. And he was definitely going to bring Laura home within the week.

When the caseworker visited the home again ten days later, the baby was still not home, but living conditions in the apartment had been improved. The place was less disordered and some painting had been done. The worker repeated her offer of temporary placement for Laura so that the Buteras might better prepare for her homecoming and for homemaker service for the family. Butera again rejected the idea of placement but appeared receptive to homemaker service. His wife could really use the help, he said.

Laura came home, at last, on July 14, almost two months after her birth. Within days afterwards, a nurse from the Visiting Nurse Service of New York, who had visited the family once before, in May, observed that the child seemed to be getting poor physical care and that she was listless. The home, too, was in poor condition. Whatever small improvement there had been by early July had evaporated before the end of the month.

Homemaker service began and ended abruptly one day in August. The caseworker arrived at the Butera home with a Veterans Social Service Center representative, a homemaker, and the homemaker's supervisor. The main purpose of the visit was to be sure that everybody knew everybody and what each was supposed to be doing to ensure all-round cooperation and goodwill. But Butera became angered by a remark to the effect that the reason for homemaker service was that the children were being neglected, and ordered all the visitors to leave immediately and permanently.

Attempts by the bureau caseworker to reestablish contact and reactivate all offers of help were ill-received by Butera. (If Mrs. Butera seems to fade into the background throughout all this, it is largely because of a language barrier which made it necessary for Mr. Butera to do the talking. He was very much the more dominant of the partners.) When the caseworker tried to persist, Butera said he was becoming upset by the interference and the caseworker told him that court action might have to be initiated, Butera countered by saying that he was being persecuted. The caseworker offered help with the children's school and health problems; Butera refused it. The caseworker again suggested the use of placement or homemaker services and asked to be permitted to visit the family. Butera turned down all her offers and her request to visit, and said that he did not want her or anyone else to interfere with him or with his family. The caseworker said again that there might have to be court action. She got nowhere. Butera was adamant and very angry.

The caseworker again visited the school and found that the older children were attending rather more regularly. But Mr. Butera had, according to school officials, been extremely upset by the caseworker's approaches, and when the school authorities attempted to persuade him to accept the bureau's offers of assistance, they were turned down cold.

Court action seemed to be the only course. A neglect petition was filed on January 6, 1971. Both Buteras had been informed of the court date, but neither was present in court. The hearing was adjourned until February 2, and the bureau worker was asked to inform the parents of that date. She did. Mr. Butera came to that hearing accompanied by his attorney. The caseworker was also present, as was the Butera children's school attendance teacher with the children's attendance records. After Mr. Butera's accusations that the caseworker was trying to injure him, his attorney requested and was granted an adjournment until March 23. Both Mr. and Mrs. Butera were notified of that court date.

But on March 23, they were not present in court. A new date was set. On that date, April 6, they were again absent, although the caseworker and the attendance teacher were there. A warrant was issued by the court at that time and executed by the warrant squad on May 5. Butera was actually brought into court, apparently having been picked up independently of his common-law wife and children. However, the worker was unaware of the execution of the warrant and was not informed of the Buteras' appearance in court. This time, therefore, she was among the missing. The case was adjourned to May 25. On that occasion, the parents did not present themselves as required. There was another adjournment. The next hearing was to be held on June 22, and a warrant was stayed for that date. On June 22, the Buteras again failed to show up in court, and the presiding judge ordered execution of a warrant.

But something had happened in the meantime. Tom Butera allegedly attacked the attendance teacher near the school, causing him to suffer broken ribs and a head wound that required eighteen stitches. Butera was arrested on criminal charges but released on his own recognizance. He was ordered to appear in criminal court on June 11, but he did not. A bench warrant was issued for his arrest.

Neither, as noted, did he appear in family court on June 22, when both the bureau caseworker and a caseworker from the Veterans Social Service Center were present.

Now two warrants were out for Tom Butera, the criminal court bench warrant of June 11 and the family court warrant of June 22.

For all our investigation, the record here gets a little muddy. On the one hand, it is said that the bureau's representative requested that the family court warrant be executed forthwith, that is, on a *rush*, top priority basis, but that the judge stated he was unable to issue a rush warrant. On the other hand, it is said that the warrant issued *was* a forthwith warrant, demanding the immediate attention of the warrant squad. The point is probably academic in view of what happened.

It is also said that a warrant officer was personally approached to expedite service; that he stated he could not say when he might be able to serve the warrant; that he suggested that the Bureau of Child Welfare serve it. The caseworker replied that she had been advised by her office that staff members do not serve warrants. As a social services department spokesman put it afterwords: "There is real danger connected in pushing these matters unless a police officer accompanies the caseworker. They have been threatened and beaten when they go in alone."

It is true, and perfectly understandable, that caseworkers are not in a position to serve warrants or removal orders.

It is true that, in this case, the subject of most of the attention was Tom Butera, and that he had become increasingly resistant and sullen in the face of the caseworker's attempts to intervene. He had also, according to the school attendance teacher's account, committed a criminal assault, probably out of anger over that teacher's "interference" in presenting himself at family court with the Butera children's attendance records.

It is also true that no evidence was brought to court that would show that any of the Butera children were in immediate danger. Neglected they were, but not apparently physically abused. Not even the concerned caseworker could predict that Tom Butera would erupt into violence against one of his own children, although it had become increasingly evident that he was a violent man.

Here, in spite of the terrible thing that happened to Laura four days after the unexecuted family court warrant was issued, it is difficult to pinpoint fault. It may not even be particularly productive. Pointing the finger at one person or one agency or one department or one judge and then applying corrective measures is simply to deal with the symptoms. That something went wrong is only too obvious. But the caseworker tried unceasingly to help the Butera children. The family court judge, at each hearing, could only work with such data and persons as were available to him or her. The warrant squad was not equipped for the job it was expected to do, but the outcome of a case that had been steadily building over the course of many months can hardly be ascribed to a single failure to serve a single warrant.

Thus Laura was found beaten to the point of death, and she died. A report from the medical examiner indicated that she showed evidence of malnutrition and battering, of bruises, and of second-degree burns on her wrists. Her three-and-a-half-year-old sister, Charlene, was hospitalized for multiple bruises and severe malnutrition. Of the six other children, placed in shelters, at least one, five-year-old Clarissa, also showed signs of possible physical abuse. She had bruises on the arms and a scar on her cheek.

When had the beatings started? Why?

We never will have answers to these questions. As to the larger question of how we had managed to let another child slip through our fingers, it was once again a matter of the cumbersome system, of delays and information gaps between the various pieces of people-operated machinery involved with child protection. But this time it seemed that the machinery itself was more to blame than the operators. What more could have been done to force assistance upon the Buteras? What tangible evidence was there to present to the court? And in what form, and by whom?

After the fact it is easy to find oversight and error, but surely not negligence, indifference, ineptitude, or an attitude of someone-else-will-do-it. The people were there, willing and concerned. It was the machinery that was not in proper working order. It was still too complicated to work efficiently, and even in its complexity, it was not properly programmed for what it was supposed to do. New courses of action and new procedures had to be built into it.

The mayor's task force studied the Butera case with a view to seeking better coordination between the various city child-protection agencies and lost no time in forwarding recommendations to Commissioner Jule Sugarman for prompt consideration and, we hoped, implementation. The recommendations addressed specific factors in the Butera case that appeared to have contributed to Laura's death. What happened to Laura, even more than what happened to Annemarie, showed us where the system was letting us down. We found the familiar pattern of fragmentation of responsibility for the case among several agencies, and we also found a lack of clearly defined responsibilities for the various individuals involved.

One of the several flaws in the handling of the Butera case was the nature of the neglect petition presented to the court. The task force found that it did not contain enough information to enable the court to perceive the emergency of the situation. The task force therefore urged improvement in the quality of petitions presented to the court in abuse and neglect cases; and, to that end, recommended in-service training for caseworkers and legal staff members so that they might be better equipped to make the most of such evidence as would most effectively support the charges.

The repeated adjournments of the court hearings, due to the nonappearance of the Buteras, constituted another vital factor in this case. Our recommendation was that, if the parents should miss two consecutive hearings without good excuse, the attorney for the department of social services should move for a finding without prejudice, that is, obtain a ruling that neglect or abuse be established as of the second failure by the parent or parents to appear. This, we felt, would cut down on court delays and expedite action.

We could do nothing about expanding the warrant squad, but we did feel that certain procedures could be adopted whereby the serving of warrants could be made more expeditious and more meaningful. Therefore the task force recommended that, whenever a caseworker felt there there was an urgency about a situation due to immediate circumstances or inability to gain access to the family, the caseworker should inform the judge and request the issuance and execution of a "rush" warrant. The caseworker would then provide the liaison warrant officer with all information pertaining to the family, to changes in address, and so on, that might assist in the speedy execution of the warrant. (In regard to the June 22 warrant issued in the Butera case, a police spokesman said that the address given on the warrant was wrong.) Again, in the case of a "rush" warrant, the name of the caseworker, and the telephone numbers at which she and her supervisor could be reached, should be given to the liaison warrant officer. It would then be his responsibility to alert her when the family was being brought into court, and to make sure that the judge was asked to hold the family in waiting for the arrival of the caseworker. (The caseworker in the Butera case had been unaware of the execution of the April 6 warrant on May 25 or the hearing of the latter date and was, therefore, not present in court on that one crucial occasion.) This three-way knowledge-sharing and cooperation between caseworker, judge, and liaison warrant officer should, we felt, expedite the execution of the warrant and ensure the presence in court of caseworker and family at the same time.

It was also our opinion that any lawyer, from, for example, legal aid or the department of social services, involved in a particular child maltreatment case should have recent and personal knowledge of the child or children in the case, so that he or she might be in a position to present such material to the judge. We further recommended that, if material concerning the condition of the child was not presented in court, the family court judge should request specific information. These measures, we thought, would help in determining the whereabouts and true condition of the children involved in these cases. This was to prevent recurrences of the situation in the Butera case, in which those present in the courtroom on May 25 had been unaware that the children were downstairs in the court nursery.

Again, we recommended that, in the public sector, one bureau have responsibility for all abuse and neglect cases, and that one caseworker be assigned to follow each case, with full support from the responsible bureau in the event of delays or obstacles effecting resolution.

We were aware that teachers and other school personnel were in a position to observe the condition of their young charges and capable of evaluating, to some degree, the likelihood of child abuse or neglect; we were also aware that many teachers had been threatened with bodily harm after reporting suspected cases or becoming petitioners. We needed this source of information. In some instances, it was the only one we had. Therefore we recommended the development of a procedure whereby the school principal would take responsibility for reporting neglect and abuse cases, thus maintaining the confidentiality of the original source.

For its own part, the task force undertook to review each case in which a child's death is suspected by the medical examiner to have been caused by abuse or neglect. This after-the-fact investigation would not help the dead child, but it might very well identify faults in the machinery that still required correction.

By September, 1971, implementation of most of these recommendations, in addition to our earlier ones, was well under way.

And yet, instances of child abuse and neglect have continued to multiply. From 1,800 cases in 1969 and 3,000 cases in 1970, the count rose to nearly 6,000 in 1971 and more than 10,000 in 1972. We know that these climbing figures are due in part to the inclusion of neglect as well as abuse cases in the totals, in part to the inclusion of reports from mandated and nonmandated sources. But the figures are, nonetheless, staggering. Are they due only to better reportage, or are they due also to an actual increase? And in view of our improved information-gathering techniques, why is it that we still see so many children when it is too late to save them?

I believe we are seeing an actual increase, and that the reported figures have not yet caught up with the facts. We are too late to save too many children either from death or a dismal future because we do not yet have adequate reportage, because we have not yet developed early-warning techniques, parent-child treatment programs, and also because the crime of maltreatment is committed within the sanctity and secrecy of the home, and its symptoms are not always apparent to outsiders. The perpetrators of violence against children are often the only witnesses. Witnesses other than the perpetrators, or witnesses of the visible symptoms, are reluctant to accept the evidence of their own eyes and, frequently, even more reluctant to report.

Our protective agencies, *all* our public facilities, including our courts, are underfinanced, understaffed, and overworked in spite of all stopgap measures.

This is a national problem: not only the disease of child maltreatment, but the lack of any sort of national program to tackle it. Our priorities are out of joint. Are we so used to violence and injustices and horror and blatant discourtesies and crimes of all kinds that we no longer seem able to cope with them or even to care? Do we let them overwhelm us and sigh with despair?

## CHAPTER EIGHT
# Our Forgotten Children: Who Cares?

IN SPITE OF ALL I have said about individual national apathy, there are a good many individuals and organizations who care very much for the children. But people who care often think only of the quick and easy solution, which is to separate the child from the home in which he is being abused.

It is my firm belief, too, that children known, and I stress the word "known" to have been abused or neglected can best be protected by temporary removal from the home. This must be done quickly or it might just as well not be done at all.

The decision for removal can only be made by the family court judge. We have seen what has happened in some cases where the judge, for one reason or another, did not rule for removal. But there is another side to this coin. It is no simple matter to take a child from his home and drop him neatly into some "better place."

Margaret Mead has said in her book *Blackberry Winter: My Earlier Years* (New York: Morrow, 1972) that the society that stops caring about children, or segregates them from adults or adults from them, is a society "greatly endangered." I think our society *is* greatly endangered. She says: "Everyone needs to have access both to grandparents and grandchildren in order to be a full human being." Each of us needs the wholeness of a home that is our own, and each of us needs the continuity of a parents-children-grandchildren family life as a base from which to function as a complete person. Man belongs in a family; and, in a sense, he and his family do belong to each other. The belonging is, or should be, mutual.

That is one reason why the social agencies and the courts are very reluctant to remove a child from a home in which he has purportedly been neglected. They want to keep the families intact whenever possible. The main thrust of New York's Family Court Act, for example, is that removal should be resorted to "only in grave and urgent circumstances." (This directive is a problem in itself. It requires a Solomon-like capacity for decision-making and a genius for timing. When is a situation "grave and urgent" but not too late?) I would be the last one to subscribe to the doctrine that the child belongs to the mother or father under any and all circumstances, although he may theoretically belong with them, but I do agree that the family as a unit must be encouraged to stay intact if there is no clear and immediate danger and if the parents want help and are responding favorably to rehabilitative treatment at the same time. Sometimes intensive retraining, or even basic training, is needed to turn a parent into a mother or father. The biological act of becoming a parent is a simple one to perform, but the performer does not automatically become endowed with the necessary knowledge and understanding of self or child. When the parenting ability is insufficient or lacking, it must be provided—if it can be. Preferably, it should be provided within the framework of the family.

Another good reason why children are not snatched from their parents' arms at the first signs of abuse or neglect is that these signs may be misleading. They may have been misread in the first place; or they may be minor, one-time, or occasional occurrences precipitated by a fleeting circumstance. One line of argument that may be employed here is that the parent who mistreats a child should never be permitted to take another crack; he or she should be punished for the lapse by having to give up the child. But one slip, or even a couple, is not a way of life. We all err.

Neither is punishment the point at issue. Removing the child from the home is not intended to be a punitive measure. It is intended to protect the child. *If* the child can be protected within the home while the parent undergoes treatment, then home is where the child should stay.

In New York City, about thirty to forty cases of child neglect and abuse come before family court every day. In only a very small minority of these cases is there any real danger to the child or the likelihood of future danger. Of course, a lot of very real cases don't come to court at all.

Furthermore, neglect and abuse cases are very difficult to prove. Judge Nanette Dembitz of the New York Family Court, writing in the New York Bar's *Record,* volume 24 (December 1969), pp. 613-527, has said, "During the writer's two months in the New York City child-abuse term, there were very few, if any, cases in which the evidence clearly established that a serious injury—in the sense of an injury causing permanent or long-term impairment of a physical function or disfigurement— was inflicted by the charged parent by nonaccidental means." Accidents do happen. Also, bruises fade, wounds heal. Tempers cool, too; and love, where it exists, triumphs over anger. And, oddly enough, even when there is a fair indication that abuse is being practiced, the child himself will often deny it and cling trustingly, or perhaps protectively, to the suspected parent.

So it is none too easy to reach a Jehovah-like hand into a home and pluck out the child. Furthermore, once the child is removed, we don't know what to do with him. Foster parents are not lined up in droves waiting for someone else's cast-off child, least of all a child whose color doesn't suit them, or isn't cute, or who's too old or too young, or is sickly or retarded, or disturbed, or difficult to get along with. Foster parenting just isn't that marvelous a deal. And among foster parents, too, there are people who are not emotionally equipped for or trained in the art of mothering. A foster mother isn't a fairy godmother; she, too, is only human, and she, too, may have urges to strike out.

Where else is there to put the child? With relatives, perhaps, but far more often a child is placed in one of those institutions we call "homes" or "children's centers" or "youth houses" or "shelters." Shelters they may be; they do keep out the rain. But that's about all many of them do. Most of them are overcrowded, grim, and prisonlike places. Often, perhaps more often than not, a youngster who is temporarily consigned to one of these cellblocks sinks to the bottom of the heap, forgotten. He may wind up being institutionalized for seven, eight, nine, ten, even fifteen years. In many cases when he comes out, he comes out a hardened criminal. Our jails and our shelters are much alike. Incorrigibles and innocents are all dumped in together. The innocents don't have much to teach but a lot to learn. Many of the children confined to these unhomelike shelters are put there too late to save them from what they have already become. Picture them: doomed children, quick with the switchblade, already experienced with soft or even hard drugs, deprived of love, full of hate, totally incorrigible, crammed into a crowded jailhouse of a "home" that cannot fill any of their needs, cannot make up for anything they have lost, cannot retrain them away from the evil they have learned, cannot prevent them from corrupting their more innocent fellow inmates. Nor are the staff members of these institutions always what they should be. It is not unique to find them committing physical or sexual abuse on their charges. Some children find life in these places intolerable. Sometimes they try to kill themselves. On the whole, it cannot be said that there's much evidence of caring in these institutions.

As the judiciary committee report noted:

> Removing a neglected child from his home does not ensure that the child will receive the love and care necessary for proper development. . . . The court is often disposed to conclude that leaving a child with once-neglectful parents is far preferable to placing him either in an overcrowded institution or in a series of foster homes. . . . It sometimes appears more desirable to leave the child in the home while providing counseling and other services to assist the family to overcome the problems presented by the neglect petition. When a child is removed from the home and placed in the custody of an authorized agency, every effort is supposed to be made to rehabilitate the family for the return of the neglected child to his parents as early as possible.

Though such effort is "supposed to be made," the hard fact is that there is not one community in America fully prepared to handle the constantly increasing incidence of child maltreatment. Few if any communities have sufficient facilities, staff, or funds to do the dual job of child protection and parent rehabilitation; not a single one has a total, start-to-finish program of action beginning with *prevention* and ending with *cure*.

Yet this is a community problem and should be handled as such. This is not to say that each community must be left to work out its own programs and solutions without government help; but the specifics of the problem vary from community to community, and direct action must be taken on a local level. We have to get to the root causes of the problem in our own communities, learn to identify the potential trouble spots, and act *before* cases reach the courts and *before* children vanish into institutions. Unless the people of a community become personally involved, there will not be much success in stamping out this disease. Certainly one of the things that all communities can and must do is to press government into action. Community leaders must take every opportunity to make their legislators on a city, state, and federal level recognize that child maltreatment is a pressing national problem of major proportions and come up with the necessary appropriations to establish programs for coping with it. All of us should raise our voices loud and clear to demand appropriate services and support for the child-care agencies in our own communities, including the money and trained staff to keep them going. But let us also look down our own streets. We, as individuals in whatever community, are solely responsible for doing something about the problem on the human level. Our personal intervention is the first line of defense and is a *must*.

Not all the people who do care about maltreated children and their unhappy parents are in a position to obtain funds, to set up task forces and study groups, to plan pilot or demonstration projects for child protection and parental rehabilitation. But there is something that every individual can do, and that is to care personally. Caring means human involvement, and it means helping.

To become involved and to help, we have to know what to look for. I am sure that we would all like to have a part in preventing the tragic life experiences that are played out daily in the homes and hospitals of our own communities. We are not interested in punishing parents; we are, or should be, interested in preventing tragedies.

Do you have reason to suspect that someone next door, across the street, within the school community is abusing or neglecting a child? Many of you, I'm sure, have such suspicions. But if you don't hear the screams, how can you really tell?

Physicians have been provided with diagnostic guidelines, indices of suspicion. Here are guidelines for the nonphysician who would like to know how he or she can recognize possible cases of abuse and neglect in order to help the parents.

Abuse and neglect may be present when several of the following factors are in evidence:

The child seems unduly afraid of its parents.

The child is unusually fearful generally.

The child is kept confined, as in a crib or playpen (or cage), for overlong periods of time.

The child shows evidence of repeated skin or other injuries.

The child's injuries are inappropriately treated in terms of bandages and medication.

The child appears to be undernourished.

The child is given inappropriate food, drink, or medicine.

The child is dressed inappropriately for weather conditions.

The child shows evidence of overall poor care.

The child cries often.

The child is described as "different" or "bad" by the parents.

The child does indeed seem "different" in physical or emotional makeup.

The child takes over the role of parent and tries to be protective or otherwise take care of the parent's needs.

The child is notably destructive and aggressive.

The child is notably passive and withdrawn.

The parent or parents discourage social contact.

The parent seems to be very much alone and to have no one to call upon when the stresses of parenthood get to be overwhelming.

The parent is unable to open up and share problems with an interested listener and appears to trust nobody.

The parent makes no attempt to explain the child's most obvious injuries or offers absurd, contradictory explanations.

The parent seems to be quite detached from the child's problems.

The parent reveals inappropriate awareness of the seriousness of the child's condition (that is, of the injury or neglect) and concentrates on complaining about irrelevant problems unrelated to the injured/neglected appearance of the child.

The parent blames a sibling or third party for the child's injury.

The parent shows signs of lack of control, or fear of losing control.

The parent delays in taking the child in for medical care, either in case of injury or illness, or for routine checkups.

The parent appears to be misusing drugs or alcohol.

The parent ignores the child's crying or reacts with extreme impatience.

The parent has unrealistic expectations of the child: that it should be mature beyond its years; that it should "mother" the parent.

The parent indicates in the course of conversation that he/she was reared in a motherless, unloving atmosphere; that he or she was neglected or abused as a child; that he or she grew up under conditions of harsh discipline and feels that it is right to impose those same conditions on his or her own children.

The parent appears to be of borderline intelligence, psychotic, or psychopathic. (Most laypersons will find it difficult to make a judgment here. It might be better for the observer to note whether the parent exhibits the minimal intellectual equipment to bring up a child; whether the parent is generally rational or irrational in manner; whether the parent is cruel, sadistic, and lacking in remorse for hurtful actions.)

It is my belief, a belief in which virtually all my colleagues concur, that a large proportion of abusive and neglectful parents do not willfully harm their children. *Willfully* is the operative word. They know they are doing damage. They know they are neglecting. They know a cry of pain when they hear one. But many would like to stop themselves if only they knew how, and they don't. They are inadequate, frightened people, incapable of parenting, and they don't like what they are.

Just as it is nearly impossible for them to change themselves without help, so it extremely difficult for them—emotionally frozen and isolated people as they are—to seek it. Therefore, it is at this level that we must start: on a purely personal, humane, reaching-out level. *Anyone* can try.

Suppose you have a next-door neighbor who you know to be a widow. She has three young children, and her husband was killed in Vietnam. She never goes out except to buy groceries. So far as you can see, she has no visitors. She exchanges greetings with you but does not encourage friendship. Often you hear the sounds of shouts and beatings from her home, and often you hear the long drawn-out painful sobbing of a child afterward. When you catch sight of the children, which is very seldom, they seem nervous and subdued. Something, you are sure, is wrong. What is your impulse? Call the police? No, not if you can avoid it. Certainly not at this stage. Call the child protective unit in your community? Not just yet. Have the number handy in case of need, but don't dial it in haste. Try, instead, to make personal contact with the mother.

No doubt you already have enough to keep you occupied, but this is your opportunity to practice plain old-fashioned neighborliness. If it seems to you that your neighbor is reaching the end of her rope with her children, and perhaps with herself, it is time to step in. Engage her in conversation whenever you can. Stop by and ask her over for a cup of coffee, or offer to baby-sit with the children once in a while, or just drop in and give her the opportunity to talk.

The chances are that she will not be particularly receptive to your friendly advances. She may ice you out. She may slam the door in your face. I didn't say it was going to be easy.

But it won't hurt you to keep trying, to keep on being concerned, to keep on reaching out without seeming to butt in. She needs someone to talk to, someone to listen to her, someone who will be undemanding, informal, uncritical, and understanding. Deep down inside she has a hungry yearning for someone to give her the very support you are offering, a chance for mutual trust, a chance to get a break from the kids, a chance to be herself in communicating with a fellow human being who cares.

In time she may gradually let down her guard and avail herself of your friendship. If she does, you will have helped her enormously, and, in all likelihood, she will turn to you in moments of stress instead of losing control. But if she doesn't, and if you are convinced by your observation of various telltale signs that the child needs protection and the mother needs help, it is time to call upon the community's child protective services.

It often seems that an individual can do so little. In this case an individual can accomplish a great deal by just being human. Teachers and other school personnel are in the best position to observe the symptoms of child maltreatment. They see their charges day after day and often for hours on end, and normally they also see the parents on occasion. The only action school officials need, and must, take on suspicion of abuse is to report what they observe to their community's child-protective unit or other designated agency. The children's division of the American Humane Association has developed a list of "indicators of a child's need for protection," directed toward teachers, school administrators, nurses, and counselors, which are paraphrased here because they can be of great value to all school personnel *and* children.

Take note of:

A child who is frequently absent or late. Whether his problem is at home or in school or within himself, known to his parents or not, his habitual lateness or absence strongly suggests a maladjustment.

A child who arrives at school too early and hangs around

after classes without apparent reason. He may not be welcome or cared for at home; he may hate his home, or be afraid of it.

A child who is unkempt and/or inadequately dressed. If he is dressed inappropriately for the weather, if his clothing is dirty and torn, if he is habitually unwashed, if other children don't like to sit near him because they think he smells bad, he is clearly neglected.

A child who more than occasionally bears bruises, welts, and other injuries. Will he say how he got them? Does he complain of being beaten at home? Or is he always fighting?

A child who is hyperactive, aggressive, disruptive, destructive in behavior. He may be acting out his own hostility. He may be reflecting the atmosphere at home. He may be imitating his parents' behavior. He may be crying out for attention and help.

A child who is withdrawn, shy, passive, uncommunicative. He *is* communicating. Whether he is too compliant or too inattentive to comply at all, he has sunk into his own internal world, a safer one, he thinks, than the real world. His message is in his passivity and silence.

A child who needs, but is not getting, medical attention. He may have untreated sores. He may have an obvious need for dental work. He may need glasses to see the blackboard.

A child who is undernourished. What is the reason—honest poverty, or uncaring parents?

A child who is always tired and tends to fall asleep in class. Either he is not well, his parents are neglecting to regulate his routines, or his is simply unable to get to bed and to sleep because of family problems.

The parent who becomes aggressive or abusive when approached with a view to discussing the child's apparent problems.

The parent who doesn't bother to show up for appointments,

or is so apathetic and unresponsive that he might as well have stayed at home.

The parent who is slovenly, dirty, and possibly redolent of alcohol.

The parent who shows little concern for the child or what he is doing or failing to do.

The parent who does not participate in any school activities or come to any school events.

The parent who will not permit the child to participate in special school activities or events.

The parent who is not known to any of the other parents or children.

The parent whose behavior as described by the child is bizarre and unusual.

The parent whose behavior is observed by school personnel to be strange, bizarre, irrational, or unusual in any way.

In time to come, it is hoped that the schools, as educational institutions, will take on a very much more active role in the war on child abuse. Curricula can surely include, for appropriate age groups, classes in family life and responsibility directed chiefly toward children who are deprived of suitable examples at home but surely useful for all children; lessons in the meaning of love, compassion, human understanding, and caring for others; and courses in the subject of child maltreatment itself, its causes, its manifestations, its possible cures. Maybe in this way, our children will learn to be more protective and less punitive then we.

But until such time as our entire educational system teaches that violence begets violence, that neglect breeds neglect, that hatred spawns more hatred, that corporal punishment which is still practiced in many schools is primitive, degrading, ineffective as a disciplinary practice, harmful to the child and dangerous to our future, we will have to deal with child maltreatment on the personal level wherever we observe its symptoms: in our schools, in our consulting rooms, in our public clinics, in our immediate neighborhoods, and next door.

If the idea of neighbor helping neighbor or running next door to offer coffee and sympathy seems old-fashioned and banal in these sophisticated times, it is nevertheless a good one. It often works. No one is more helpless than a child, and we are bound to reach out to those we can help. Furthermore, this business of being neighborly isn't just being a do-gooder. It's practical; it's commonsense. People need people, and that's why it works even when people don't always admit right away that the concerned interest of another person is what they have been yearning for. Any approach to child protection must include the proposition that the abusing parent needs understanding love, unlovable though he or she may seem to be.

The first organized attempts at the love-thy-neighbor approach have been made in Denver, a pioneer city in the field of child protection primarily because of the presence there of Dr. C. Henry Kempe and his colleagues. Due to Kempe's impetus, and the efforts of Doctors Steele and Pollock, it has been demonstrated that home visits by social workers and laymen who make themselves available as friends on a twenty-four-hour-a-day basis can go a long way toward meeting the mothering needs of abusing parents and changing their attitudes. Lay therapists, acting as surrogate parents to maltreating parents, have long been active in the Denver program with extremely encouraging results.

More recently, the Pediatric Service at Colorado General Hospital has enlarged on the concept of the lay therapist as parental figure for the abusing parent and given the lay therapy program a two-pronged approach. They utilize the services of foster grandparents, all of them over 65 years old, as stand-in grandparents for hospitalized children. This service is not primarily for abused children but does include them; it includes every child whose parents are unable or unwilling to spend much time with him during his hospital stay. The grandparent cuddles, judiciously spoils, and generally acts like a real grandparent to the assigned child while he is in hospital. In the early stages of the program some of the foster grandparents assigned to battered children could not relate at all to the parents, but a number of them not only grandparented the children but mothered the parents as well. In some cases this relationship continued beyond the hospital stay into the home, with beneficial results for the whole family. This success suggested that parent aides of all ages might be utilized in a larger-scale program. The second part of the Denver approach involves the use of parent aides ranging in age from 24 to 60. These are men and women with no formal training as therapists but with plenty of informal training as warm, sympathetic human beings because of their own upbringing in stable homes by loving, effective parents, and their own successful experience as parents. The focus of the parent aid is not on the child but on the confused, unhappy parent. They visit the families, listen, pay only fleeting attention to the children, and behave like mothering adults towards the parents. As Doctors Helfer and Kempe stated in their book *The Battered Child* (Chicago: The University of Chicago Press, 1968): "Flexibility, patience and compassion, a willingness to listen and be nondirective and noncritical, are the basic requirements for a successful parent aide. The qualities are those of a mild and loving individual who is not easily upset by an ungrateful, suspicious, and often initially unwilling client."

Question: Are there not dangers involved in letting amateurs venture where perhaps even some psychiatrists may fear to tread?

Answer: No. The aides are carefully chosen and work under the supervision of social workers and in consultation with pediatricians and psychiatrists. Furthermore, they are not usually dealing with dangerous people or highly volatile situations. According to Kempe and Helfer, fewer than 10 percent of the people who mistreat their children are psychotics or psychopaths. The majority are hurt, lonely, guilt-ridden, insufficiently mothered people who would like to do the right thing but don't know how, and who erupt with pent-up frustration when they fail. In the Denver program, the entire family structure is carefully evaluated and the parent or parents psychiatrically tested before any sort of therapy is initiated. The ill receive treatment, and the immature get motherly visitors.

It may be wondered if home visits are truly protective of the child. If the aide is successful in establishing a supportive relationship with the parent, if she is able to build up the parent's self-esteem and sense of personal worth, if she is able to develop a relationship of mutual trust, if she is able to ease the parent through crisis situations and truly understand the parent's feelings, then she is not only helping the parent but the entire family and protecting the child in the most effective way possible.

The parent-aide idea is not being advertised as a patented magic cure for child abuse. Success is not measured by the transformation of sinner into saint or the friendless home into the neighborhood clubhouse. Success is a situation in which the once-damaged child can return home and live in an intact family without being reinjured; in which the child is recognized as a human being with individual charateristics, a person who can actually be enjoyed; in which the parents have outgrown their dependency on the aide as an emotional prop and are able to reach out to others in the community on a mature, give-and-take basis; and in which the parents are able to look ahead realistically to spot a crisis in the making before it overwhelms them and then make their own plans for coping with it.

Success of a sort is also when a mother who cannot learn to care for her child and fears her own lack of control, recognizes her problem and requests placement for the child on either a foster care or adoptive basis. The Denver team is acutely aware of the many cases in which death and injury have resulted after parental requests for child placement have been refused. They believe that "any parent who requests that a child be removed from the home should be seriously heeded." If a weekend foster home or crisis nursery facility is available, where a child can be left for a few hours or a couple of days during periods of great stress, there may very well be less need for long-term placement and greater opportunity for the parent to obtain relief and regain control.

Denver continues to contribute to our knowledge of child abuse and the whole-family approach to treatment. We have long needed a center, and possibly several, located in various parts of the country devoted to study every aspect of child maltreatment: why it occurs, what sort of child it strikes, what sort of parent is responsible, what can be done to predict and prevent it, and what can best be done to handle the total situation once it occurs. Now, it seems, we will have just that in Denver. In November 1972, the Robert Wood Johnson Foundation announced a grant of $588,000 for the establishment of the National Center for the Prevention and Treatment of Child Abuse and Neglect at the University of Colorado Medical Center. This new study center, which began operating January 1, 1973, has a fine foundation on which to build: the many years of practical research, hard work and innovation by Colorado University's child protection team under the leadership of Dr. Kempe. The team of pediatricians, psychiatrists, public health nurses, and social workers, already provided with blueprints for action, will further test a coordinated approach to parental child abuse.

I think they will approach their work in the spirit expressed by Doctors Brandt F. Steele and Carl B. Pollock:

Too often in the past, severe abuse of children has been managed by separating the child from the parent and placing it in a foster home, and the problem is considered to be solved. While separation is useful and often necessary intervention, it does not in any way deal with the basic issues involved. Sooner or later will arise the question of whether the child can be returned to parental custody. Also, the abusing parents already have or may have in the future other children who can be mistreated. Therefore, effort must be directed not only to handling the immediate situation so as to protect an infant from further abuse, but also toward investigating the total pattern of parent-child interaction in a family and instituting remedial measures. . . .

Our philosophy of the value of treatment is twofold; first, it deals in the most humanitarian and constructive way we know with a tragic facet of people's lives; second, therapeutic intervention in a process which seems to pass from one generation to the next will hopefully produce changes in patterns of child rearing toward the lessening of unhappiness and tragedy (Ray E. Helfer and C. Henry Kempe, eds., *The Battered Child* [Chicago: The University of Chicago Press, 1968]).

It has been said that it is almost impossible for abusing parents to help themselves. However, a few years ago a California mother discovered that it *is* possible for such parents to help themselves by helping each other. Parents Anonymous may yet turn out to be the only type of organization capable of reaching into every kind of home on any social or economic stratum in which children are being maltreated or are in danger of maltreatment.

P. A., as it is known, is a self-help, help-each-other organization modeled along the lines of Alcoholics Anonymous and similar groups. It was founded in Los Angeles in early 1970 and called Mothers Anonymous until its organizers realized that many fathers need help too. Its premise is that people with common problems can work together to save themselves, each other, and their children. Older members take responsibility for newcomers, and as the newcomers mature into the group they in turn become responsible for others. These parents, unable to share their feelings with uncomprehending outsiders, are able to talk to each other. They air their feelings and exchange experiences knowing that they will not incur anger or condemnation for their thoughts or acts. And when they feel the stresses building up, they know where to go for help. "Help" is a combination of group therapy sessions, ego building, and the availability of a twenty-four-hour-a-day "hot line" crisis-intervention system. When a mother feels that her inner tensions are about to explode into violence against a child, she can phone a fellow member with whom she has exchanged telephone numbers. If necessary, the mothers may even exchange children because an abusing mother does not express her hostilities by whomping borrowed children. Most P. A. parents soon find that it is even more rewarding and therapeutic to receive a call for help and be able to deliver the needed understanding and compassion than it is to make a call to an understanding friend and pour out their own troubles.

It was an anonymous, now-famous dynamic, articulate young woman known as Jolly K. who brought the group into being. Her training for the role of mother included brief stays at some 100 foster homes and 32 institutions, a fifth-grade education, rape at the age of 11, a career in prostitution, countless unfortunate experiences with men in her personal life, and two disastrous marriages. Her third marriage was more fortunate.

But as a parent of two little girls she was, unsurprisingly, not a success. Twice she came close to killing the target child, "beating the little slut I brought into this world." "Little slut" was a revealing term. "My mother always said I'd be a slut," Jolly K. has been quoted as saying, "and damned if I didn't believe her." And damned if she didn't see herself in her daughter.

She tried for three years to get help, and all she found was that there was almost no place to go. But she did have one confidant and supporter, a psychiatric social worker with whom she had gone into therapy, and after she had blown her top about the absence of services for people such as herself, he asked her what she thought could be done about it. Mrs. K. suggested that she might be able to start her own therapy group composed of mothers like herself. Her social worker thought it was an excellent idea and gave her every encouragement to go ahead. Sensing her dynamism and leadership abilities, but aware that her own poor self-image would permit her to drop the idea unless he could get her to become committed, he promptly rounded up the first candidates for her group. Before long, through his own activism and persuasion, he managed to gently maneuver Mrs. K into such a position that she was bound to go ahead. And so, with misgivings and plenty of guts, she did.

Her psychiatric social worker was right. Mrs. K. had the energy and leadership qualities to make the group work for herself and her fellow members. With his continued support, she built the group into a vital force. P. A. today is a very much enlarged organization that still reflects the no-nonsense, down-to-earth attitude of its founder.

From the Parents Anonymous Manual:

You are entitled to your anger, to your rage. Everyone has those emotions. Everyone! The only difference between you and that sweet little perfect mother down the street (if she really is) is that you are not quite able to handle the actions of your anger. And that's just what Parents Anonymous is all about—how to handle your anger and many other negative feelings, so that you do not take it out on your kids! . . .

Parents Anonymous was not begun by a group of Ph.D.'s or psychiatrists or social workers, who had theories, educated guesses and evaluations in mind; it was begun by ordinary parents from all walks of life (rich and poor, blue-blood and mongrel) who were ready to admit they had a problem in dealing with their children, and who felt that if they shared their emotions and their experiences they could help each other to overcome it. . . .

P.A. is *not* a "show and tell" program. If you want to tell your group what you did to your kids just to get it off your chest, that's fine, but you don't have to—ever. We are not here *just* to swap child-abuse stories, we want to get at the solution of how to stop our abusive tendencies and abusive behavior. . . .

Just knowing that you were actually "taught" to be a child abuser aids greatly in overcoming your own fears and tension. As an adult, you do not do every single thing your parents taught you to do. . . . and there's no reason why you must abuse your own children either. Understanding yourself and why you abuse children is more than half the battle.

P. A.'s aim is not to give lessons in how to be a parent but to achieve behavior modification. Its founding mothers believe that abusing parents must, first of all, learn to reach out for help before, during, and after crises; and that they must, in time, learn how to handle their negative feelings and redirect their destructive attitudes and actions into constructive channels.

There is a beautiful directness about P. A., a straight-from-the-shoulder kind of talk, that makes one hope for its continued success as an organization and for the salvation of its members as individuals:

We encourage members to phone other members, especially if a member is at a panic-point of stress. There will undoubtedly be times when a member will need you, in person and in that member's home, to avoid abusing a child. They have to phone someone for help, someone who not only can get over to their place right away but who also *understands* what they are going through—they can't very well phone the fuzz. There will be times you yourself will need to phone a member, and knowing there is someone who really cares about *you* and *your* problems might make all the difference between an unpleasant memory . . . and a manslaughter charge. It's only fair to give to other members what you expect them to do for you.

Members of P. A. know better than anyone that professional help is hard to find, that waiting lines for parents requiring treatment are long, and that crises don't wait for their turn on any waiting list. They know that the total situation, the safety of the target child, the treatment needs of the mother or father, the entire family structure—needs *do-it-now* attention. They also know that child abuse is likely to perpetuate itself endlessly unless there is effective intervention, the least and last part of which consists of putting a parent in jail. Therefore one of P.A.'s most important functions is to break the generation-to-generation chain of maltreatment by promptly giving support to today's parent and today's child. In their view, it is both impractical and unfair to shuttle a child into a foster home while the mother gets or waits for counseling. More practical and more fair to all is to treat the total situation before severe crisis occurs.

P.A. does not suffer from any goggle-eyed reverence for professionals. Its members have been exposed to them through punitive, hostile, and judgmental agencies, but P.A. does not hesitate to call on professionally trained people for support and advice. A chapter sponsor, they suggest, should be a professional but a nonmoralizing, nonpatronizing one. The parent chapter itself, located in Redondo Beach, California, has a distinguished board of directors including physicians, psychiatrists, social workers, nurses, attorneys, and former abusing mothers, plus the advisory services of Dr. Ray E. Helfer.

One of the great difficulties in tackling the complex problem of child abuse is the stigma that society has attached to it.

Even the professionals, and sometimes, I think, *particularly* the professionals, have a disgust or contempt or even hatred for abusing parents that often blinds them to the fact that they are dealing with unhappy human beings in terrible need. They forget that few parents get through the experience of child rearing without sometimes becoming so upset with their children that they react to their actions with extreme anger. They forget what stress can do to people; they forget that the majority of abusing parents' problems with their children are shared to a lesser degree by all parents. They forget how easy it is to "snap" and overstep the thin line between discipline, in the form of corporal punishment, that is acceptable to most, and abuse. They forget that the difference between "normal" parents and a great many abusing parents is that the latter simply go too far, that they lack control over their potential for violence. And they forget that these parents do this because of their own built-in wounds, wounds that render them terribly vulnerable to all the barbs life throws at us. It is in this area that such organizations as Parents Anonymous can make one of their greatest contributions. They can help remove this stigma. In helping each other as they do, they can teach us all a lesson. We too should be helping, instead of throwing up our hands in horror. Nonabusers are basically no better than abusers, they've just been a whole lot luckier in life.

None of us is in a position to cast any barbs at the troubled parents among us. Many parents who neglect their children or abuse them physically are really saying, "I have problems I cannot handle that I am taking out on this child." Whatever the immediate source of difficulty, the parent feels overwhelmed, frustrated, and helpless like a child who doesn't know where to turn. It may not take much to pull a parent through a crisis situation and set him on the right track. Often little more than support, understanding, a listening ear, a friend to call is needed. But the support, to be of more than fleeting value, is required on a ready-at-all-times basis, and must be given without moralizing and thus further undercutting the troubled one's self-esteem. And that is why Parents

Anonymous may prove to be one of our valuable tools in breaking the chain of child abuse.

P.A., a nonprofit, self-made organization, doesn't have all the answers, but it has been extremely effective for many parents. It has one thing going for it that no other type of preventive-protective organization has: it is a self-propelled organization of, by, and for abusing parents who take delight in "sharing our new found abilities with one another, helping while we are being helped; getting involved, caring, reaching out." Its members are motivated by a healthy self-interest, and they are not going to turn *that* off every afternoon at five. For more information about Parents Anonymous and how to start community chapters write: Parents Anonymous, Inc., 2009 Farrell Avenue, Redondo Beach, California 90278. Since P.A. asks no fees or dues, it can always use nominal contributions to cover the cost of handling inquiries.

In New York City, a temporary shelter-home program for the treatment of abusing and neglectful mothers is currently under way at the Foundling Hospital. It is a pilot project employing a multi-disciplinary medical-social approach which provides, in as comfortable and homelike a family atmosphere as we have been able to create, all the therapeutic and preventive services necessary to alleviate the root problems of the maltreating parents and to help them nurture their children. Like so many other pilot programs, it is limited to a small number of clients, but it is a beginning.

It was my feeling, early in 1972 that we in New York had done enough talking about child abuse, and that it was time to do something very positive about the problem in our own community. Plans were drawn for a project that was initially thought of as a crisis-intervention type of program easily accessible to mothers or families needing immediate relief from acutely overwhelming situations. There was, at that time, very little a desperate mother could do to get help. If the family court, for example, were to place her child in protective custody and tell her that she must be under psychiatric care before the child could be returned, the parent would be faced with a long separation, not necessarily helpful to either parent or child, while waiting five, six or seven months to get an appointment and start treatment. Such treatment should be available at once. Or, if a mother not under the eye of a public agency were to reach a crisis point and feel in imminent danger of doing harm to her child, she would have scarcely anywhere to turn because immediate-help facilities were simply not available for parents in crisis. We had an obvious gap in our system that urgently needed to be filled. It was possible to start filling it by providing a facility to which a mother in crisis could be referred on a voluntary basis, or to which she could come on her own volition, wherein she could immediately get the help of a psychiatrist as well as any other help needed.

I proposed a demonstration program specifically designed for early intervention in cases of neglect and abuse. This program would utilize community-based services, in order (as the proposal put it) to: (1) prevent separation of parents and children; (2) prevent the placement of children in institutions; (3) encourage the attainment of self-care status on the part of the mothers; and (4) stimulate the attainment of self-sufficiency for the family unit.

A certain amount of space could be made available at the Foundling Hospital. It wouldn't be much, but the facilities would be able to support, at any one time, eight to ten mothers and ten to fifteen children, five mothers commuting on a daily basis, and two emergency cases. Each program would last for three months, after which the participating mothers would be followed-up for a year. Any other closely involved person, such as the husband, boyfriend, father of the child, or other member of the family, could be included in the program of treatment. Initially, until mothers in need started walking in off the streets and asking for help, as I hoped they would in time, we would receive our referrals from the family courts, from the Bureau of Child Welfare Protective Unit, and from various members of the community working with, for example, Head Start and day care programs, people in a position to detect children in trouble or potential trouble and mothers in need of help. The Foundling Hospital would then provide the shelter home-setting and a total treatment program, including psychological, psychiatric, medical and social services, and nursing care.

I presented the proposal to Human Resources Administrator-Commissioner Jule Sugarman, chairman of the Interagency Council on Child Welfare, and Mrs. Barbara Blum, assistant commissioner of special services for children and youth and staff director of the Interagency Council. (This body had been set up by Mayor Lindsay in December 1970. Its goal was to improve protection and services for children in foster homes, shelters, training schools, and other public and private institutions.) It was fortunate for the future of the shelter home program that the mayor's task force, of which I was chairman, had recommended, coincidentally, that a program of this type be supported, and that I was a member of the executive committee of the Interagency Council. This naturally made it easier to communicate with Commissioner Sugarman and Mrs. Blum. A close working relationship with them made it possible to enlist their support for the program and obtain the approval of the Interagency Council. With this, the first hurdle was crossed; the temporary shelter-home program had the backing of the city of New York.

Next came the difficult task of obtaining state and federal approval. To get any program off the ground, it must be properly financed. The State Department of Social Services would be required to do a certain amount of funding, and the federal government under Title IV of the Department of Health, Education, and Welfare would also have to give monies. Neither funds or approval are easily obtained for an experimental project. It would take a great deal of pushing to get the program approved, but no one could have known it was going to take as much as it did.

The program ran head-on into bureaucracy: interminable stumbling blocks and delays, innumerable meetings, countless criticisms, and a great many questions, most of which could not possibly be answered until a program such as our demonstration project had actually been attempted and completed.

Perhaps the answers, which we were looking for ourselves, wouldn't be available even then. At this point, a lot of the questions seemed pointless and obstructive. We couldn't guess how our program would turn out or what it would prove or how to evaluate its accomplishments before it even existed. One had to expect a certain amount of caution and perhaps even skepticism, certainly some genuinely pertinent questions, and possibly even some constructive comments. But there was so much resistance and such a runaround that it seemed the bureaucracy was hoping to discourage us so we would drop the whole thing.

What gave our efforts a great deal of muscle was the support given by the Foundling Hospital and its friends. Early in the planning stages, I had described the proposed program at the annual meeting of the board of managers of the New York Foundling Hospital. The day the presentation was made, the weather was abominable, and less public-spirited citizens would have stayed at home, but a good eighty percent of the board of managers was nevertheless present. Among the friends of the Foundling attending the meeting was Mrs. Vincent Astor, a great friend of Cardinal Spellman during his lifetime and also a friend of His Eminence Terence Cardinal Cooke.

In describing the program, the hope that the proposed program could be started at the New York Foundling Hospital was voiced. Already existing was a temporary shelter for unwed mothers that was not being used. This would be a fine place for a program of the type proposed, since the facilities and professional staff were already available there. The X-ray, laboratory, and all requisite medical facilities, and, of course, the rooms to house the mothers and their children, as well as the necessary kitchen and laundry facilities, were there. Neither time nor money would be required for blueprinting and constructing a building. Nor would it take six months to get people together, as it so often does for programs of this sort. The psychiatrists were there, the psychologists were there, the social workers were there, the internal medical people were there; and, although we would need to recruit additional staff, essentially it was a ready-made setup that could go into operation almost immediately. The services we intended to offer and how we planned to run the project were explained in detail.

Mrs. Vincent Astor was extremely interested, and she had jotted notes as the presentation was being made. The next day a call came from the Vincent Astor Foundation. How much money, the caller wanted to know, would be needed to begin the program? I was more than happy to answer. The Vincent Astor Foundation gave us $50,000 to get the project going, and it was this $50,000 which gave us the opening wedge. Such monies, if given to the city for the type of demonstration project we had in mind, can be tripled by federal funds.

Well, now we had what, for want of a better word, I am obliged to call our grubstake, and we had the program fully spelled out on paper. Then followed weeks and months of re-drafting and resubmitting our proposal for the State Department of Social Services and for the regional office of the Department of Health, Education, and Welfare; a multiplicity of telephone calls, letters, meetings, questions, answers, re-writes, reassurances, arguments, obstacles, frustrations, and a great deal of pressure and insistence on our part. It seemed that the rewriting and the questioning and the explaining would never come to an end.

Fortunately, we received a great deal of consideration and support from Abe Lavine, commissioner of the State Department of Social Services, plus the backing of the New York Foundling administrators, and the active support of the Arch-diocese in the person of Monsignor Arpie. Eventually, in spite of all doubts, questions, and resistance, the program was ap-proved. It must be said that it was due to the intensive efforts of Barbara Blum, Jule Sugarman, and Monsignor Arpie that approval was finally given. Pat Bologna took on the important job of coordinator of the Temporary Shelter Home Program.

The program, now fully in operation (though it has only been funded for one year and we have no assurance that we can be equally persuasive a second time around), is unique in that it brings together the best aspects of all other ap-

proaches to the problem of child abuse and neglect. It is
pointed toward treatment of the psychiatric as well as the
social and environmental factors of the disease; and the treatment is given within the context of the disorder, that is, we
are treating each mother in the context of her problem, which
is her relationship with her child.

The mothers who live in the shelter and those who come to
spend the day receive treatment daily on a one-to-one basis.
This includes psychiatric treatment, medical treatment, and
consultation with a registered nurse. There are also group-
therapy sessions twice a week during which the mothers get
together, "let down their hair," and openly discuss their
problems. Pediatric services are available for the children—
services that include large doses of love and gentle handling.
Although each mother is responsible for the care and feeding of her child, she must often be taught the basic necessary techniques of child care, so part of the day is spent
in the baby's room observing and helping the child-care
worker.

The major emphasis of the program is on the strengthening
of the mothering capabilities of these women; on preserving
the existing family unit, and on making each mother responsible for her own child within a protective setting. At the same
time, the program is designed to provide crisis management
for mothers and children in a highly vulnerable state. Those
already in the program have help available instantly. Those
not in the program also come in without notice. Those who
have completed the program need only call in, whenever they
feel life's pressures getting too much for them, to receive immediate support.

The temporary home-away-from-home offers mother and
child some distance from each other without actual separation;
there is a cushion of space and protective people between
them. The ultimate aim of the program is to pull together our
various resources and services, usually so hopelessly frag-
mented, in an attempt to make an impact upon the cycle of
generationally repeated violence. If we find that through this
coordinated, homestyle, and compassionate approach we are

able to modify the behavior patterns of these mothers, we will have come a long way toward breaking the cycle.

We have adapted Kempe's parent-surrogate idea and provided each mother with her own personal social-worker assistant, in each case a mature woman who has been a successful mother, to be a friend to her, to work with her, to go shopping with her, to do the laundry with her, cook with her, and teach the mother to mother her child. This close personal contact is kept up in a follow-up program after the mother's discharge from the shelter home. The mother knows that she can call this friend at any time before or during crisis and will get a helpful, supportive response. Thus we have a hot line service, similar to that of Parents Anonymous and C.A.L.M. (Child-Abuse Listening Mediation) of Santa Barbara, California.

But the educational program extends well beyond the mothering services of the social worker. The parent must be gradually weaned away from her dependence on the aide toward a new reliance on herself. We have courses on child rearing, on nursing, on children's medical problems, on homemaking, on shopping, on consumerism, on venereal diseases, on alcoholism, and on drug addiction. In the meantime, the mothers are getting a clean room, good food, friendly attention, and the psychiatric and psychological intervention that is necessary for them to gain insight into their own problems. We are also trying, through the various city agencies, to see that a mother, upon discharge, will be able to go to a better environment than the one she left before coming to us. We would like to see each mother getting better housing in a better neighborhood, so that many of the triggers that caused her to strike out can be removed.

We don't know how successful the program is going to be. We are watching and learning. The great benefit of the living-in part of this approach is that we can watch the interaction between mother and child. We can observe them together on a minute-to-minute basis. This can be quite revealing.

One young mother, for instance, persists in neglecting to raise the side of her infant's crib. In the course of my rounds I have gone into her room time and time again to find the side of the baby's crib down in spite of my repeated cautioning that this could be dangerous. "He can't fall out," she says. "He's too young. He can't crawl or move around." "But you can't tell," I say. "Children develop from one second to the next. Overnight, he could start crawling around and falling out. That crib side should be *up*." This mother, in keeping the side down, is probably doing it unconsciously for some reason, but we wouldn't have known she was if she and her child had been at home.

Another young woman reveals an unfortunate habit pattern when feeding her child. When the child isn't willing to eat, the mother immediately and instinctively slaps her in the face. We have noted that the child appears to associate eating with being slapped. Her mother is conditioning her not to eat. Again, we wouldn't have seen this if the mother and child had been in their home instead of the shelter.

We have also had one mother whose day-by-day, minute-by-minute actions convinced us that she was quite badly damaged psychologically. We saw her slowly losing contact with reality. It was fortunate that we did see her close-up, because surely her beautiful two-year-old child would have been terribly hurt at some future date. At is was, we were able to separate the mother and child while there was still time to save them both. The child was removed to safe custody and the mother accepted the suggestion that she be admitted to a psychiatric institute for intensive treatment. That mother, if she had not entered the program, would not now be getting psychiatric help. She would probably still be walking the streets with her child or disintegrating at home, and, perhaps, there would have been another headlined child-murder.

So even at this early stage we can see some value to the program. But "success" is difficult to measure and even to define. A successful program is not necessarily going to be one that has fulfilled our essential aim, which is to keep the family unit intact. It would indeed be a success if we could keep the family together in health and happiness. But it would also be a success of sorts if a mother who did not want her child were to tell us so, at the end of the assessment period, and put the child up for adoption. It would also be a success as in the case above, if a mother who was psychiatrically incompetent and beyond rehabilitation in our program were to release her child from a life-threatening situation and accept psychiatric treatment in an institution.

At the same time, we know that there are some areas in which we are not yet succeeding by any measure of success. We have failed to draw the expected number of mothers into the program. Many of the hard-core maltreating mothers are not being reported and do not come to our attention. We are redoubling our efforts to get into the community, to find these mothers through day care and Head Start programs where signs of abuse are likely to be evident, but, as yet, we are not getting the personal referrals that we anticipated. Neither are we getting referrals from the family court *or* the Bureau of Child Welfare Child Protective Unit after cases are reported. At the start of the program we were not able to fill our ten positions for mothers and our fifteen beds for children. We have had three, four, five mothers at a time. This, out of 10,000 cases of suspected child abuse and neglect recorded in the central registry in a single year! Why, out of 10,000 cases, are we unable to fill the few positions we have? There are several possible answers.

Perhaps there is some doubt as to the efficacy of the program. We have periods of doubt and pessimism. Perhaps we are not going to be able to heal those who come to us; perhaps the wounds that have accumulated through a lifetime or even over the course of generations cannot be cured; perhaps the scars leave the being permanently distorted, particularly if the patient is so tied to her damaging environment that the disease is being reinforced even while we try to fight it. There may be no way to help these parents unless we can also treat their friends, their relatives, and their neighborhoods. Even after having done our best, perhaps there is something in this illness that has not responded to our efforts, possibly because we have not reached or even recognized it, so that it has remained outside the help that we have been attempting to provide.

We do not deal with mothers whose problems are superficial or who are like the young mother who occasionally slaps her child and worries about it. Nor do we deal with parents who realize, like those in Parents Anonymous, the enormity of their action and are able to take some action toward self-help. Our young people are badly wracked by life—past, present, and possibly future. They are hard-core cases of generational deprivation and abuse, and there is little innocence left in them. All are accustomed to beating, neglect, and depravity as a way of life. They are usually sexually promiscuous largely because they have no real communication with people and seek the illusion of love; their families, for the most part, have thrown them out; they may be on drugs when they come to us; and they may, for all we know, simply be regarding the shelter program as nothing more than a temporary sanctuary from the storm. Many are so damaged that it may not be possible to rehabilitate them.

Of course this troubles us. We are especially concerned that we may not be able to teach them how to mother, the most important thing that we must teach them for the sake of their children. We look at our results to date, or nonresults, and wonder. Is anyone born with the mothering instinct? Is it developed in a child's early years? If they don't have it, is it possible to instill this instinct, if that is what it is, into young adults by education and example? We don't know the answers.

In October of 1971, Dr. Judianne Densen-Gerber began an innovative Odyssey House program for drug-addict parents and mothers-to-be. It is now located at Mabon House, a former hospital on Ward's Island in New York City, donated by the state of New York. To the best of my knowledge, it is the first drug program in the country to deal with mothers (sometimes fathers) and their children as a unit. The residents, almost without exception, have a childhood history of parental abuse, sexual molestation, neglect, rejection, or abandonment. The goal of the program is to salvage not only the present generation but the one newly born and those to come, and, if possible, to determine in the process whether mothering can be taught. For many months, the skilled staff has been trying to teach this skill to mothers who do not have it. Mabon House has its financial problems, as do all such ventures, but the greatest concern is not money. It is the question of mothering. The staff is not convinced that it is operating on psychologically valid assumptions.

Dr. Densen-Gerber made the following statement to the *New York Times*, December 18, 1972: "I wonder if the entire concept of mothering as a natural instinct is off the wall, and the supposition that it can be taught is in question. We want to see if, with proper input, it can. . . . If I had to flip a coin now, I would say that it can't. This has profound ramifications for the entire country. If mothering can't be taught, you've got to get many children away from their mothers."

We, in our program, have not yet been able to define success in our attempts to teach mothering. Other programs, in other parts of the country, dealing with different kinds of abusing parents, may be achieving more gratifying results. But, to date, my colleagues and I, in the current program as well as our previous efforts, have met with failures and successes. We have worked for months with mothers whom we thought were responding, only to find too many of them reverting to their former lifestyle in a culture pervaded by drugs, alcohol, petty theft, sexual promiscuity, and demeaning poverty. The entire concept of "mothering" gets lost in the shuffle; the children's needs are almost instantly forgotten.

Even within the shelter-home program, we find our mothers backsliding. A mother on a weekend pass often turns up a day or two late, full of apologies and stale liquor, disheveled and only half coherent. She's been out with a boyfriend and gotten too drunk or drugged to come in on time. Another takes drugs on the quiet but denies it strenuously because she's afraid she might be thrown out of the program, deprived of the clean room and the care and the food, to go back to the one-room, rat-infested apartment with the child who has become the butt of her problems. Then there is another who has her boyfriend visit her, and who has sexual relations on the couch with him without thought to whoever might happen to walk in and see them. I have known at least one apparent success who suddenly abandoned her child, as well as the program, to go off with a man with whom she can apparently share a fleeting love far greater than her love for her child.

Pat Bologna, coordinator of the shelter program, noted in a personal communication to me that:

Perhaps the most common characteristic found among New York City's poor parents who neglect or abuse their children is their sadomasochistic relationship with one another and their children. Having been subjected to the poor social and economic conditions of the ghetto along with the high degree of violence and crime, these parents tend to associate ego satisfaction with punishment. Their total life experience has been such that they have been conditioned to act out as a way of gaining attention and recognition. Having a weak self-image as result of this form of conditioning, such parents tend to be attracted to people with similar characteristics, thus a vicious cycle is formed which reinforces their already weak ego.

There are problems with every program. But I do think our program offers something for the future, no matter how we measure success. These hard-core cases are the ones we must try urgently to solve or, at least, to alleviate. Parents and children are all people who must be given every possible chance to lead normal lives. We are making a positive effort, however, and, though we do get discouraged when we find that we are not making measurable progress with our patients and with this complex disease, all we can do is try and keep trying to find some of the answers.

I like the way Dr. Judianne Densen-Gerber put it, in regard to her doubts about her own drug program: "This doesn't mean that Odyssey House doesn't work. Like cancer, you don't give up because people are dying of it. You simply work harder."

That's the way it is with people who care. All of us are simply going to have to work a whole lot harder and not give up.

# CHAPTER NINE
# Where We Still Fail

SHE WILL BE HOME AGAIN, perhaps, by the time you read these words, or perhaps she will be in the care of relatives. I hope the latter. She is now in the pediatric ward.

"She" is a little three-year-old Chinese girl, one of several maltreated children who were brought in recently. It is seldom that we see a Chinese child under these circumstances. Child abuse is not part of the modern Chinese family culture pattern. But perhaps the culture lines become blurred when one culture meets ours. Or it may be just another manifestation of what's happening in our times; and it may be that no culture is any longer exempt from the disease of child abuse.

This little girl is three years old and weighed fifteen pounds when she was brought in. Her little body was nothing but skin and bones and bruises. The complete right side of her face was swollen, and the eye was closed and black. The pathetic little body just lay there: limp, contused, almost lifeless, the gaunt ribs all but thrusting through the skin. The mother had struck out at the child, and the father had brought her in.

The wheels of protection went into motion, once again almost too late. We took color photographs and began treating the child at once. Following the procedure in these cases, the pediatric resident reported immediately to the New York City Emergency Children's Service (or Child Protective Unit) of the Bureau of Child Welfare. Within twenty-four hours of the telephone notification we followed with a written report to the central registry.

Immediate concern, after ascertaining that we were doing everything possible for our small patient, was to see if there were any other children in the family who might be in any conceivable danger. A social service investigations worker went to the home and found that there was one other child. We had her brought in for physical examination. She looked perfectly fine, and thorough examination bore this out. Unlike her sister, she was well nourished, showed no signs of physical abuse, and appeared to have no problems. More often than not, it is the case that only one child in the family is the abuser's whipping post, but there are enough exceptions to this rule to warrant a prompt visit to the home to check on the siblings and provide for their care and protection.

On that same day, three other children were brought into the children's emergency room. One was the child of a drug-addicted mother. He had black and blue marks all over his body and a skull fracture. The other two were brought in after having been abandoned and left to starve by alcoholic parents.

At St. Vincent's Hospital of New York there are almost always one or two maltreated children in the ward. That week, there were several, three of them on a single day. An eighteen-month-old child had been brought in the week before, dead on arrival with fifty percent body burns. A twenty-two-month-old baby girl had been brought in the week before that, strangulated, also dead on arrival.

Our little Chinese girl is slowly beginning to get better. She's gained six pounds in this past week. She smiles. She looks beautiful. She's even walking, and she walks as if she's just beginning to learn how to walk—learning to walk, at three years old. Everybody loves her, and she's become the pet of the pediatric ward. And when she goes to the courts, she is going to look absolutely gorgeous. We do have the "before" pictures to present as part of the medical testimony. But who else besides the doctors and nurses who saw her when she first came in can possibly have any idea of the flesh and blood suffering of this little being? A picture is only a picture. This little girl is real. Her pain and her fear are real. *How* can one get the agonizing reality across? At least she is alive.

Where are we going? What are we accomplishing? Are we making any progress against the disease, or in getting through to people? These are some of the thoughts that go through our minds.

My colleagues and I talk endlessly about child abuse to physicians, to teachers, to lawmakers, to social workers, to students, and to the public. We talk about the little signs that indicate insidious neglect and abuse in the making; about the need to recognize children in imminent danger; about the cases we see in our hospital beds, the ones that were not brought in as maltreated children but may turn out to be just that; about the need to protect hurt children from further hurt, and protect their brothers and sisters, and help the parents without reendangering the victims; and about the flesh-and-blood reality of the beaten baby.

We often show color slides of battered and neglected children who have come under our care. And, of course, the viewers react because the pictures are not pretty. They are appalled and repelled. And then it's all over. They have seen the horror pictures. They know what the kids look like flashed on a screen in multicolor. But can they relate this to life and death experience? Can they identify? Can they grasp, in their minds and hearts, that this is real, that this has happened to once-whole children, and that it has happened at the hands of the parents?

It is very difficult for them, and even more difficult for people outside the social professions, to truly understand and accept the reality of what they are hearing and seeing.

If we talk about a mongoloid child, you know what a mongoloid child looks like. You know about mongolian children because somebody in your family, a friend, a friend of a friend, or somebody in your neighborhood has a mongolian child. You know that a child can have cerebral palsy, and you know what that child is like, because your neighbor has a child with cerebral palsy. You know about polio, muscular dystrophy, leukemia, hemophilia; there have been many public appeals on behalf of the sufferers and a great deal of sympathetic publicity. You can relate to these afflicted children. You should; we all should. We can understand their afflictions as the misfortunes of fate, and our sympathies go out toward these children. What has happened to them is an unhappy accident of nature.

And so we have a Cerebral Palsy Foundation, we have a Multiple Sclerosis Foundation, we have a Polio Foundation; we have all these foundations for children, and many more, to raise money for research and treatment. But we have nothing comparable to help abused and neglected children, even though abuse is the most common cause of death in children and a heavy contributor to permanent mutilation and deformity. We can accept that nature has dealt out dreadfully unfair blows to children whose diseases we can comprehend, and we can visualize these children and feel for them because we have all seen them. But we have not seen, and are unable to visualize, the child whose disease is abuse. We are not, as individuals, *able to see* the battered child, to accept the fact that it is the parent who is dealing out the unfair blows or even accept the fact that these awful things we occasionally read about really happen.

I would like to take you on a guided tour, not only to show you a few of the children we see in the course of our daily work in the hospital but to provide a glimpse of the frustrations and human failures we encounter.

It is shortly after two o'clock in the afternoon and we are on the pediatric ward making the rounds. The little boy who came in last week with multiple fractures, the little boy whose sister died a few months ago, a victim of apparent battering and broken bones, is doing nicely. He is eating well, and he no longer cringes when the nurse or doctor reaches out to touch him.

The resident calls from the emergency room. There is a child downstairs dead on arrival, strangulated, possibly as a result of abuse.

We go downstairs at once and into the children's emergency room. Though the general emergency area is large there is only a small area for children. It is a four-bed room partly screened off from the waiting area. There is another room, separate from the four-bed room, that is not completely closed off, but it is kept private. This is where the more seriously ill children are treated.

We walk through the main children's area. It is filled with children, most of them crying, and with mothers who look worried, irritated, or tired. They are waiting for the interns and residents to see them. They may have quite a long wait; it is a busy day. But their emergencies are not of an immediate life and death nature. It is impossible to tell what the problems are as we pass, but we can assume that there are colds, perhaps a case of pneumonia, scratches, maybe a puncture wound, almost certainly at least one case of falling-off-a-bicycle.

We leave the crying behind and enter the quiet room in the back. The dead child is a beautiful blonde baby girl. She was twenty-two months old, well-nourished, even chubby. But she has markings around her neck; and whatever caused those markings caused her death.

During the examination the resident tells us that the mother had brought her in. The mother's story is that the baby had been in her crib, and that in the crib with her was a little mirror with a string attached to it. The mother had turned away for a moment, leaving the child playing happily in her crib, and when she came back she found the child with the string around her neck. Apparently the baby had been playing with the mirror and string and had somehow managed to wrap the string around her throat tightly enough to strangle herself.

This story seems unlikely. These things can happen, but what are the chances of something like this happening to a child who is almost two years old? The child is large for her age, and it is doubtful that a string the size ordinarily used around a mirror could have done this.

In the meantime, the resident has finished telling what little he can about the parents. The mother had been very quiet when she came in with the child, very apathetic, apparently not at all concerned. The father had come in a little while later. He also seemed cool, barely interested. All he asked was, "Is the child dead?" All these things indicate that this is not just a simple case of strangulation.

We complete our examination, take the pictures, and just look at the child, this beautiful blonde baby with the marks around the neck. But we have no emotions. We are all without feelings. There we are, the nurses and the doctors; there is a child, dead. We are numb. Have we become desensitized by the many similar scenes in which we have stood grouped around a tiny body like one-dimensional non-characters in a photograph? Our reaction is, "Okay, that's it. The sooner we get this body out of here, the better." We notify the child protective unit to report the death.

We also want to find out if there are any other children in the home and be sure the child protective unit is alerted so that someone can get out to the home immediately and, if there are other children there, make sure they're all right. The police are also informed so that they can get a detective to the home if necessary. The police should know that some abuse is suspected. I will talk to the medical examiner's office after they've seen the child. They are alerted immediately.

After leaving the emergency room, there are rounds to be finished and calls to be made. There is nothing we can do now to help this baby.

When all the ward patients have been seen, I call the precinct and talk to the detectives whom I *hope* will investigate this case. I want them to know that I feel this case is highly suspect, that to me it is a probable case of abuse and inflicted injury that should be looked into. I come on strong. I do so to get more than a "Yeah, sure, we'll try to look into it" reaction. The immediate concern is that somebody really does go to investigate the home circumstances and make sure that there aren't any other children there who are being abused or neglected. The police say they'll check and they thank me for calling.

I put through a call to the medical examiner's office to make sure that they have our initial call and its substance on record.

They have, and are aware of suspected abuse. They say they will call back after they have made their examination.

The child's body is still in the little room in back of the children's emergency area. Downstairs we walk through the pediatric emergency room, threading our way between the mothers and the children. The dead baby is wrapped up and ready to go. We have a problem here, but before we can get to it the resident tells us he has called the child protective unit again. They still can't find any record of our report, they can't track it down. One of the workers there was very incensed by the fact that we had demanded anything or requested anything. He said he doesn't need us to tell him what to do. But he also doesn't know anything about anybody going to the home, and he can't track down who took the report. He says he'll call us back. (He does not.)

Our immediate problem is how to take the dead child out of the emergency room, past all those mothers and children. We don't want to scare or upset anyone. It is a terrible, traumatic experience for mothers or children to see a child being brought out dead. If we take her out completely wrapped as she is now, they will wonder and they will guess, and the whispers will spread. But we cannot take her out unwrapped. We decide to loosen the coverings a little so that the face and hands are not completely hidden but do not show too much, pediatric emergency room, threading our way between the X ray.

We carefully rearrange the coverings. As the nurse gently carries the child out and I walk along with her, a little boy says to me, "What's the matter with that baby? Where are you taking it?"

"Oh," I say, "she's going up to X ray. We just have to make sure she doesn't catch cold along the way so we have to keep her warm."

"Oh," he says, understandingly; and nods.

I call the child protective unit. They still don't seem to know about the telephone report. We will have our written report ready within twenty-four hours, but I want them to know *now*. In addition, there is a rule to call at once. I talk to somebody there who says he will look into it, and he asks me to hold. There is chitchat and laughter at the other end of the phone.

The worker comes back to the phone and tells me that since it is now getting close to five o'clock they will not be able to get anyone to the home until tomorrow. There simply isn't anyone available to go out. Oh yes, they will definitely do something about it in the morning.

The police precinct is called. A police detective has gone to the dead child's home to see if there are any other children. We leave word asking him to call me back in the morning.

It is getting close to the end of the day, but there are still many calls to make, private patients to see, reports and papers of various sorts to write or at least get started on. My secretary, Anne Dougherty, and I have been at it since 7:30 in the morning. There have been letters to dictate, the normal morning and afternoon rounds to make, the meetings to attend; there have been discussions with the interns about the insidious signs to look for in possible cases of child abuse, and how to treat the frightened little patients with compassion. More letters come in, and the phone keeps ringing.

In the day's mail is a letter from another New York hospital. A nurse writes to ask me what can be done about the case of a child who had been treated there. The child had had old fractures as well as new ones. To the doctors it was obvious from the X rays that the child had been injured repeatedly over a long period of time. Their findings were consistent with the battered-child syndrome. The doctors and nurses felt very strongly that the child had been abused. The child recovered and went to the courts. Medical testimony wasn't even asked for, and the child was returned to the parents. What to do? The nurses are extremely upset about this. Because they are so concerned about the child's life and because they don't know where else to turn, they write us. This matter is referred at once to the mayor's office, specifically, the Interagency Council on Child Welfare which is known to us with a great deal of affection as "Barbara Blum's office." We know we can refer to that office, and we know we can get *action*. They do something, and we do get an answer back.

Another call is made to another agency on another case. *Are* they pursuing the case of the little boy brought in with his belly hideously swollen with malnutrition? Have they found the mother? Will they let me know when they do? They say they will. The detective on that case is also called. He is still out on another case. I know that he is overloaded with cases of one kind or another.

The next letter bears the letterhead of the United States Senate. It is from Senator Hubert H. Humphrey, and he writes for an opinion on the proposal introduced by Mario Biaggi of New York for child-abuse legislation and for suggestions to aid Senator Humphrey in proposing effective child-abuse legislation in the ninety-third Congress. We are pleased to hear from the Senator and only too happy to offer opinions and suggestions, but at the same time I wonder why it has taken all these years for our legislators to get started. We have been telling them about child abuse for the last ten years and give the answers to the best of our ability, but they are still at the stage of asking the basic questions. Would we still be getting these questions if the men and women who have begun to ask them could only see what we see in our emergency rooms?

A doctor calls in desperation from another city hospital. He has, in his care, a child whom he strongly suspects to have been seriously abused. The child is now recovered. He has notified the child protective unit that he believes that the safety and well-being of the child demand that he remain in the custody of the hospital until the child's case can be taken to court. The social agency, he explains, is petitioning on behalf of the child; but in the meantime an attorney is petitioning on behalf of the mother, and the doctor is very much afraid that the mother is going to succeed in taking the child home. He is *very* much afraid for the life of the child. He is unable to get satisfaction from the various agencies he calls. Would we intercede for him?

This again, is a case for "Super agency." The case is referred at once to Barbara Blum's office for children's services.

At the same time Anne, my secretary, who is now an authority on child abuse, is getting a round of similar calls. Many of hers are from laypeople: "The woman next door is beating her baby. What shall I do?" "My niece is neglecting her children, but I don't want to get her into trouble." "My downstairs neighbors left their children alone two days ago and haven't returned." "My brother-in-law is an addict, and he's beating the kids with a belt. What should I do? Please do something. Please help."

She helps. First, she gives them the address and telephone number of the Emergency Children's Service or the Society for the Prevention of Cruelty to Children. Then she suggests that if they get no satisfaction when they call, if they find that nothing is being done, they call us back. If the worried callers do call back, she refers them directly to the office for children's services. Interestingly, they do not often call back.

There are still administrative details to take care of. We finish these up and, at eight o'clock, exhausted and somewhat numb, call it a day.

The next morning, I do my dictation, which consists largely of letters to doctors who have referred patients to me, and miscellaneous matters pertaining to the task force, the interagency council, and various committees and subcommittees on child abuse. Then I go to the ward. Our little Chinese girl is even more beautiful today. She is still not fully awake, but smiling sleepily. The little boy with the multiple fractures is also progressing. However, the recovery of the child whose skull was fractured by his drug-addict mother and the condition of the two abandoned children is not satisfactory. They look like frightened little animals. They are going to need a great deal of loving care.

Sandwiched between other duties are my own inquiring calls. I am waiting for word from the medical examiner's office. I do not get it, even though this office is usually reliable. The detective on the case does not call back and cannot be reached, but at least he has been to the home of the little strangled girl. In spare moments, a call is made to the child protective unit to find out what they have on the case, and if there is anything further they have turned up about the homes and families of the maltreated children that are lying upstairs in the ward.

Late in the day, we indirectly learn that the medical examiner's office does not support the suspicions of abuse in the strangulation case. They have decided that the strangulation was indeed accidental and that there were no signs of sexual molestation. This is the end of that particular case. When a medical examiner makes a statement of this sort, the police have no grounds for pursuing an investigation.

The detective still does not call back. Perhaps, now, there is no reason why he should. But we wish that he had, and we wish that one of the medical examiners had considered it worthwhile to at least discuss the case with us.

I wonder how is it that the medical examiner's findings do not match mine. I suppose that his observations were different from mine because he saw the body several hours later in slightly changed condition; and because his interpretation of what he saw was not colored by surrounding circumstances such as the attitude of the father and mother. When I saw the body the rectum was open, looked as though it had been penetrated, seemed to be oozing liquid material; and there were those black and blue marks on the vulva that seemed to me to have been inflicted, to have been traumatic. By the time the body reached the autopsy table, it was ten hours old. It was relaxed. It was cold. It was blotchy. The rectal relaxation and the black and blue marks, which appeared to be traumatic, may well have been postmortem findings. That is to say, they saw what we saw, but they saw it in a more advanced stage, a more exaggerated condition, a condition that appeared to be a normal postmortem state. And perhaps that is exactly what it was. The child had been dead for perhaps three hours when she was examined at the hospital. On the one hand, I think I had a better opportunity to observe trauma because I saw the body so many hours earlier than the medical examiner; on the other hand, since the child was dead when she came to us, what I had interpreted as traumatic might have been the beginnings of postmortem changes. So it is possible that we were wrong; it is possible that the examiner was right. But the case is not going to be pursued, and we will never be sure.

There are people walking the streets right now who have murdered their own children. The only child-murderers we know about, with very few exceptions, are the ones who confess. The others, the many others, are free. A few of them may carry the burden of a heavy conscience; but walking around with a heavy conscience is more acceptable to them than spending the better part of a lifetime in jail. And some have no conscience at all. They have simply disposed of their own tiresome property.

This is not to suggest that one or both of the parents of the little blonde girl are deliberate murderers. I certainly would not be able to prove beyond reasonable doubt that they are guilty. What happened may have been a genuine accident, but I'm highly suspicious. I hope that, if it was not an accident, the couple have no other children.

It is telephone time again. The calls come in; the calls go out. This is another one of those days when a lot of people seem utterly unable to get any sort of satisfaction from the agencies called. Only Barbara Blum and her staff seem to be on the ball. Why doesn't the detective call back on the fracture case? Did the social worker go out to the house? What became of that case record someone was going to send? Why couldn't the information be given to the resident when he called? Who took the initial report? What happened to it? Where is the child now? Have you checked the mother's record? You'll call me back? Okay. Thanks. Goodbye.

There is a dreadful sluggishness about this day. The hands are moving around the clock but nothing is happening. I am referred to one person after another; from one who knows nothing to another who doesn't want to, from one who is unpleasant to another who goes off to look for something, can't find it, and leaves the phone hanging. The whole performance seems to show a callousness, an indifference, a thick-skinned discourtesy that one is accustomed to getting from the business office of a public utility.

Far too many of our daily encounters are pitched battles with surliness, apathy, and a strange sort of resentment that comes from employees not knowing how to do a job with reasonable decency and efficiency. Often, it's the same old story of don't-give-a-damn.

But here we are not dealing with an electric light bill or a TV set that won't work. We are dealing with the lives of children, lives that may be ruined or lost through our indifference or incompetence. All the child-abuse laws in the world will be of little help if we are unable to implement them.

It is another day, a week later. Many small things have happened, but nothing seems to have changed.

The morning's correspondence includes letters to several physicians who have asked my opinion of certain symptoms they have observed in several of their young patients and a letter to an out-of-state assistant attorney-general asking me to testify in the case of a young woman accused of murder in the death of her baby son.

Then I go up to the ward and make rounds with the residents and interns. It is not unusual to see a newly-admitted child who has been maltreated, although the reason for requested hospitalization has not been given as maltreatment. But on this day, fortunately, there are no such children. Lately it seemed there had been an epidemic; so many abused children had been brought in during the last week or two. Strange, that they should be brought here, of all places; strange that is, when the parents themselves bring them in. You would think they would take the children somewhere else if they didn't want to be suspected of abuse. You wouldn't think they would want to go anywhere near St. Vincent's Hospital after all the publicity about its involvement with child abuse. Maybe they want to be suspected. This being the last place in the world a parent is likely to bring a child in abused condition, imagine what's going on in other hospitals?

There are many children to look in on, including our favorite little Chinese friend, several other maltreatment cases, and a number of new arrivals with commonplace childhood ailments. The abuse cases seem to be responding somewhat more favorably now. They've got a long way to go, and they're going to be with us for many weeks, but eventually they will physically recover.

Unfortunately, we have observed that many children who are abused tend to develop traits that make them unlovable and thus even more abusable. A child that is well taken care of reflects that care and, in turn, attracts positive responses. Abused children naturally become frightened; they often react to the abuse in various unattractive ways, which often makes it difficult for even experienced pediatricians and pediatric nurses to respond to them with the whole-hearted, loving concern that they desperately need. They may act as though they are seriously, irreversibly retarded, even when they are not; they may be animalistic in manner as well as appearance. Some are negative, cringing, pessimistic, full of bottled-up hatred. Others are aggressive in their hatred and strike out physically: they punch, they kick, they literally bite the hand that feeds them—and every other accessible part of the body attached to the hand. Many are incapable of returning affection even when it is, belatedly, poured into them. Children who are not salvaged at an early age from abusing homes carry these characteristics with them through life. In the home situation, they may develop illnesses which make them even more unattractive and difficult to handle. They grow up, if they grow up at all, with their retardation, hatred, and aggression built in. It is a job to call a halt to this process of growing up "bad." With attention, food, and love, they do improve. We have seem some near-miracles. We hope, as we go about our rounds, that we have some more near-miracles in the making.

So far, it is a good day, but suddenly there is a call from the children's emergency room. A mother has brought in what she thinks is an unconscious child. She is wrong. The child is dead.

Once again, we walk past the waiting mothers and children, through the four-bed children's emergency room, into the small room in the back.

A little boy, about eighteen months old, has burns over

half of his body. Some of the burns are relatively old; some are new; all are serious, so serious that he is dead. The child is very thin; he is emaciated.

Questions: What is the mother's story of how this happened? What was her attitude when she came in?

Answers: We don't know her story yet. She left the child with somebody while she went someplace. She came back and found him in this condition and brought him in right away. She didn't know he was dead; she really thought he was unconscious. She seemed very agitated and concerned.

The examination of the body continues. The burns are terrible, and they might very well have caused blood poisoning. The little boy must have suffered terribly for there is nothing more excruciatingly painful than a deep burn. The protective skin is gone and the flesh beneath is vulnerable, hideously sensitive without its outer protection. The marks are lurid, but the agony must have been infinitely worse. The burn marks are scattered all over his tiny, thin body: small ones, big patches, stripes. His small face reflects the torture he has endured and died of.

How terrified he must have been; it comes to mind like a stab of pain.

There is something else. This child has also been sexually molested. Whether or not the medical examiner's office confirms this, the other evidence is clear: the burns are not the result of accident.

We go through our usual procedure. The report is called in. There is no question that this is a case of abuse and neglect. The child protective unit sends out an investigator to see if any other children are involved. The police get onto the case immediately. We send the small body over to the medical examiner's office. We have done all we can. Now the wait and the phone calls.

According to the history that we receive later, the mother emphatically denies having injured her child in any way. She claims her boyfriend did it in her absence. Her story is that she had gone to Chicago to look for a job and left the child with her boyfriend in a hotel room. When she came back, she found the child in the condition in which she saw him, unconscious so far as she knew. She had brought him in immediately.

The medical examiner's report confirms our findings: the child had developed blood poisoning from the wounds, which could not possibly have been accidentally incurred; and the rectum gave sure evidence of sexual abuse. The little boy's death had been indescribably awful. The police are conducting an intensive investigation, requestioning the mother and trying to locate the elusive "boyfriend." The day ends.

The case of this little boy continues to weave its way through the crowded days that follow. At the hospital, we have no more children brought in dead on arrival; however, a newly admitted child upstairs looks like a case of neglect. The child whose skull was fractured by his drug-addict mother seems to have reached a plateau in his progress, but we are not completely satisfied with his condition. No one has come to visit the maltreated children in our ward, with the exception of the father of the Chinese girl.

During spare moments, the detective handling the case of the little boy who was burnt is called. On days like this, there are twenty or thirty calls made to find out the progress of a case. Although the police encounter some difficulty, they do find the man who is allegedly responsible. He denies charges and blames the abuse on another child that was visiting in his hotel room. This seems strange to us.

The last report from the detective indicates that they have the man in prison, but there is no proof. We have the pictures of the child, a whole series of views of the body showing the atrocity. They are turned over to the detective, and we promise to testify, if needed. We ask the detective to keep us posted, but he does not call again.

In the meantime, there is a call in connection with another case. It is not in my immediate bailiwick, but it is definitely within my field of interest. A prominent New York district attorney calls to introduce, over the telephone, one of his assistants who is engaged in obtaining evidence in a case of apparent child murder. Certain allegations have been made to him which do not, in his opinion, square with the physical evidence. He asks me to offer my opinion. The assistant district attorney describes the parents' presenting story and the injuries. He is concise but explicit, and he quotes from the medical examiner's report.

Though only tentatively, at this stage, I corroborate his suspicions. What happened to the child could not possibly have happened in the manner described by the suspect. For a child to fall and receive such injuries, she would have to fall from the top of the Empire State Building. The assistant district attorney is gratified and will call again for a definite appointment.

We have heard nothing more about the burn case. Another tragedy of these situations is that, as time passes, the immediacy is lost. There are too many child victims to keep them separate. The little individual bodies blur into a faceless group and become buried in a sort of mass grave of memory. The little burned body will be lost in the shuffle and, perhaps, forgotten. Other cases will come, piling up on top of it. Without the reminder of a questioning call or a request to testify, we will eventually forget about the boy and the strangled baby girl.

The children upstairs and in my office right now are important. Soon they are going to be even more important, because, one day, they will be healthy enough to leave here. What's going to happen to them? We want to be sure that the living are not forgotten.

At least there is one case in the Bronx that is not being forgotten. It is too late to save the child, but there is to be a prosecution. The assistant district attorney has come to see me, and I will testify.

# CHAPTER TEN

# A Child's Day in Court

THE CASE OF THE PEOPLE VERSUS Smith, began for me with a phone call from Burton Roberts, who was then district attorney in the Bronx.

"Dr. Fontana," he said, "we have a problem here, and you might be one of the people who could possibly help us out. An assistant district attorney with me, a young fellow with long hair, name of Cantor, has a case of child battering, and he thinks he can get something done about it. Would you speak to him and help him out wherever you can. And, uh, by the way, we'd appreciate it if you'd go easy with your fee and don't let Cantor's long hair turn you off."

There would be no fee, and Mr. Cantor's hair was no problem.

At this point, I spoke with Robert Cantor, assistant district attorney for Bronx County. He explained that he was preparing a case involving a child who had, he was convinced, been battered to death. He suspected the father, the mother's part-time common-law husband, was responsible, but his suspicions were difficult to prove.

The vast majority of such cases are difficult to prove. The difficulty is that they usually occur in a setting where the only witnesses are those who are actually responsible for the acts: the people on the scene, the mother or the father or the mother's boyfriend, or the mother and male parent-figure acting virtually in complicity with one another.

The man had not admitted to having committed any crime, and it was not to be expected that he would. It was his legal right to remain silent and not incriminate himself. And, apart from the suspect, there was no witness to whatever might have happened. Not even the mother had seen the so-called accident. But the child had been autopsied; and the medical examiner's findings were not consistent with the history that was related in the presenting story.

Mr. Cantor concisely, almost laconically, outlined the conflicting stories and asked if I, as a pediatrician and authority on child abuse, would be willing to testify. And, he asked, could he possibly come down and speak with me? Of course, I said, and we made an appointment.

He came down with a colleague, a detective who was working with him on the case. He described the situation to me.

But first, let me describe him: tallish and compact of build, neatly and quite conservatively dressed in a dark suit, serious eyes, somewhat brooding face, near-black hair down to his shoulders, reflective but businesslike manner, waste-free in his movements and speech, no time for smiles and amenities until the discussion is over. Then he relaxes briefly, half smiles, and goes on his way. He is the new breed of attorney. He cares very much about what he is doing. He is in the homicide bureau of the District Attorney's Office, and his job comes into play when a case becomes ripe for prosecution.

In the course of his six years with the Office, he has encountered several cases of severe child abuse, and, of course, they are severe, because it is in the homicide bureau that one finds cases of abuse that culminate in death. His agency does not have the conciliatory function of the family court; the cases it receives are beyond repair. Cantor's business is that of prosecution, and he does just that.

The case he related to me was one he considered unusual because there was no previous history in this family of child neglect, abuse or battering. It was one that I, watching it develop from somewhat of a distance, came to regard as unique, not because of its built-in characteristics, but because of the way Cantor handled it.

The mother of the dead child, I learned, was a woman of about twenty-five or twenty-six. She had been married and divorced. When she met the defendant, Philip Smith, with whom she entered a common-law relationship, she had two small children by her first husband. One was a little boy just four years old, and the other was a female infant of approximately fourteen months.

The man moved in with the woman, and they lived together for a few months. Then the full-time partnership terminated. But the man and the woman continued to see each other and have sexual relations, and the woman would sometimes use the man as a babysitter.

After a while, during which she had left the children with the man when she went out, she began to notice a change in the baby girl. The baby had been an extroverted, cheerful, happy child who loved everybody including her unofficial stepfather. People responded to her childish charm, and she was very responsive in return. Everyone who visited the house was enchanted by her friendly attitude. But now, the mother observed, this usually outgoing and loving child would become cranky and start crying whenever the man tried to approach her. Strangely, she did not act that way toward other people. Her reaction was confined to the mother's lover. The man told the woman that he had no idea why the child was acting that way; he couldn't understand it. But everyone who knew the child observed the change in her when the man was around.

One morning, late in 1970, the mother went downstairs to do the wash. (These cases take some time to come to court.) She took the little boy with her and left the baby in her crib. The little girl seemed perfectly normal and happy at the time. The man was dozing in another room.

The mother was gone from the apartment for about six minutes, the time it took to get down to the washing machine, load it, and get back upstairs. When she got back, she found the baby lying in her crib in an altered condition: her fists were clenched, she was gurgling in an oddly choked sort of way, and there was blood oozing out of her mouth. In physician's terms, she appeared to be in a traumatic state. To the mother, it must have seemed that the child had been having convulsions. But when she called out to the man, who had been alone in the apartment with the little girl, he told her that he had heard a sound in the bedroom and gone in only to find the baby on the floor having apparently fallen from the crib. He hadn't seen any signs of injury and had, therefore, simply put her back.

Yet now she appeared to be in very serious condition and in shock: and her breathing was labored and uneven. Frantically, her mother called a neighbor, and together they rushed the child to her own pediatrician. She was dead by the time they got her there.

There were no external black and blue marks on her; no indications of deep-seated internal injury. Her doctor had seen and examined her only eight days before, and, at that time, she had seemed to be perfectly fine. Now, at nineteen months old, she was suddenly dead. Of course a fall from her crib, especially if she had landed very awkwardly, might very well explain it. The pediatrician regarded it as a case of accidental death and made a tentative diagnosis of broken neck.

It was unfortunate and tragic. Everyone was in agreement on that. The mother was in a state of near-shock in her sorrow. She and her family and friends and neighbors were openly and unashamedly grieved by the death of the little girl. They mourned for her, together, and no one entertained the slightest suspicion that the cause of death was anything but accidental.

But in almost all cases of sudden unexplained death, there has to be an autopsy. Theoretically, there has to be an autopsy in every case, but in practice this does not always occur. There are many genuine "crib death" situations, wherein an infant is suddenly found dead in the crib of unknown causes, and these are incidents of terrible tragedy to the parents. (The little girl in this case was never considered to come into the crib death category, since at nineteen months she was well over the usual age for these mysterious deaths.) To add to the sorrows of an innocent parent by suggesting that there is something suspicious about the child's sudden death and implying that the parent may be responsible is not something that can be lightly done. There really should be no shame in having an autopsy performed in an attempt to determine the cause of an otherwise inexplicable death. Perhaps our attitude toward postmortem examination will change when it becomes completely standard procedure. But as it is now, there are times when an autopsy, for whatever reason, is not done, and these exceptions are unfortunate. Some of them literally permit a parent or guardian to get away with murder. If blows are inflicted and cause injuries to the underlying soft tissues and body organs, there may very well be no hematoma, no black and blue marks, no outward manifestation of violence upon the body surface, especially if the body is observed shortly after the infliction of the injuries. Thus at first glance, the tragedy may indeed appear to be an accident, and the matter is not pursued. In the presence of parental grief, and who is to tell whether it is sincere or feigned, it is difficult to believe in parental guilt. Without seeing or suspecting any outward manifestations of foul play, one is reluctant to assume that the injuries were inflicted by another human and pursue inquiries along criminal lines.

However, if an autopsy is performed and if there is a prompt and exhaustive medical examination, the chances of determining the true cause of death or the nature of the injuries and their likely source are infinitely increased. If a child dies a natural death, the autopsy will, in all probability, reveal this. If a child dies of injuries, the autopsy will reveal the nature of the injuries and will almost always determine whether they are consistent with an accident, the story usually presented by the parents, or consistent with an inflicted beating or intentional traumatization.

In the case of this little girl, there was no suspicion whatsoever. But her death had certainly been sudden and unexpected, and its precise cause was unknown. So, in what was pretty much a routine move, the little body was sent down to be autopsied by the medical examiner.

The mother thought nothing of this. Her parents thought nothing of it. Her friends thought nothing of it. It was just a question of the law, and something that had to be done in the case of any sudden, unexpected death of any healthy child; that was all. The family mourned, and they consoled each other; and they scarcely gave a thought to the specific cause of death or what the results of autopsy might be. All they knew was that the child was tragically and unexpectedly dead; and they grieved as they would have if she had darted unexpectedly into the street and across the path of an oncoming truck.

Only the lover, Philip Smith, behaved differently. No one paid a great deal of attention to this peculiarity at the time. They only realized afterwards that it might not have been what they thought. But he did seem to be going through some sort of crisis, and they understood it on their own terms: according to his own statement, he had been alone with the child when the accident happened, and now he was needlessly blaming himself. He was emotional, like everyone else, but unlike everyone else he was saying some rather strange, uncalled-for things. During the two days preceding the autopsy, he let slip a number of comments that would have been highly suspect at the time if the case had been regarded as homicide from the beginning. But, as it was, the police were not collecting statements because the fullblown investigation they would normally pursue was held in abeyance pending the results of the autopsy. Only the people close to him heard what he said, and they failed to attach any special significance to his comments. Obviously, he was very upset. That was perfectly understandable.

At the end of that two-day period of mourning, the medical examiner came up with the finding that the child's death was due to multiple blunt-force injuries. There were eight independent structures and organs in the baby that had been extremely severely traumatized. The number, positioning, extent, and severity of the wounds were not, in the medical examiner's opinion, consistent with a fall from a crib. He communicated his findings to the police.

Whatever they might have suspected before, the police had had no reason to investigate, beyond acquiring a preliminary body of information, before receiving the medical examiner's report. Now the waiting period was over for them, and they could act in full measure.

They called on the mother and her part-time paramour and brought them in to attempt to obtain their statements in the presence of the assistant district attorney on duty that evening. Both people were now prospective suspects and were advised of their rights. A stenographic statement was taken. It was very much the same as the story given when the child's death was initially reported. But the important point here is that the police already had a statement from the mother that the man had been alone with the baby, a story that the present statement brought out again and that could be backed up by what the man himself had told other people. Thus it seemed apparent that one person had unwittingly laid himself on the line as the only one present when the so-called accident occurred.

Interestingly, this is something that quite often happens. A suspect in a case of this sort frequently makes a statement that is exculpatory on its face—"I was the only one there, and I know it was an accident"—but nevertheless places himself or herself at the scene at the time in question. As a matter of circumstantial evidence, one can reasonably draw the inference that, if two individuals are together in a room and one comes out alive while the other stays there dead, and if some criminal agency has been employed, and not in a self-afflicting manner, it could only have been applied by the survivor. Certainly if the death was not due to natural causes or accident, something that can only be determined by medical examination and not always then, it is reasonable to conclude that no one else but the survivor had the opportunity to commit the criminal deed.

Thus, in the light of the doctrine of exclusive opportunity, coupled with the medical examiner's findings that the baby had been subjected to injuries inconsistent with a fall, what the district attorney's office had were grounds to proceed against Philip Smith.

This evidence was presented to the grand jury, which returned an indictment.

It now became Robert Cantor's job to prepare the case. Studying the evidence, he became convinced in his own mind that the defendant was indeed responsible. But he had to be able to prove it beyond any reasonable doubt. And the evidentiary problems were still very real. There were a great many questions to be answered: Was the medical examiner's evidence completely without loophole, was it remotely possible that the child could have climbed up on the crib and fallen out in such a way as to cause those injuries after all, exactly what had happened in those few minutes when the woman was downstairs doing the wash, what possible motive could the defendant have had, did he have any past history of abusiveness, had he actually intended to kill the child or merely inflict injury upon the child, or was the act an "accident" in another sense?

The main difficulty here, as always in these cases, was the absence of witnesses. No one else had been in a position to see what the defendant had done or hadn't done. Whatever had happened had happened within the four walls of the bedroom, and the true story could only be told by the defendant himself. And whether he would take the stand at trial and testify was anyone's guess.

But he had done some talking during those two days preceding the autopsy, and now people were beginning to remember some of the things he said. Cantor and his men went out and interviewed neighbors, friends, and relatives in depth. They learned that the defendant had made a multiplicity of conflicting statements to various people as to exactly how the child had died. Every time he described the accident to someone and how he had found the child lying on the floor, he offered a slightly different version, and some of the versions flatly contradicted each other.

On the evening after the child's death, he spent the night at a friend's home on the plea that he couldn't bear being in the place where the tragedy had occurred. He talked to his friend about what had happened and made the statement that the child had internal injuries in the stomach area. It did not occur to the friend to wonder how he could have known that. But, of course. at that stage, *nobody* could have known that. Nobody could even have guessed it, except perhaps someone who knew more about the accident than he was admitting.

At one point after the child's death and before the autopsy was completed he had said, right out of the blue, "They can't prove a thing!" To someone else he said he thought he might have done it himself during a nightmare, like the time when he was a kid and had woken up from a violent dream to find he really was beating up his screaming baby brother.

The people to whom he had made these and other comments did not think too much about what he was saying at the time. They thought he was torturing himself over the death of the child, perhaps blaming himself for not being on the scene in time to save her. But these statements, when repeated to investigators from the district attorney's office after the medical examiner's report was studied, took on a different meaning.

Furthermore, Smith was not a notably responsible type of person. In his irresponsibility, he had announced no intention of legitimizing his relationship with the woman, nor did he want to have a child by her. He had once gotten her pregnant and made her get an abortion that she didn't want. Another thing, he said he hated to hear a baby crying.

Mr. Cantor briefly outlined the case during that meeting in my office and went into detail about the age and size of the child, the height of the crib, and the autopsy findings. What he needed from me, and from other sources, was testimony to indicate that this child, because of its age and its size and its development, and particularly because of the height of the crib and other factors, could not possibly have fallen out of the crib. Question: Could this child, from the pediatric standpoint and taking into consideration all known factors about the child and the crib, possibly have maneuvered herself into such a position as to have fallen to the floor? And my answer to that had to be no. Question: But supposing, for the sake of argument, that the child had been able to climb up and that she had then fallen out, could she possibly have sustained the injuries described in the autopsy report? And my answer to that, again, was no.

Among other injuries, the child had hemorrhages of both adrenal glands, a ruptured liver, a ruptured pancreas, and a contused heart. Taking up the question of the pancreas, for example, this is an organ of the abdomen (or perhaps one might say, the stomach area, in the defendant's phrase) that is far back and deeply insulated in the body. It takes a great deal of pressure or impact to rupture it. This is not something that just happens; rupture of the pancreas does not occur because of a fall from a crib unless the crib is five stories high, which cribs are not. As for the contusion of the heart, this, perhaps more than anything, emphatically showed the extent of the trauma. The heart is protected by a shield, the breastbone; and for a heart to receive such damage, the impact must be severe indeed. There had to be a difference between the defendant's statement and what actually happened. The autopsy revealed a child who had received a great deal of trauma, a considerable impact that would be consistent with a fall from a great height or being hit by something like a truck.

There could be no doubt about it. I told Cantor that the damage the child had sustained certainly could not have happened as a result of a fall from a crib, even if the circumstances had permitted such a fall, which they had not.

This, essentially, is what he wanted to ascertain. He asked me, then, if I had access to an anatomical model showing the positions of the body organs. Such a model would be helpful to him in demonstrating to the jury and the court the exact locations of the traumatized organs in the child's body and showing that the damage revealed in autopsy far exceeded any trauma that could possibly be sustained through a fall from a crib.

Unfortunately, I didn't know the whereabouts of any such model and could only suggest that he try a medical school or a hospital such as Mount Sinai.

He nodded and said he'd keep trying until he found one.

The medical examiner was going to testify, and his testimony should have quite a striking effect if illustrated by a model of the human body. Another pediatrician was also going to testify. The medical testimony in this case was absolutely crucial, and Cantor was determined to pound it home with all the energy and ingenuity at his disposal.

Then he left. I was impressed. I liked his thoroughness; I liked the way he went about his job, as if it really was important to him to pin the responsibility for the death of the child squarely where it belonged. In a way, it seemed as if he were the dead child's advocate.

He kept in touch; he called several times to reassure himself that I would be available to testify when needed. I told him that I would be; all he'd have to do was call me several hours before he wanted me, and I would certainly find my way up to the court. In the meantime, he was still pursuing various lines of inquiry.

He had a strong case, perhaps about as solid a circumstantial case as it is possible to get in a matter of child homicide. He was fully aware that medical testimony, though always vital, is not always convincing, and he knew he had to show in the most vivid and graphic way that the deep, severe damage to the child could not possibly have been incurred as claimed. That is why he persisted in his search for the model: so that he could have the medical examiner demonstrate in court, in front of the judge and jury, on an anatomical structure, exactly how deep-seated the injuries were; so that he could actually take out the movable parts and show that, for example, the pancreas is located behind the lower part of the stomach and is thus literally shielded by it, that the liver is in the front of the body, and the adrenal glands are in the small of the back; and it would have to be a very strange fall indeed, an impossible fall, to cause this combination of injuries which also included the traumatization of the esophagus and the heart.

So he had to find the model. And he did. To his enormous gratification, the Flower-Fifth Avenue Hospital was good enough to lend him an anatomical structure worth hundreds of dollars to help him prove his case.

When the case came up for trial, Assistant District Attorney Cantor had a lot going for him. He was able to show the conflicting statements Smith had made, the consciousness of guilt exhibited in some of them, and the man's exclusive opportunity to commit the crime; he brought out the defendant's own admissions of nightmares and fits, insofar as they were interwoven with the death of the infant; and he refuted the defendant's claim that the baby had fallen out of its crib.

He called me toward the end of the trial, explaining on the telephone that he had purposely kept my testimony for the end so as to lend impact to the testimony already presented. Now he was ready for me. I went up to the courthouse and was promptly called to the stand.

Cantor introduced me as his witness and asked me to state my credentials. I did so. He then showed the jury a copy of my first book, *The Maltreated Child*, in order to further establish me as an authority on the subject of child abuse, and stated that I was in the process of writing another. With my credentials established and the preliminary statements out of the way, he got down to business.

The crib was in the courtroom. He gave me its measurements, including the height of the rails; he told me the age, height, and weight of the child and described the state of growth and development at the time of death; and then asked me if such a child could possibly have fallen off her crib or climbed out. I said no. He gave me the medical examiner's report to read. I refreshed my mind: the major injuries were the bilateral adrenal hemorrhages, the rupture of the liver, the rupture of the pancreas, the contusion of the heart, and the hemorrhages of the peritoneum. Yes, I said, these were all signs of deep, severe impact.

The defendant's lawyer asked me if the child could possibly have stood on top of the crib rails and dropped off. This was an attempt to suggest that the greater height might account for the severity of the injuries. I said, no, I did not think the child could *possibly* have been able to stand up on top of the rail. But could not the injuries described in the medical examiner's report have been sustained if the child *had* fallen off the crib? And I said, no.

My testimony took only a few moments, and I left immediately after giving it because I had other things scheduled. But I took with me a mental picture of the empty crib in that courtroom; and the defendant sitting there listening to me and watching. He was clean-cut, neatly dressed in conservative suit, shirt, and tie, wore horn-rimmed glasses, and generally looked fine. I assumed that this wasn't quite the way he had been dressed when picked up. Now he was cleaned and fixed up to make the best possible impression on the jury. They would look at him and ask themselves: Could that nice man have done that terrible thing? Could anybody deliberately hurt a child that way?

But then, they had also seen the medical examiner's demonstration, and they heard pediatric testimony from me and another physician. Perhaps the medical evidence, tied in with the defendant's own damning statements, would make them realize that he might not be all he seemed to be in his good suit and behind his dignified glasses.

Mr. Cantor called me the next day, thanked me for appearing, and told me that the trial was over. The defendant had pleaded guilty, not to murder, but to manslaughter in the first degree.

If I might recap for a moment: After establishing, through witnesses, the demeanor of the defendant and his statements at the relevant times, the prosecution chose to refute the defendant's assertion that the baby fell out of the crib. They did succeed in showing that a child of that size, age, height, and so on could not fall out of the crib and damage itself; they did succeed in showing that, as a normal child with normal coordination, the child could not have climbed out of the crib or climbed up on the rails and fallen off.

Then, to undermine the credibility of the defense case, they had to make the assumption that she could have. Supposing she could have, could she possibly have sustained such injuries? No, she could not. Expert pathological testimony, including that of Dr. John Devlin from the medical examiner's office, proved beyond any doubt that she could not. But supposing she had fallen, and supposing she had fallen onto a toy that was claimed by the defense to have been lying on the floor, could she then have sustained such injuries? Again, it was shown beyond any doubt that the severity of the child's injuries was not consistent with a fall from a crib even if she *had* fallen onto a toy, and the prosecution proved that the toy had not been where the defendant said it had been and that the child could not have fallen onto it.

Faced with overwhelming expert testimony and with the statements previously made by the accused himself, the defense asked if he could plead guilty to manslaughter in the first degree.

The mandatory minimum sentence for murder in New York is between fifteen and twenty-five years. The mandatory maximum is life. Assistant District Attorney Cantor had prepared such a solid case that the defendant was in line for a murder rap. And yet he and his colleagues did not think, in spite of all the evidence, that a murder rap was completely justified or necessary. They had evidence that he was guilty, but there was still a perceptible doubt in their own minds as to whether he had really intended to kill the baby. There was no hardcore body of evidence of his intent to kill. Nor was the man a hardened criminal. He was not a recidivist. A sentence that might seem light to a hardened criminal would seem very rough to him. Therefore, when the defense attorney sought to strike a bargain, the prosecution agreed to offer the defendant a plea of manslaughter in the first degree, which carries a penalty of from zero to twenty-five years, but to ask the court to treat the man severely, when pronouncing sentence, within the limits of first degree manslaughter.

The defendant accepted the offer and entered a plea of guilty. It should be noted that he did not admit to anything. He simply pleaded guilty to first degree manslaughter after assessing the strength of the prosecution's proof and offered neither confession nor explanation nor regret.

No one knows even now exactly what did happen or why it happened. But it seems that, on the day prior to the baby's death, the man had had a cyst removed. It might have given him pain. Medication was administered. He may have had an uncomfortable night, but when morning came he was sleeping soundly. He was, apparently, a heavy sleeper anyway. The crying of the older child, the boy, awakened him. This infuriated him. Still groggy, he "blew his stack" and made a terrible scene. Later, when the woman went downstairs to do the laundry, the little boy was apparently too scared to stay in the apartment with him and went down with the mother. The baby was drowsing in her crib. One could reasonably conclude from the prosecution's case that perhaps the baby might have started to cry while her mother and brother were gone; and that the man, still in a bad mood and trying to catch up on his sleep, could have gone into a fit of anger and taken his rage out on the crying child.

But unless Philip Smith eventually decides to get the whole story off his chest, we will never know if there is any substance to this guess. Most child-abuse cases are essentially secret crimes, and even this one still has hidden elements. If it had not been for the autopsy report, it would probably have remained secret altogether and been buried with the child; and if it had not been for the doggedness of one assistant district attorney, the convicted killer might even now have been in a position to destroy another child.

As for the mother of the dead baby, she seems to have been the unhappy victim of circumstances. By all accounts, she was a good mother. Unlike many other partners of abusing parent-figures, she did not stand idly by and permit the abuse to occur. She didn't know it was happening. She was puzzled by the child's changed attitude toward the defendant in the weeks before the tragedy, but she had no reason to suppose that there was anything serious underlying it. The child's own pediatrician had found the little girl fit and well only eight days before her death. This was not a case in which violent acts perpetrated over a period of time eventually took their toll. This was a case in which the one violent act resulted immediately in the death of the infant, to the deep shock and sorrow of the mother.

The worst that can be said of her is that she was a lonely woman who sought solace in the company of a man who appealed to her because of his aura of "manliness." She was young, tied down by two children whom she loved but who kept her from all outside social life and longing for companionship. Some time after the death of her child, she met another man, to whom she is now married, and she is currently pulling the pieces of her life together.

What impressed me about this case was the persistence of the young assistant district attorney. He cared about what had happened to the child. Before he began his investigation, he knew as well as anyone, and better than most people, that cases of this sort are extremely difficult to prove because of their secret nature. But he went ahead and dug deep, asked questions, listened, took the trouble to find out who might be in a position to give expert testimony in the area of child abuse, searched for an anatomical model to give impact to the medical evidence, and put together his case with painstaking care. He was convinced he had a valid suspect and spent his entire time and energies for several weeks on proving his case, and would not stop when it was suggested to him that he might better be spending some of his time on more positive ventures. To him, this was a positive venture; he made it one; his diligence paid off. What was important to him was the fact that the child had died of inflicted injuries, that someone was responsible, and that the guilty individual must not be permitted to get away with it.

So far as Robert Cantor is concerned, he was simply doing his job and was lucky enough to have the resources to do it thoroughly. He shrugs of the suggestion that he gives more of himself and has perhaps a more dynamic approach to his work than many others in similar positions. Ignoring any attempted pats on the back, he points out that "the D.A.'s office could not proceed in cases of this sort without the cooperation of pathologists like John Devlin of the medical examiner's office and pediatricians like Dr. Fontana." He is grateful that we took the time to go to court and testify. "We need such people," he says. "In cases such as this one, without pathologists and pediatricians willing to put their experience on the line, we've got nothing."

I realize the truth of this. I wish that more individuals in the medical field would be willing to stick their necks out occasionally and slice a little time out of their regular schedules to offer the courts the benefits of their expertise. Too many of us simply cannot be bothered. But in regard to this specific case, I am convinced that it was only the persistence of this one nonmedical individual, the assistant district attorney, that produced results in the case of *People* versus *Smith*. It points out the fact that *one person* can do something if there is a determined effort to become involved. Cantor spoke for the child. He was her advocate. Though she was dead, she had her day in court.

# CHAPTER ELEVEN
## Children's Rights: The New Crusade

WHO, IN OUR SOCIETY, speaks for the children? Who speaks for them while they still live? Not many people. Not very many people are in a position to. But even if they were, they would be talking into the wind. They can scarcely insist on upholding rights that do not even exist. Our cultural and legal traditions virtually deny the child's right to be heard or to have a spokesman, particularly in questions involving the principle of parental rule.

Our constitution and our laws guarantee us certain human rights, but it seems to be our tacit assumption that only adults are human and, therefore, have exclusive claim to these rights. The Supreme Court, in 1967, had occasion to declare that "neither the Fourteenth Amendment nor the Bill of Rights is for adults alone," something that should have been too obvious to need pointing out but that unfortunately needs pointing out again and again.

Attitudes toward the rights of children under law and under the parental thumb have gradually changed throughout the centuries, but the change is more a matter of degree than essence.

The old Roman law of *patria potestas*, providing that the father had absolute power over his children even in such matters as selling them into slavery or slaughtering them, is no longer officially recognized. But a continued belief in the concept seems to be embedded in our culture and in the parental heart. The doctrine of *parens patriae*, conceived in the Middle Ages and born in the United States in the eighteenth century, acknowledged that parents have responsibilities as well as rights and asserted the power of the state to assume the role of parent in cases of parental failure to fulfill these responsibilities. It was a step in the right direction, but it has not yet proved to be a particularly effective one. In practice, the parent can still do pretty much what he pleases with his child; his rights are virtually sacrosanct, and the performance of his duties as a parent is seldom questioned unless and until he fails to meet his parental obligations, such as keeping his child alive, fed, clothed, and reasonably clean, in the most blatant and public way.

When the first frenzy of shock over the existence of child abuse in our country swept the nation in the sixties, the result was the rapid passage of laws in all fifty states relating to the reporting of suspected cases of child abuse. These laws bear only indirectly on the question of children's rights, and since they have reference only to the reporting of abuse and neglect cases, they can hardly be said to attack the problem at its core. They have not had and cannot have any direct effect on children's rights per se.

The haste with which these laws were enacted bore witness to the sudden, widespread recognition of the maltreatment problem, and the public demand that somebody do something about it. Somebodies in all states did something about it. They quickly drafted and passed the reporting laws, but then everybody's conscience relaxed, as if the passage of these limited laws had solved the problem of child abuse.

But we know now that the reporting laws are only the most basic beginnings of an approach to a problem that is extremely complex; a problem that not only involves questions relating to the spotting and reporting of suspected cases of child abuse but also questions intimately related to parental versus children's rights, to societal stresses, to human depravity, to the deep root-causes of the disease, to the possible means of preventing it, and to effective methods of treating it. These laws can only provide a means of initiating rescue operations in individual cases of maltreatment wherein the child is in a life-threatening situation. If there is no machinery to effect the rescue, if there are no adequate preventive, protective, and curative facilities, and if there are not enough trained people to carry out the mandate, the laws are empty words and nothing more than window dressing. Perhaps what we need is a law *against* child abuse: a very specific law spelling out crimes against children and the penalties which could be enforced. Possibly there are still people who fail to realize that starving, whipping, burning, or killing a child is just as illegal as starving, whipping, burning, or killing an adult; possibly they will be deterred by the knowledge that a sentence awaits them. And, perhaps, we need another law mandating that complete preventive, protective, and treatment facilities be available in every single community in the United States.

In an article in *Children* (March-April 1966, volume 13), p. 48, Dean Monrad Paulsen of the University of Virginia Law School expressed his concern over the reporting laws as a solution: "Reporting is, of course, not enough. After the report is made, something has to happen. A multidisciplinary network of protection needs to be developed in each community to implement the good intentions of the law. The legislatures which require reporting but do not provide the means for further protective action delude themselves and neglect children." He adds: "No law can be better than its implementation, and its implementation can be no better than the resources permit."

To me, this is a most important statement relating directly to the core of the problem of child-abuse legislation in this country. In many instances, the resources are miserably inadequate, and, in many instances, the human spirit required to do the job, to implement our laws, and to provide the resources, is just as woefully lacking.

Certainly, in the last decade, the acuteness of our need to mount a counterattack against child abuse has been recognized through the passage of the reporting laws. However, a reluctance on the part of the physician to become involved, the yielding by the courts to traditional parental authority, overlapping of investigations by social service agencies, inadequate training of social workers and allied personnel in the field of child abuse, and very poor communication between the various disciplines responsible for protecting the abused child (including the legal profession), has resulted in a notable *lack* of protection and has given abusing parents the opportunity to continue their cruel actions which result in so much pain, so much fear, and so many unnecessary deaths of defenseless children.

In the course of my own involvement, I have personally seen and experienced the many gaps and loopholes and pitfalls that exist in every area of the child-protective system. All too often, physicians, nurses, social workers, teachers, and others in a position to identify and report suspicious cases are extremely reluctant to do so. The reasons are many, some acceptable and others not. They are not always sure of their suspicions, therefore they bury them. They fail to understand the seriousness of the problem. They are unaware of their own responsibility to report. They don't want to antagonize the parent-suspects and thus lose contact with them. They don't want to become personally entangled in a delicate and difficult situation. They have an unfounded fear of legal liability. They don't want to become involved in court proceedings. They are afraid of alienating patients in private practice and exposing them to court hearings. So, justifying their inaction by telling themselves that their suspicions are probably groundless, they do nothing. If, with time, the matter fails to surface and thrust itself uncomfortably close to their unwilling eyes, it will be forgotten; it will simply disappear while they're not looking. Thus, unknown numbers of cases go unrecognized and unreported, law or no law.

Reporting in itself is not as easy as it may seem. Calling the emergency number in the community, if there is one, can mean instant, efficient action or complete chaos possibly ending in disaster, depending on who answers the phone. It's an unfortunate fact, but sometimes there is an incompetent at the other end of the line. And the one person answering the phone can discourage, anger, and disillusion the caller, can destroy right then and there the entire reporting procedure. The one weak, rotten link subverts the entire chain. It is too bad that a child-protective system should be so fragile that it can collapse because of one weak link; but that, regrettably, is the way it is.

But supposing the call is intelligently handled: what happens next? We have already seen what can happen, what has often happened. Other links in the chain give way, and the child, duly reported, may still be lost. The chain, the machinery, the child protective system by whatever name, is cumbersome and faulty, and the people whose job it is to make it work are not perfect and sometimes frighteningly inept.

This must be changed. Only through cooperative planning between the various agencies that are responsible for child protection and cooperative effort on the part of physicians, social agencies, and courts, can endangered children be properly cared for and parents rehabilitated. Protection of the child, his rights, his person, his future happiness and health, and the protection of parental rights at the same time should be the ultimate aim of all these various disciplines. Physicians, hospital administrators, social workers, legal advisers, and other child-caring personnel should all have specific guidelines to direct them in delineating responsibility in the management of child-abuse and neglect cases. The decisions involved are of critical importance and cannot be based on the personal feelings or bias of any one physician, social worker, or judge, *or* the uncooperative, uninformed, untrained know-nothing answering the telephone. All humans are potential victims of error when encountering complex problems and difficult decisions; in this grave disease, such error may seriously affect the welfare of the child, may result in his reinjury or even death. This is an area where there should be absolutely no room for error, where there should be no errors made. The individuals involved in these decisions need special training, and they need that quality called "dedication." The protective system demands absolute cooperation between all individuals and agencies and should have a built-in fail-safe component as a backup against the error of any single individual.

The future of the abused child is dependent on the education and enlightenment of all people concerned with child care, upon the upholding of the laws of the various states as well as our nation's constitution, and upon our finding means of reporting that will make protection of the child and subsequent investigations of child-abuse cases more realistic and more efficient. Further progress toward the prevention of this disease can only be made through proper interdisciplinary, cooperative educational programs, delineating the responsibilities of the specific disciplines involved and offering a realistic follow-up of all cases not only to ensure the safety of the children but to determine the effectiveness of the system.

And so the reporting laws, vital though they may be as the first link in the chain of child protection, are only a minuscule part of it. Furthermore, they only begin to touch on the overall question of children's rights. Do children really have any legal rights in our society? Precious few. Theoretically, as people and as citizens, they enjoy all the rights and protections accorded to adults. In actuality, as children, they do not, simply because they *are* children. The rights of children are not as easily legislated as those of adults. In legislating for children, one runs the risk of chipping away at parental rights and even the very concept of the family. On the whole, the family unit is a fairly successful one. The majority of parents somehow manage to bring up their children adequately and without infringing too heavily on their rights. The growing child is not mature enough to run his own life. He needs parental guidance and loving discipline—discipline in the sense of controls properly exercised. It is therefore no easy matter to define children's rights as against parental rights and no easier to obtain them.

There has been some trend toward increased rights and protection for children. We have seen the enactment of child labor laws, and the development of the child protection movement in the form of the Society for the Prevention of Cruelty to Children, the Children's Bureau in Washington, the Children's Division of the American Humane Association, the Child Welfare League of America, the Head Start program and the day care movement. In recent years, there have been two important Supreme Court decisions affecting the constitutional rights of minors: the 1967 *Gault* relating to due process of law in juvenile proceedings and the 1969 *Tinker*, upholding the right of suspended students to have worn black armbands in school in memory of the men killed in Vietnam as a protest against the war.

These are both far-reaching decisions, but as yet they are mere drops in the bucket. Adult or parental rights still take precedence in parent-child confrontations. Deny it as we may, there is still something in us that persists in regarding children as parental property or chattels.

According to a statement made in *Parade* (July 27. 1969) by Joseph Reid, executive director of the Child Welfare League of America, "We need a complete and radical reexamination of our whole philosophy on parental rights. We need a hard evaluation of judicial decisions and interpretations of statutes. Perhaps most of all, we need an educational campaign to establish the rights of the child as paramount, even above the rights of parents—certainly equal to the rights of parents. Parenting needs more than fathering or giving birth to a child. If a parent abandons, neglects, or abuses a child, his rights to the child should be terminated."

But this is not a simple thing to do, even if it were always the right thing. There is the difficult question of proof of abuse, then there is the question of existing tradition and law. Robert Cantor stated in a personal communication to me:

You get into problems of ascertaining or proving whether the origin of the injury is accidental or intentional. Our assumption is that the child must be brought up according to the dictates of his or her parents; the parents' rights vis-à-vis the child's are superior. But who are the spokesmen for the children? It comes down to this: we have this archaic view, this traditional concept or principle, that there is an inherent right vested in the parents to bring up their children in whatever manner they deem proper. And if that means certain discipline, why, that should even surmount the child's rights. A lot of these types of cases have gone so far as the United States Supreme Court, cases of parents having raised their children in a manner that's considered somewhat bizarre—as when certain religious or social doctrines are being subscribed to by the parents but which foursquarely and adversely affect their children's physical safety and general welfare. It's a very difficult and thorny area. In New York State, as a practical matter, it's only when the actions of a parent actually bring about the death or grievous injury of a child that criminal prosecution arises. You've got to balance on the one hand the parents' rights to bring up their children according to their own religious or ethnic or social scruples with the rights of society in seeing that all of the children of this particular society are raised in a healthy fashion—at least physically healthy, if not spiritually.

It is indeed a difficult area. There are laws dealing with child neglect, but they are broad and subject to conflicting interpretations, differences based not only on the vagueness of the laws but on very real moral, religious, cultural, and disciplinary beliefs. Nobody openly denies a child's right to parental affection, support, care, education, guidance, and discipline. We all give lip service to this basic right, even when it is not accorded. But there are many interpretations of "discipline," "guidance," "education" and, even "care," particularly when it comes to cultural and religious practices. Also, there are "rights" that fall outside the affection-through-discipline grouping, and these are extremely muddy.

Does a child have a right to medical care, or to obtain it for himself if his parents' beliefs forbid it? Does a child have the right to go to school with his peers, or may his parents deny him a formal education? Does the child have the right to receive what an adult would regard as fair treatment from those in authority, or is he bound to do as he is told? Does the child have the right to be heard, or does he have to shut up and listen? Does the child have the right to continuity of residence in a divorce case or express his wishes regarding custody? Does the child have the right to work or refuse to work? Does the child have the right to keep his own earnings or allocate them as he pleases? Must the child be obliged to dress in a manner atypical of the population at large, or may he choose not to look different from his peers? Similarly, must he submit to wearing conventional clothes when he wishes not to? Is the child obliged to fit himself into the religious pattern demanded by his parents? Does the child have a right to what nutritionists regard as a balanced diet, or do his parents have the right to restrict him, for example, to seaweed and nuts? Does a child have the right to be regarded as a person? Does a child have the right to respect? Does a child have the right to protection from abusing and neglectful parents or caretakers?

Again, one is forced to conclude that children have very few rights under law. Some are lucky enough to have decent parents who make available to them the rights they do not have on paper. Others aren't.

Mrs. Helen L. Buttenweiser, a New York City attorney, has stated:

> There are no statutes that specifically state what a child is entitled to. Adult rights, on the other hand, are stated very specifically and clearly. There should also be statutes stating a child's legal rights— to a good home, education, health care, affection, love, and security. As it stands, a child is really in limbo. In law and in court actions, society can only step in after an allegation of abuse or neglect. The burden of proof is on society. I say that the burden of proof should be on the parents. Children should be considered as people, not as things.

At least one family court judge agrees. In a case that has drawn surprisingly little comment since it went to court in 1965 but which I regard as highly significant, Judge Harold A. Felix of the Family Court of the State of New York circumvented certain difficulties in an abuse case by applying the doctrine of *res ipsa loquitur*. The court stated that, in view of the difficulties in obtaining witnesses for a crime such as child abuse and the critical nature of the battered-child problem, it would permit the circumstantial evidence to put the burden of proof, or "satisfactory explanation" of the child's condition, upon the parents. It was up to the parents, Judge Felix declared, to explain how the child came by his injuries:

[The proceeding] was initiated undoubtedly by a consensus of view, of medical and social agencies, that the child Freddie, only a month old, presented a case of a battered-child syndrome. Proof of abuse by a parent or parents is difficult because such actions ordinarily occur in the privacy of the home without outside witnesses. . . .

Therefore, in this type of proceedings affecting a battered-child syndrome, I am borrowing from the evidentiary law of negligence, the principle of *res ipsa loquitur* and accepting the proposition that the condition of the child speaks for itself, thus permitting an inference of neglect to be drawn from proof of the child's age and condition, and that the latter is such as in the ordinary course of things does not happen if the parent who has the responsibility and control of the infant is protective and nonabusive. And without satisfactory explanation, I would be constrained to make a finding of fact of neglect on the part of a parent or parents. . . . This is the court's responsibility to the child.

Here at last is an influential spokesman for the child. Perhaps this is what child power is and where it lies: in a responsible, compassionate, thinking adult speaking out on behalf of the helpless young and thereby influencing other adults. In 1970, the presumption of "the thing speaks for itself" in neglect cases before family court was enacted into law in the state of New York.

Dean Paulsen adds a comment: ". . . . Leaving in his home a child who bears the marks of unusual injuries which seem to have been intentionally inflicted is taking a chance with the child's life. Not all doubts should be resolved in favor of parents. . . . Parents have a right to their children, but their children have a right to live."

To me, it is clear that we must further reflect on our traditional social and legal values. We must recognize the best interests and welfare of the child, versus the parents' rights over the child and to the custody of an endangered child. Many a child may be sacrificed if we continue to follow, as we do for the most part, traditions and precedents that defer to parental rights. Certainly the law cannot insure that a child will receive the love and affection that it needs for physical and psychological survival in its own home or another home;

but surely it should recognize that a child must not be sacrificed in order to uphold the presumed rights of parents who have failed to preserve the family unit when it has gone beyond preservation.

Again let me quote Robert Cantor:

I sometimes wonder whether there shouldn't be a reexamination of this concept of entrenched or inherent rights of the parents to raise the child in their own way. Maybe there should be something that's been termed the Child's Bill of Rights. Maybe there should be someone to stand in *loco parentis* for the children, to act on behalf of them, some guardian or appointee of the state to raise a voice on their behalf. We deal with some very outrageous, repugnant acts toward children, sins of omission as well as commission. And the callousness and lack of remorse shown by the parents is sometimes staggering to the imagination. That they can talk about the death of an infant as if it were such a mundane matter is utterly amazing to me. I find it absolutely loathsome. It's as if one were discussing a transaction dealing with a piece of furniture such as a kitchen table. It may be that the individuals are numbed, that the fact of death hasn't sunk in, that the perpetrators are blocking out things, that people faced with arrest will sometimes deny everything. And it's their absolute right to remain silent. But I'm just utterly amazed by the facility with which they discuss acts which to me are the most heinous and barbaric . . . as if the destruction of a child meant no more than the disposal of a piece of furniture!

To some of these parents, with all their rights, the snuffing out of a baby's life is no more than the snuffing out of a candle; and the drowning or strangling or smothering of an infant no more dreadful than the disposing of excess kittens at birth or the disposal of a trivial piece of property.

In recent years, a number of minority groups have begun to come into their own. But the one minority group that encompasses all ethnic and religious backgrounds, the "minors" themselves, has no national movement or lobbyists working for it. And this is very strange, since each member of this group is tomorrow's full-fledged, adult citizen. Must they all be second-class citizens until they reach the age of eighteen or twenty-one when, perhaps, their citizenship is too late to do them any good?

It is true that a number of recommendations for strengthening the rights of children have lately been put forward, but none has yet come to fruition. The Joint Commission on Mental Health of Children has proposed a national advocacy system; several groups and individuals are in favor of an ombudsman for children; many others have proposed, and some have even drawn up, a bill of rights for children.

One such bill, published by the New York State Division for Youth, includes these rights to be enjoyed by every child, regardless of color, race, or creed: the right to the affection and intelligent guidance of understanding parents; the right to be raised in a decent home in which he or she is adequately fed, clothed, and sheltered; the right to a school program which, in addition to sound academic training, offers maximum opportunity for individual development and preparation for living; the right to receive constructive discipline for the proper development of good character, conduct, and habits; the right to be secure in his or her community against all influence detrimental to proper and wholesome development; the right to live in a community in which adults practice the belief that the welfare of their children is of primary importance; and the right to receive good adult example.

Other rights might well be added, rights to be exercised should the preceding basic rights be traduced, including the right of the child to be released from a home that does not provide these necessities; the right of the child to be freed from a hopelessly deteriorated parent-child relationship; the right of the child, no matter what his age, to bring suit against parents who violate his constitutional rights as a person and a citizen.

Such a bill must not be just another piece of window-dressing, another sop to conscience. It must be not only a noble declaration but a legal instrument which incorporates the means of enforcement. And then it must be enforced.

But, as of now, we have done little to provide our children with any legal rights at all. Only some individuals, some courts, and some court decisions, have taken steps to protect our children and their rights as human beings—in a nation that proclaims justice for all.

In search of a quick and easy solution to the ugly reality of child abuse, a great many people have come up with glib answers based on the pill and other birth-control devices, planned parenthood, vasectomies, and abortions for the asking. Abortion is the favorite theme of the moment. The thrust of the argument is, of course, toward the prevention of child battering, neglect, and abuse through the prevention of children. This method of solving the maltreatment problem would also have the virtue of giving us fewer children with chicken-pox, few children with measles, fewer children with meningitis, fewer children to get knocked down by automobiles, fewer children to fall out of trees, fewer children to skin their knees in the playground, fewer children to grow up well and strong and loved. There would be fewer children and, therefore, fewer problems all round. It might be a wonderfully neat solution, if it were not quite so sweeping and simplistic, or if it were only valid.

The fact that it is a stopgap measure and one that treats only the symptoms of the disease rather than any possible causes is a large objection to the birth-control-abortion solution, but it is not *the* largest. It is unfair, uninformed, and, I believe, dangerous, to preach the doctrine that abused and neglected children are unwanted children and to imply that unplanned or unwanted children are going to be maltreated. The assumption that every battered child is an unwanted child, or that most or even a large proportion of abused children are unwanted children, is totally false. This myth maligns not only the thousands of parents who desperately want children and then find themselves incapable of parenting, but also the thousands of parents who accept their initially unwanted children with wholehearted warmth and love. Certainly, some maltreated children are the results of unwanted pregnancies. But these, in my experience, are in the minority.

Why, in a family of four or five children, is the second or

third child maltreated. Was that the unwanted child? Why, in a family of two children, is the first child maltreated and not the second, or the second but not the first? Which one was unplanned, and why is the other acceptable? Why do proper middle-class parents carefully plan a family of three children and then coldly neglect the lot of them? Didn't they know what they wanted, or weren't they pleased with what they got? Why do parents with access to birth-control devices not use them and wind up with several children whom they abuse in turn? Do they enjoy abusing them? Why do stepparents, paramours, foster parents, and other guardians abuse and neglect children with whose conception they had nothing to do and for whom they are not obligated to make themselves responsible?

Many maltreated children are children who were very much wanted before birth. Perhaps they were wanted for the wrong reasons: to prove to the mother that she is capable of doing something, anything; to prove to the man or woman that he or she is normal and able to have a child; to give the mother something of her own to love and give her love in return; to cement a couple on the verge of separation; to present a picture of a conventional family unit because for one reason or other that is the expected or respectable thing to do. Immature people, lonely people, emotionally starved people, abused people, neurotic people, retarded people, disturbed people, deprived people, more often than not, sincerely want their children. It is only after the children arrive that the doubts set in and the problems surface. It is not just a question of saying ahead of time, well, this one isn't wanted; let's not have it. It's just not that easy. People's motivations are much too complex for the problem to be solved in this way; and their own assessments of themselves, their needs, their wants, and their capabilities are often sadly wrong. Who is to know and who is to tell them how wrong they are, and that they must not have their wanted children? We should also remember that a good many parents, in the act of abusing their children, are in the grip of an uncontrollable anger and a love-hate emotion that has nothing to do with wanting the children or not wanting to love them. Their reasons for striking out are as distant from the unwanted-child theory as it is possible to be.

It makes a great deal of sense to plan families, particularly if the planned parenthood and family planning agencies can reach and suitably educate the people who most need their services. But let us not offer the prevention of children as a cure-all for the problem of child abuse as at least one pharmaceutical company, peddling its contraceptive pills, has been wont to do in one of the most offensive pieces of self-promotion I ever hope to see.

The problem of child abuse goes far beyond the conception and birth of the child and deep into the roots, environment, and daily discords of the parents and often their parents and *their* parents before them. It is a medical, legal, social, moral, and psychological problem that is not treatable by any one-dimensional approach. A practical approach must take into account all the factors that have made the abusing mothers and fathers what they are; it must get to the etiology of this particular disease. There are no shortcuts, such as abortion, that lead to the answer. Even as emergency measures, these superficial, quickie solutions bypass the stated goal. Most middle- and upper-class parents-to-be who know they do not want children also know what to do about it, either before or after conception. But many of the young and scared, the poor, the uneducated, and the minority groups know nothing of the pill or intrauterine devices or the legal abortion services available. Some who do know about them cannot afford or do not care to avail themselves of the existing contraceptive measures or consult family-planning agencies. Among the ghetto dwellers and the minority groups, there are a great many people who are suspicious of the family-planning programs in their communities, largely, I suspect, because of their usual experiences with social agencies.

Therefore, while there is a place for family planning, it has not yet become part of the solution and is unlikely ever to be a large part of it. I am afraid that all efforts taken toward zero population growth will not help alleviate the multiplicity of social and environmental factors responsible for this major health and life-death problem. Here we literally have a situation in which people recommend throwing the baby out with the bath water; and, as a solution, it does not make any human sense. Surely it would be a far better thing to improve the quality of life for all the living, to work at changing social conditions, than to reduce the number of human beings. Surely every human being should have the same rights and comforts enjoyed by some of us. Regardless of what some ecologists are saying, there is room for all of us. As Dr. Frederic Wertham says in his book, *A Sign For Cain,* "Human beings do not suffer from hunger or live in misery because there are too many of them, because they do not possess anything which would enable them to work and supply what they need. . . . It is not the quantity of the people, but the quality of their social environment, in the widest sense, which explains their condition. . . . It is most likely that if we want to carry out all the tasks of civilization that lie ahead for mankind, the number of people will have to be greater and not smaller." The more productive people we have to improve our world and work at finding solutions for our countless problems, the better off all of us will be.

In the meantime, we are still faced with the prospect of thousands of children growing up unhappy, maltreated, and deprived. They show no signs of becoming the productive citizens we need. But they are *here.* We cannot undo their existence. Are we, therefore, going to permit them to continue on their present course, and tell ourselves we should have known, they should have been aborted, and that we'll know better next time (which we won't)?

It is pointless to go on in this self-destructive fashion. Let us be selfish in another way. Let us persuade ourselves of the truth that if parents cannot give their children the kind of life that is the right of every human being, then our government must step in and do so. That is to say, *we* must step in. This would mean subsidization for maltreated children; this would mean another tax. Question: Why should I subsidize someone else's children? Answer: Because my children are going to have to live and grow up with those children, and their lifestyle must be improved or *my* children are going to suffer.

But whether we are selfish or unselfish, it has got to make more sense, if there is any humanity in us, to find ways to improve the quality of human life and enrich it for all of us with every means at our disposal rather than abort it so that we will have fewer human beings to worry about and answer for.

Personal concern and involvement must encompass government action. Our government is supposed to be a government of and for the people. It is, therefore, not too much to ask, of these our own representatives, that they concern themselves with a matter that is the concern of every citizen. We have to reach the people who are presumably working for us and get them to turn their attention to our most basic needs.

I must admit that I fear the red tape and dehumanization of the bureaucracy on all government levels. I fear the inability of our public officials to heed the needs of our maltreated children and their unfortunate parents—all unhappy human beings, our brothers and our sisters and our children in the human family. I personally dread the frustrating, often fruitless, encounters with the various government agencies that must be approached in order to secure the funding and support necessary to institute child-abuse programs throughout the communities of our country. I know I am reaching for pie in the sky when I tell myself, hopefully, that government help might be forthcoming if our highest officials were only to become aware of the magnitude of this terrible social ill, even though every day I see funds being siphoned away from vital social services and diverted into programs of considerably less significance and urgency.

But, if I could push the right buttons and magically produce the desired effects, I should like to see instant government interest and knowledge of the child-maltreatment problem at the White-House level. I should like to see federal legislation, starting from the top, aimed at protecting the rights of children: a complete package of very specific, enforceable laws covering all aspects of minors' rights but with particular emphasis on child abuse and neglect. It is time, I think, for us to pour some of the national outrage we seem to have reserved for such questions as pollution, and some of the enormous interest we have lately shown in conservation, into a crusade for the rights of children. I should like to see a centrally organized, fully funded study-and-action program go into effect at once. I wouldn't mind at all seeing the establishment of a private foundation dedicated to a study of child abuse and the means of combating it, but I do believe that since this problem is of major national concern it must also be of major government interest. And by all means, let there be more such child-abuse centers as the one in Denver, philanthropically funded. That first one is a giant step. But I think it is vital that we have a fully staffed and funded national child-abuse institute with its headquarters in or near our nation's capital, equivalent to the National Institute of Mental Health but dedicated to the investigation and dissemination of information on every aspect of the child maltreatment syndrome.

I should like to have this center study all existing programs and proposed techniques for the identification, prediction, and management of this syndrome; to devise teaching programs and to educate physicians, social workers, child care workers, teachers, members of the legal profession, and community leaders in the proper method of handling it from their respective points of view; to distribute training programs for use in colleges, medical schools, universities, nursing schools, and so on; to serve as an information center for interested members of the general public; to develop criteria for the establishment of research-treatment centers in other parts of the country.

Realistically, this center will not mushroom into existence overnight. When it does come into being, I would hope to see it proliferate: I would like to see branches throughout the country, and I would like to see funds and programs funneled right into each community. In the meantime, I think there is a great deal we can proceed with on a community level, including setting up smallscale study-and-treatment programs and demonstration projects for which we might very well be able to obtain at least some federal funding.

But quite apart from study groups and pilot projects, there are things we can and should be working on right now. In our own small way, within the limits of the agencies with which we are now working and within the limits of ourselves as people, we must try to develop an early warning system to tip us off to latent trouble, a predictive *sense* rather than a formal program that will enable us to look into our own communities, using our educators, physicians, social workers, day care workers, and various community people as our eyes and ears, to spot potential or incipient maltreatment of children. From what areas are the child-abuse cases likely to come? From what homes? From what parents? From what pregnant mothers? We may not, ourselves, in the community, be able to develop such predictive tools as questionnaires. But the Denver group has reserach to this end well in hand, and I would certainly hope that my proposed National Institute for Child Maltreatment would also work on the development of sophisticated methods of identifying potential abuse situations and potentially abusive parents, as well as on the steps to be taken to prevent potential from becoming reality. In the meantime, the commonsense and alertness of professionals in a position to observe and the cooperation of the various agencies providing services to people can, together, form quite an effective prognosticative force. We'll see a lot more once we use our eyes to see, use our ears to hear, and stop turning our heads away.

Physicians are going to continue to be on the front line. Unfortunately, some private physicians are still reluctant to admit even to themselves that parents can and often do inflict serious damage upon their children; hospital residents, interns, and nurses are unwilling to recognize or accept the evidence of their own eyes, or the idea that a parent might be responsible. Aware physicians must take it upon themselves to speed the educational process of bringing this syndrome to the attention of medical students, hospital trainees, interns, residents, and even general practitioners; to give personal, on-the-spot instruction whenever and wherever they can to make up in part for the existing shortcomings in the curricula of medical and nursing schools; to encourage their medical societies to disseminate information to all physicians concerning the syndrome and the steps that the physician can take to protect maltreated children from further abuse; to push for the inclusion, in medical schools, of courses in the diagnosis and management of the maltreatment syndrome.

Physicians no longer bear the full brunt of responsibility as once they did. But since the maltreatment syndrome and the battered-child syndrome are medical diagnoses, the physician will often find himself the one on the spot, the one person in a position to report suspected instances of child abuse to the responsible agency or individual and to validate the diagnosis by presenting evidence in court.

Furthermore, physicians in private practice, as well as in hospitals, should make themselves responsible for following up maltreatment cases that come to their attention. Their human responsibiliy does not cease when they make their report. Sometimes it is *only* the continued interest and prodding of the physician that ensures coordinated action (or any action) by the various agencies and subagencies involved in child protection and parent rehabilitation. This is an unfortunate truth, but it is a truth; and the fact that following up each case can be time-consuming, frustrating, and sometimes enfuriating does not absolve the physician of this human responsibility.

The private physician will not see enough of these cases in a lifetime for his follow-up efforts to seriously interfere with his practice; the hospital seeing at least a score or so of maltreatment cases per year would be well justified in having its own specialized child-abuse team to handle and follow up all cases, or one fully trained child-abuse consultant on its staff to serve as coordinator between the hospital and the various outside agencies. It is my belief that every major metropolitan hospital should have immediate access to a trained consultation team consisting of physician, social worker, and coordinator to review all suspected cases of neglect or abuse and follow through with therapeutic programs where these prove to be required.

It is, in turn, the responsibility of each community to provide for an effective central reporting agency and make sure that it is fully equipped with trained personnel and other resources to take prompt and efficient action on receipt of any child-abuse or neglect report. That one agency in each community, the agency of prime responsibility, must have the capacity to process each case from start to finish, from receipt of the report to investigation to emergency action to court proceedings and, when necessary, to long-term protection of the child to rehabilitation of the family structure; *or* the capacity to coordinate all other community agencies in the handling of the total problem. This is where personal involvement really counts. This is where the responsible members of any community can get together and push, through their local legislators and representatives and through their own personal efforts, for the necessary social services. This is where a citizens committee can function as a watchdog group to see that the agencies providing these services function together as a unit to follow each case through to a satisfactory end.

To every concerned member of every community I have this to say: When you get together with other concerned individuals, when you make the effort to find out what is being done in your community and what remains to be done, when you raise your voices loud and clear so that your local officials can hear them, you will get action. Personal activism is the way to get it: action breeds more action.

Community members with a legal bent can carry their watchdogging activities to the juvenile and family courts. These courts, in each community, must be made even more cognizant of the concept of parental delinquency. They need to reevaluate the traditionally accepted idea that the child belongs to and with its parents in the light of our present knowledge that some parents do not belong with their children; that returning a child to a problem home may sometimes be detrimental to the child, its parents, and the entire family; and that we cannot wait for evidence of serious injuries before stepping in to rescue the victim. We like to think that maternal love will triumph, but we have to admit that it does not exist in all mothers. We like to think that a father or surrogate father takes pride in his child and will give it what it needs in spite of an occasional lapse, but this is not always the case. We must admit to ourselves, through our courts as well as our other institutions, that each child's right to life and happiness is just as important as each parent's supposedly God-given right to the child. The child is helpless in this adult world. We must watch out for him, speak for him, and personally safeguard his rights.

In every state, the designated state agency should keep a central registry of all maltreatment cases, with free access and a give-and-take flow of information to all people with a right to know. In time, I would hope to see a system of cross-checking between all the state registries and, eventually, a national registry keeping a record of all maltreatment cases reported throughout the country; but until that probably far-off day we must bend every effort to the establishment of statewide registries so that suspected abuse cases can be checked out immediately and acted upon without delay in spite of all parental efforts at hospital-hopping. Provision should also be made for the removal of reports from all registries when it is proved beyond doubt that the suspected abuse did not in fact occur. Suspicions do prove false on occasion, in which case they must be wiped from the record.

I should also like to see the establishment, in all the larger urban areas, of clinics for the diagnosis and treatment of the maltreatment syndrome. I envision these as being part of a network of centers operating under the aegis of the national headquarters; but since my dreamed-of national institute may be a long time in coming I think we have to lobby at a local level to get our state legislatures and our community-based philanthropic foundations to come up with the funds to enable us to get these centers going without delay. Each, in its own community, should provide centralization of resources and centralization of expertise; each should provide facilities in which all the needed disciplines may work together in a cooperative, coordinated way. Such a clinic might be attached to a health center, a community hospital, or a child care facility. It should be *the* child-abuse center of the community;

the community center for research, diagnosis, treatment, and management of the disease we call child maltreatment.

Such a center's overall program should include a "crisis management" program offering immediate emergency support to families needing prompt relief from acutely overwhelming situations. The crisis program should offer a full range of options to parents in urgent need of support, from a telephone "hot line" service to homemaking help, and from parent aide visits to shelter or day care facilities that may be utilized at any time by parents who feel they must separate themselves temporarily from a possibly endangered child.

Because of the probability that a single center will be unable to contain on its premises or under its immediate supervision all the facilities required, and because it may not be conveniently located for all families in need, I further believe that each community must take upon itself the responsibility for providing more and better day-care services, more and better training, and higher pay, for child-care workers, more temporary shelter facilities, more lay therapists and parent aides and foster grandparents and homemakers. And I would certainly encourage the establishment and support of new chapters of Parents Anonymous.

Essentially, it is all a question of caring. Do we care enough to do these necessary things to save our children and ourselves and our society? I hope we do. I do not believe that our government is giving anything like the necessary attention and financial support to child welfare, and I do not believe that we who claim to care are doing enough to make our needs and wishes known. It is up to us as citizens to stand up and be heard. We must insist on "child power" legislation and that our federal government allocate funds for an all-out attack on the crippling and often fatal disease of child abuse. We must get the people who represent us on a national, state, and local level to recognize this wound in our society and dedicate themselves to healing it. When we all accept the fact that child maltreatment is as important a problem and as frequent a cause of death as cancer, leukemia, cardiac or pulmonary disease, cystic fibrosis, or muscular dystrophy, then we will have taken the first step toward saving the lives of thousands of children and improving the lives of perhaps millions of others. But it will be difficult to achieve even that first step until we enlist the aid of what columnist Harriet Van Horne (*New York Post,* January 31, 1973) describes—in another but only slightly different context—as "the only agency having the power to heal in the massive way that is required—the federal government."

And I think, for our own sakes, we have to remember that the effect of childhood maltreatment very seldom wears off as the abused child, if he lives, grows into adulthood. We must be concerned with the effect of today's battering and neglect upon tomorrow's adults. What we, in our present inaction, are doing is permitting our neighbors and our peers to not only mistreat their children but produce a new generation of criminal misfits who are going to turn around and attack us and our children. The violence in our society can only continue to increase so long as we think of child battering and neglect as something rather unfortunate and sometimes horrendous for the child in question but nothing to do with the rest of us. Child maltreatment has a great deal to do with all of us. It is an ugly symptom of our times, but it is more than that; it is inextricably linked with unbearable stress, with impossible living conditions, with material or spiritual poverty, with distorted values, with disrespect for human life, and with the drug addiction, alcoholism, assaults, armed robberies, murders, and other ills in the midst of which we live—and for which we must find massive healing. It is born of this illness and violence, and it will breed more of the same. If we cannot feel for the children who are even now being savaged and scarred, at least let us feel for ourselves and the kind of future we are shaping for ourselves and our own children.

# Epilogue

## DOUGLAS J. BESHAROV
### Assistant Professor of Law
### New York University

## The Missing Legal Framework*

IT IS DIFFICULT to write about the law of child abuse and neglect without discussing all aspects of the child-protective process because so much of it is established and regulated by statutory law. And it is naive to present the system of law without explaining its actual operations. Successful child protective legislation must be properly implemented.

Many children suffer further injury and maltreatment after coming to the attention of the authorities. In early 1972, the New York State Assembly Select Committee on Child Abuse completed a detailed study of the fifty-four suspected child-abuse fatalities that were reported in New York City in 1971. Forty-eight of these families were known to the city family court or to other agencies before the children died.

Although generalizations are always tenuous, it is fair to say that there is a pervasive inability on the part of child-care agencies to respond both programmatically and administratively to the needs of the children they are meant to serve.

*Douglas J. Besharov, J.D., LL.M., is also executive director, New York State Assembly Select Committee on Child Abuse. This epilogue was prepared with the assistance of Susan H. Besharov, M.S.W.

Part of the explanation is the suffocating bureaucracy, the callousness, and insensitivity that the system encourages and our inadequate understanding of how to influence human behavior. But more fundamentally, there is no one and no one agency in government who speaks solely for the needs of children. From the highest to the lowest levels of government, no one speaks on behalf of the overall needs of the child. The thousands of children who rely upon our child-welfare complex for care, treatment, and protection are unrepresented in government planning circles.

Presented here are the various approaches that New York and other states have adopted in their quest for effective child-protective systems.

## 1. There Must Be a Strong Reporting Law

The early recognition and reporting of suspected child abuse or neglect is the first essential step in preventing further maltreatment. The victim of child abuse is most often too young or too frightened to seek help on his own. Society, therefore, must perform this function for children by providing adequate and workable reporting processes. If a case of suspected child abuse is not reported, a protective caseworker cannot investigate the child's situation and the report cannot be recorded in the state's register of child-abuse cases.

The laws of all states require the reporting of suspected child abuse and maltreatment from a variety of officials and professionals. Unfortunately, substantial numbers of children have injuries suggestive of child abuse or maltreatment and are seen by physicians, nurses, social workers, or teachers, and yet are not reported to the authorities.

The single most effective method of encouraging fuller reporting is to educate professional personnel who are mandated to report under the law. Child-care professionals, including physicians, nurses, social workers, and teachers, must be sensitized to the occurrence of child abuse, must be trained in its identification, and must be instructed in reporting procedures. An educational program would also seek to explain that child-protective procedures are not punitive in nature, that their purpose is the protection of the child and the rehabilitation of the family.

Nevertheless, the appalling lack of sensitivity and callous disregard of the law exhibited by those who continue to violate their legal obligation to report cases of suspected child abuse cannot be continenced. Therefore, although it is absolutely appropriate that persons who report in good faith should be free of any liability, it is equally appropriate that officials and professionals mandated to report who willfully fail to do so should be civilly and criminally liable for that failure.

Another way to encourage fuller reporting is to allow "non-mandated" persons, for example, friends and neighbors, to report.

It is true that many reports from neighbors will prove to be unfounded—indeed, a large number of reports from mandated sources also turn out to be unfounded—hence provision should be made for amending, sealing, or expunging unfounded or untrue reports.

## 2. There Must Be an Effective Central Register of Child-Abuse and Maltreatment Reports

The maintenance of a central register of reported cases of child abuse and maltreatment is an important part of any child-protective program.

The purposes to which the central registry can be put largely depend upon the material it contains and the method of its dissemination. By receiving and processing reports immediately, it provides a fool-proof method of insuring that investigations are performed and services provided. It can also monitor the provisions of such services by other agencies, and it can operate as a research tool to determine the incidence of abuse and the most effective means of prevention.

But most importantly, a central register can assist in the diagnosis and identification of child abuse by locating previous reports on the same child or his siblings. This is especially important in child protective cases because the repetition of suspicious injuries is strongly indicative of child abuse or maltreatment. However, the families in such cases often move from jurisdiction to jurisdiction. Without a statewide or, perhaps, even a regional register, it is impossible for an individual child-protective agency to know if a child has been previously reported.

Every state should have one central register system, with a single telephone number to receive all reports of child abuse and maltreatment from any and all sources. New Jersey already has such a central register system, and there is no reason why such a system should be beyond the capabilities of any other state (*New York Times*, March 6, 1972). The information contained in the central register should be available to all persons with a "need to know." The register should be responsible for notifying the appropriate local authorities to perform an investigation and would be responsible for monitoring the delivery of protective services to the child and family involved.

### 3. There Must Be a Specialized and Highly Qualified Child-Protective Agency

In theory, a "protective service agency," whether it is a department of social services or a Society for the Prevention of Cruelty to Children or other similar type agency, receives reports of parental misconduct from the courts, police, hospitals, other agencies, and private citizens. It then performs an "investigation or intake procedure" in which staff persons determine if the case is appropriate for further agency involvement. The social workers in these agencies may contact schools, neighbors, relatives, and police to obtain as complete a picture as possible. On the basis of these findings as well as interviews with family members themselves, the social workers then make a psychological evaluation of the family.

In some cases, the agency concludes that no intervention is appropriate. The reports may have been inaccurate or unfounded, or the parental neglect may be insufficient to warrant intervention. In some cases, no action is taken because the agency is unable to locate the necessary parties after the family moves or because a father or paramour against whom the charges have been made disappears.

When the protective service agency's investigation indicates that a situation of abuse or neglect warranting action exists, it then, again in theory, determines what action is necessary, from immediate removal to supervision, and attempts to have the parents agree to accept such services. In the absence of voluntary acceptance, the agency resorts to the juvenile or family court for its mandatory procedures. Under New York law, a designated employee of a local department of social services can remove a child from his home or a doctor may retain custody of a child he is treating if the child is in "imminent danger." (Of course, if such a removal or retention is made, the family court must be notified "forthwith." [New York Family Court Act, section 1026]) In this way, the social workers can rescue children in jeopardy.

Since most abused children are too young or too frightened to relate what happened, and since most acts of abuse and maltreatment take place in the privacy of the home, without an identifying motive, the gathering of evidence in such cases is probably more difficult than the proof of adult murder. Therefore, those who are given the grave responsibility for such investigations must be highly qualified. Unfortunately, the reality of child-protective services is often sharply divergent from this theoretical model.

Investigative caseworkers appear to have difficulty in getting genuine information about families. Some records have no official information from other agencies involved in the case, and the only available information comes from the statements of relatives or from the parents themselves. Often no attempt is made to verify these assertions, which are accepted as fact. In fact, caseworkers often have trouble in finding parents or surviving children after a child has died.

In uncertain cases, workers often accept the parents' version of the injury and accept, as collaboration of the parents sketchy story, the fact that the police or district attorney did not have enough evidence for criminal charges (as if lack of sufficient evidence from criminal prosecution were proof of no neglect or abuse). Fully one third of the New York City Department of Social Services' investigators interviewed by the staff of the New York Task Force on Child Abuse and Neglect admitted difficulty in diagnosing both abuse and neglect (New York City Mayor's Task Force on Child Abuse and Neglect, *Final Report* [1970] p. 95).

This table, prepared from information supplied from the New York State department of social service, reveals the large number of cases in which no action is taken because of a "lack of evidence."

RESULTS OF CHILD-ABUSE INVESTIGATIONS

| Type of Result | 1969 % OF TOTAL | 1970 % OF TOTAL |
| --- | --- | --- |
| *Abuse Confirmed* ........ | 44.3 | 42.0 |
| Social Investigation .... | 33.4 | 33.4 |
| Court Decision ........ | 10.8 | 8.6 |
| *Abuse Ruled Out* ........ | 21.1 | 28.1 |
| Social Investigation .... | 20.1 | 25.6 |
| Court Decision ........ | 1.0 | 2.5 |
| *Abuse Uncertain* ........ | 34.6 | 29.9 |
| Lack of Evidence ..... | 25.0 | 23.1 |
| Case pending in court . | 9.7 | 6.8 |

Present practice is for a case to be closed when there is a "lack of evidence." Besides indicating the weakness of investigative technique, these figures also indicate an ignorance of Section 1046 (a) (ii) of the New York Family Court Act, enacted into law in 1970. It provides:

[P]roof of injuries sustained by a child or of the condition of a child of such a nature as would ordinarily not be sustained or exist except by reason of the acts or omissions of the parent or other person responsible for the care of such child shall be *prima facie* evidence of child abuse or neglect, as the case may be, of the parent or other person legally responsible.

Much of the problem lies in the fact that child protective workers do not clearly understand that their primary role and responsibility is to protect children from further injury and maltreatment, and in too many cases information critical to the safety of a child is known to one agency and is not shared with the agency charged with protecting the child.

## 4. If Court Action Is Necessary, the Court Must be Equipped to Perform Its Function

Although most reported child-abuse cases do not reach the court, the juvenile court is nevertheless the lynch pin upon which the entire out-of-court system depends. Only if social agencies can ultimately turn to the court can we realistically expect their offer of assistance to be accepted. Moreover, the cases that do reach the juvenile court are often the most severe and require speedy and firm action.

Although child abuse and neglect are crimes, the criminal court can only protect the child by jailing the offending parent. While this is sometimes necessary and appropriate, in most cases the abuse or neglect arises from and is exacerbated by a constellation of familial relations and tensions. In such cases, the remedial actions of the juvenile court are much more effective than those of the criminal court in preventing future abuse or neglect. The juvenile court protects children by providing social and psychological assistance, albeit often involuntarily imposed, to families and households in order to "assure that the home satisfies at least the minimal requirements of a suitable place for a child to grow" (Committee Comments to 1962 New York Act, repealed Section 334). This is a reaffirmation of the notion that the problems of child abuse and neglect are primarily social and psychological, and that they are therefore subject to amelioration through social and psychological assistance. Unfortunately, as many recent studies in New York and other states make clear, our juvenile courts have not been able to transfer this ideal into reality.

That we tolerate this level of functioning is a sad comment on our values. For, juvenile courts deal with the lives of our young. They deal with the future of those before them and of society itself. In any one day, a juvenile court judge can decide that a neglected or abused child should be placed in foster care for years, that a child should be placed in a state training school, that a father or mother should be prohibited form returning to a home, that a child's custody should be transferred from one parent or relative to another, that a child's parternity has not been established, that a parent's rights over a child should be permanently terminated, or that a child should be adopted. These decisions are of immense importance to the individuals before the court and society as a whole. These decisions involve the most intimate, the most intricate, and the most delicate of family matters. A hasty, ill-conceived or expedient ruling may have an adverse impact that is felt for generations within the family and the community.

Although courts could benefit from additional funds, there has been noteworthy improvement in the administration of a number of family courts in New York State through the assertion of authoritative judicial administration. Too often, where such leadership has been asserted, it has resulted from a child-abuse tragedy: e.g., the report of the *Judiciary Relations Committee [First Department] on the Handling of the Roxanne Felumero Case* (1969); Office of the Directors of Administration of the Courts, First and Second Departments, *A Study of the Family Court of the State of New York Within the City of New York and Related Agencies and Recommendations Concerning their Administration* (1969); Hon. Harry D. Goldman, presiding justice of the Appellate Division, Fourth Judicial Department, *Report on the Investigation of the Onondaga Family Court* (1970); Isaacs, et al., *Report to the Presiding Justice of the Appellate Division, Fourth Judicial Department, and the State Administrator of the Judicial Conference, Recommending Improvements in the Operation of the Family Court in Onondaga County* (1971).

Juvenile courts traditionally have been considered of secondary importance to which priority resources need not be assigned; the importance of its work underestimated and its personnel demeaned.

The juvenile court is, in many ways, a unique court, de-

pendent upon numerous outside agencies to make its processes effective. From adjudication to disposition, the judge
is "dependent upon the cooperation and assistance of other
municipal agencies and private social agencies, so often understaffed and ill equipped to meet even the minimum needs and
demands of this court, [contributing] heavily to its inability
to become the social forum it was designed to be" (*Report
of the New York State Senate Judiciary Subcommittee on the
Family Court*, March 3, 1970, p. 2).

The juvenile court can only act upon cases which are
brought to it. It depends on local departments of social services, police, and other agencies and interested parties to
bring cases of abuse and neglect to its attention. Likewise, the
adjudicatory process is dependent upon the evidence discovered by the investigations of these agencies and their effective presentation in court.

In 1971, twenty-six percent of all child-protective proceedings initiated in New York State were dismissed by the
family court; twenty-one percent were withdrawn before a
hearing. We can only conclude that forty-seven percent of all
cases brought before the family court either (1) should never
have been brought because they were unfounded or (2) were
dismissed because insufficient proof was presented to the
court. In either event, it is clear that something must be done.
For those cases that should not have been brought, an effective
screening mechanism should exist to save the court from
expending its limited time on unfounded cases. For those cases
that failed because of inadequate preparation, it is of utmost
importance that more effective legal services be provided.

For these reasons, it is imperative that a special attorney or
staff of attorneys be assigned the responsibility for the effective investigation and presentation of *all* child protective cases.

## CONCLUSION

Every year, hundreds of children are brutally killed by their parents; some of these deaths are unavoidable. For, to an extent, at least, child abuse and maltreatment will be with us for as long as we refuse to reorder our social priorities. However, many of these children, perhaps three-quarters of the total, could be saved by an effective and efficient child-protective system. We may not be able to prevent the fundamental causes of abuse, but once discovered in a family, we should be able to prevent future abuse by protective social action or removal of the child. We do not have such a system today.

According to the conventional wisdom, the failure of our institutions is caused by a dreadful lack of facilities, of social workers, of judges, of shelters, of probation workers, and of all sorts of rehabilitative social and psychiatric services. Undoubtedly, if we poured more millions of dollars into existing programs, the picture would be less bleak. But existing facilities and services, if properly utilized, could go a long way toward filling the need for service. In fact, unless existing services are first put in order, additional sums of money could not be properly utilized. Most states have expensive, mismanaged or unmanageable child-welfare systems that only imperfectly fulfill the important child-protective responsibilities assigned to them.

Generalizations are always unfair, and it is true that there are many judges, attorneys, probation officers, social workers, and clerks who are vitally concerned with and dedicated to the children and families involved in court process. However, they make up far less than a majority of their colleagues, and the constant demoralization they face embitters and discourages many of them. It is hard to convey the sense of the dehumanization and frustration engendered by the present system. It is not only the child who is caught up in a largely futile process. Every person in the "system" works with the knowledge that he is most often helpless in meeting the needs of those who come before him. Our child-protective system is a fraud.

The illusion of help misleads and mollifies the public. The plight of these children, the victims of deprivation and physical attack, must be exposed in all its grim reality. Only in that way will society, you and your neighbors, demand that these children receive the protection they deserve.

But if humanitarian feelings cannot mobilize sufficient resources to really help these children, perhaps a consideration of the social costs in failing to provide sufficient care for abused and maltreated children will. We tend to think of abused and neglected children as only injured physically, but the emotional damage may be equally severe and may have more long-lasting consequences for the child and for society. Professionals agree that such children have extremely high potential, when older, to engage in socially deviant and criminal acts. Unless the cycle of child abuse from generation to generation is broken, the social deviance that is its heritage shall recur without end. Abuse turns the child toward aggression, violence, and crime. We must break this vicious cycle. The abuse and neglect of children must be recognized as a major factor in the production of criminals. There is an urgent need, largely unmet, to treat such children before they become the criminals of tomorrow.

From a cold dollars-and-cents point of view, it is less expensive to protect and rehabilitate a child then it is to endure the social costs of his later deviant behavior.

# Index

protective procedures are not punitive in nature, that their purpose is the protection of the child and the rehabilitation of the family.

Nevertheless, the appalling lack of sensitivity and callous disregard of the law exhibited by those who continue to violate their legal obligation to report cases of suspected child abuse cannot be continenced. Therefore, although it is absolutely appropriate that persons who report in good faith should be free of any liability, it is equally appropriate that officials and professionals mandated to report who willfully fail to do so should be civilly and criminally liable for that failure.

Another way to encourage fuller reporting is to allow "non-mandated" persons, for example, friends and neighbors, to report.

It is true that many reports from neighbors will prove to be unfounded—indeed, a large number of reports from mandated sources also turn out to be unfounded—hence provision should be made for amending, sealing, or expunging unfounded or untrue reports.

## 2. There Must Be an Effective Central Register of Child-Abuse and Maltreatment Reports

The maintenance of a central register of reported cases of child abuse and maltreatment is an important part of any child-protective program.

The purposes to which the central registry can be put largely depend upon the material it contains and the method of its dissemination. By receiving and processing reports immediately, it provides a fool-proof method of insuring that investigations are performed and services provided. It can also monitor the provisions of such services by other agencies, and it can operate as a research tool to determine the incidence of abuse and the most effective means of prevention.

But most importantly, a central register can assist in the diagnosis and identification of child abuse by locating previous reports on the same child or his siblings. This is especially important in child protective cases because the repetition of suspicious injuries is strongly indicative of child abuse or maltreatment. However, the families in such cases often move from jurisdiction to jurisdiction. Without a statewide or, perhaps, even a regional register, it is impossible for an individual child-protective agency to know if a child has been previously reported.

Every state should have one central register system, with a single telephone number to receive all reports of child abuse and maltreatment from any and all sources. New Jersey already has such a central register system, and there is no reason why such a system should be beyond the capabilities of any other state (*New York Times*, March 6, 1972). The information contained in the central register should be available to all persons with a "need to know." The register should be responsible for notifying the appropriate local authorities to perform an investigation and would be responsible for monitoring the delivery of protective services to the child and family involved.

## 3. There Must Be a Specialized and Highly Qualified Child-Protective Agency

In theory, a "protective service agency," whether it is a department of social services or a Society for the Prevention of Cruelty to Children or other similar type agency, receives reports of parental misconduct from the courts, police, hospitals, other agencies, and private citizens. It then performs an "investigation or intake procedure" in which staff persons determine if the case is appropriate for further agency involvement. The social workers in these agencies may contact schools, neighbors, relatives, and police to obtain as complete a picture as possible. On the basis of these findings as well as interviews with family members themselves, the social workers then make a psychological evaluation of the family.

In some cases, the agency concludes that no intervention is appropriate. The reports may have been inaccurate or unfounded, or the parental neglect may be insufficient to warrant intervention. In some cases, no action is taken because the agency is unable to locate the necessary parties after the family moves or because a father or paramour against whom the charges have been made disappears.

When the protective service agency's investigation indicates that a situation of abuse or neglect warranting action exists, it then, again in theory, determines what action is necessary, from immediate removal to supervision, and attempts to have the parents agree to accept such services. In the absence of voluntary acceptance, the agency resorts to the juvenile or family court for its mandatory procedures. Under New York law, a designated employee of a local department of social services can remove a child from his home or a doctor may retain custody of a child he is treating if the child is in "imminent danger." (Of course, if such a removal or retention is made, the family court must be notified "forthwith." [New York Family Court Act, section 1026]) In this way, the social workers can rescue children in jeopardy.

Since most abused children are too young or too frightened to relate what happened, and since most acts of abuse and maltreatment take place in the privacy of the home, without an identifying motive, the gathering of evidence in such cases is probably more difficult than the proof of adult murder. Therefore, those who are given the grave responsibility for such investigations must be highly qualified. Unfortunately, the reality of child-protective services is often sharply divergent from this theoretical model.

Investigative caseworkers appear to have difficulty in getting genuine information about families. Some records have no official information from other agencies involved in the case, and the only available information comes from the statements of relatives or from the parents themselves. Often no attempt is made to verify these assertions, which are accepted as fact. In fact, caseworkers often have trouble in finding parents or surviving children after a child has died.

In uncertain cases, workers often accept the parents' version of the injury and accept, as collaboration of the parents sketchy story, the fact that the police or district attorney did not have enough evidence for criminal charges (as if lack of sufficient evidence from criminal prosecution were proof of no neglect or abuse). Fully one third of the New York City Department of Social Services' investigators interviewed by the staff of the New York Task Force on Child Abuse and Neglect admitted difficulty in diagnosing both abuse and neglect (New York City Mayor's Task Force on Child Abuse and Neglect, *Final Report* [1970] p. 95).

This table, prepared from information supplied from the New York State department of social service, reveals the large number of cases in which no action is taken because of a "lack of evidence."

RESULTS OF CHILD-ABUSE INVESTIGATIONS

| Type of Result | 1969 % OF TOTAL | 1970 % OF TOTAL |
|---|---|---|
| *Abuse Confirmed* ........ | 44.3 | 42.0 |
| Social Investigation .... | 33.4 | 33.4 |
| Court Decision ........ | 10.8 | 8.6 |
| *Abuse Ruled Out* ........ | 21.1 | 28.1 |
| Social Investigation .... | 20.1 | 25.6 |
| Court Decision ........ | 1.0 | 2.5 |
| *Abuse Uncertain* ........ | 34.6 | 29.9 |
| Lack of Evidence ..... | 25.0 | 23.1 |
| Case pending in court . | 9.7 | 6.8 |

Present practice is for a case to be closed when there is a "lack of evidence." Besides indicating the weakness of investigative technique, these figures also indicate an ignorance of Section 1046 (a) (ii) of the New York Family Court Act, enacted into law in 1970. It provides:

[P]roof of injuries sustained by a child or of the condition of a child of such a nature as would ordinarily not be sustained or exist except by reason of the acts or omissions of the parent or other person responsible for the care of such child shall be *prima facie* evidence of child abuse or neglect, as the case may be, of the parent or other person legally responsible.

Much of the problem lies in the fact that child protective workers do not clearly understand that their primary role and